SCIENTISTS:

The Lives and Works of 150 Scientists

SCIENTISTS:

The Lives and Works of 150 Scientists

Peggy Saari and Stephen Allison, Editors

VOLUME 2

G–O

U·X·L
AN IMPRINT OF GALE

Scientists: The Lives and Works of 150 Scientists

Edited by Peggy Saari and Stephen Allison

Staff

Carol DeKane Nagel, *U·X·L Developmental Editor*
Thomas L. Romig, *U·X·L Publisher*

Shanna P. Heilveil, *Production Assistant*
Evi Seoud, *Assistant Production Manager*
Mary Beth Trimper, *Production Director*

Kimberly Smilay, *Permissions Specialist (Pictures)*

Tracey Rowens, *Cover and Page Designer*
Cynthia Baldwin, *Art Director*

Linda Mahoney, *Typesetter*

Library of Congress Cataloging-in-Publication Data

Scientists : the lives and works of 150 physical and social scientists / edited by Peggy Saari and Stephen Allison.

p. cm.

Includes bibliographical references and index.

Contents: v. 1. A-F – v. 2. G-O – v. 3. P-Z

ISBN 0-7876-0959-5 (set); 0-7876-0960-9 (v. 1); 0-7876-0961-7 (v. 2); 0-7876-0962-5 (v. 3)

1. Physical Scientists–Biography. 2. Social scientists–Biography. I. Saari, Peggy. II. Allison, Stephen, 1969– .

Q141.S3717 1996
509'.2'2–dc20

[B]

96-25579

CIP

Contents

Albert Einstein

VOLUME 2

VOLUME 3

Scientists by Field of Specialization

Italic type indicates volume numbers.

Ruth Patrick

Archaeology

Astronomy and Space

Astrophysics

Atomic/Nuclear Physics

Botany

Chemistry

Climatology

Computer Science

Reader's Guide

An Wang

Budding scientists and those entering the fascinating world of science for fun or study will find inspiration in these three volumes. *Scientists: The Lives and Works of 150 Scientists* presents detailed biographies of the women and men whose theories, discoveries, and inventions have revolutionized science and society. From Louis Pasteur to Bill Gates and Elijah McCoy to Margaret Mead, *Scientists* explores the pioneers and their innovations that students most want to learn about.

Scientists from around the world and from the Industrial Revolution until the present day are featured, in fields such as astronomy, ecology, oceanography, physics, and more.

In *Scientists* students will find:

- 150 scientist biographies, each focusing on the scientist's early life, formative experiences, and inspirations—details that keep students reading

- "Impact" boxes that draw out important information and sum up why each scientist's work is indeed revolutionary

- 120 biographical boxes that highlight individuals who influenced the work of the featured scientist or who conducted similar research
- Sources for further reading so students know where to delve even deeper
- More than 300 black-and-white portraits and additional photographs that give students a better understanding of the people and inventions discussed

Each *Scientists* volume begins with a listing of scientists by field, ranging from aeronautical engineering to zoology; a timeline of major scientific breakthroughs; and a glossary of scientific terms used in the text. Volumes conclude with a cumulative subject index so students can easily find the people, inventions, and theories discussed throughout *Scientists.*

Acknowledgment

Aaron Saari was an important asset to this project. In addition to conducting research, he wrote the biographical boxes and several main entries.

Suggestions

We welcome any comments on this work and suggestions for individuals to feature in future editions of *Scientists.* Please write: Editors, *Scientists,* U•X•L, Gale Research, 835 Penobscot Bldg., Detroit, Michigan 48226-4094; call toll-free: 800-877-4253; or fax to: 313-961-6348.

Timeline of Scientific Breakthroughs

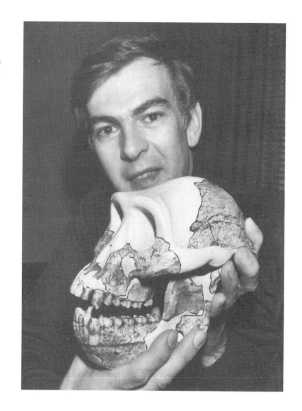

Donald Johanson and Lucy

1730s **Charles Townshend** introduces innovative farming methods that help spur the Industrial Revolution in England.

1769 **Richard Arkwright** patents the water frame, a spinning machine powered by a water wheel.

1769 **James Watt** patents his design for the steam engine.

1774 **Joseph Priestley** reports the results of his experiments with oxygen, gets credit for discovering the gas.

1789 **William Herschel** completes his revolutionary study of the nature of the universe.

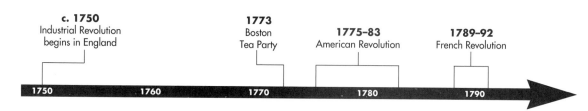

c. 1750 Industrial Revolution begins in England

1773 Boston Tea Party

1775–83 American Revolution

1789–92 French Revolution

1750   1760   1770   1780   1790

1789 **Antoine Lavoisier** describes the role of oxygen in animal and plant respiration.

1799 **Carl Friedrich Gauss** discovers the root form of all algebraic equations.

1808 **John Dalton** publishes his view of the atomic theory of matter, marking the beginning of modern chemistry.

1808 **Humphry Davy** invents the carbon arc lamp, initiating the entire science of electric lighting.

1823 **Charles Babbage** begins to build his Difference Engine, predecessor of the modern digital computer.

1831 **Michael Faraday** confirms that electricity and magnetism are a single force.

1847 **James Prescott Joule** publishes his calculation for the mechanical equivalent of heat.

1848 **William Thomson, Lord Kelvin** develops the Kelvin scale of absolute temperature.

1854 **Louis Pasteur** begins his experiments with fermentation that lead to the widespread sterilization of foods.

1856 **Henry Bessemer** patents the converter, a device that will revolutionize the steelmaking industry.

1859 **Charles Darwin** publishes *The Origin of Species by Means of Natural Selection,* "the book that shook the world."

1864–73 **James Clerk Maxwell** devises equations that prove that magnetism and electricity are distinctly related.

1865 **Gregor Mendel** presents his basic laws of heredity.

1867 **Alfred Nobel** patents dynamite.

1869 **Dmitry Mendeleev** formulates the periodic law.

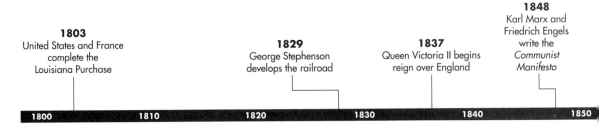

1803
United States and France complete the Louisiana Purchase

1829
George Stephenson develops the railroad

1837
Queen Victoria II begins reign over England

1848
Karl Marx and Friedrich Engels write the *Communist Manifesto*

| 1800 | 1810 | 1820 | 1830 | 1840 | 1850 |

1871 **Luther Burbank** develops the Burbank potato.

1872 **Elijah McCoy** patents the lubricating cup for steam engines that eventually becomes known as "the real McCoy."

1876 **Alexander Graham Bell** patents the telephone.

1877 **Thomas Alva Edison** invents the phonograph; two years later he demonstrates in public the first incandescent lightbulb.

1884 **Svante Arrhenius** formulates electrolytic dissociation theory, explaining how some substances conduct electricity in solutions.

1887 **Nikola Tesla** perfects the use of alternating-current electricity in his polyphase motor.

1887 **Granville T. Woods** patents the railway telegraph, allowing communication between moving trains.

1892 **Rudolf Diesel** patents an internal-combustion engine superior to the gasoline-powered engines of the day.

1895 **Wilhelm Röntgen** discovers X rays.

1896 **George Washington Carver** joins the Tuskegee Institute, beginning his career in scientific agriculture.

1897 **Guglielmo Marconi** patents the wireless radio.

1898 **Marie Curie** and **Pierre Curie** publish the first in a series of papers on radioactivity.

1899 **Sigmund Freud** lays out the basic principles of psychoanalytic theory in *The Interpretation of Dreams*.

1900 **David Hilbert** sets an agenda of twenty-three problems for mathematicians to solve during the twentieth century.

1900 **Max Planck** formulates the quantum theory, taking the science of physics into the modern age.

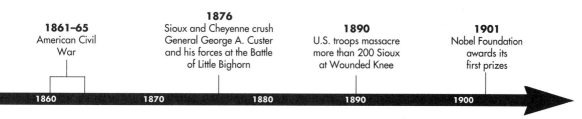

1861–65
American Civil War

1876
Sioux and Cheyenne crush General George A. Custer and his forces at the Battle of Little Bighorn

1890
U.S. troops massacre more than 200 Sioux at Wounded Knee

1901
Nobel Foundation awards its first prizes

1860   1870   1880   1890   1900

Scientific Breakthroughs

1900 **Florence R. Sabin** commences her studies of the human lymphatic system.

1903 **Bertrand Russell** unites logic and mathematics in *The Principals of Mathematics.*

1903 **Wilbur Wright** and **Orville Wright** achieve the first sustained flights in a power-driven aircraft.

c. 1903 **Arthur C. Parker** conducts his first formal archaeological excavation on the Cattaraugus Reservation.

1905 **Albert Einstein** formulates his special theory of relativity, changing forever the way scientists look at the nature of space, time, and matter.

1906 **Lee De Forest** patents the audion tube (triode), crucial to the development of the modern radio.

1910 **Annie Jump Cannon**'s method for classifying stars, known as the Harvard system, is adopted by the astronomical community.

1910 **Ernest Rutherford** determines the structure of the atom.

1912 **Alfred Wegener** proposes the theory of continental drift.

1913 **Niels Bohr** introduces the quantum mechanical model of the atom.

1913 **C. G. Jung** publishes *The Psychology of the Unconscious* and is outcast by the psychoanalytic community.

1919 **Karl von Frisch** discovers that honeybees communicate through ritual dances.

1919 **Karl Menninger** and his father open the Menninger Clinic for psychiatric treatment and research.

1908
Henry Ford introduces
the Model T

1914
World War I
begins

1917
Russian Revolution

1920
19th Amendment
gives American
women the
right to vote

1923
Time magazine
begins publication

1910   1913   1916   1919   1922   1925

1920–40 **Edith H. Quimby** conducts studies of the effects of radiation on the body.

1924 **Vladimir Zworykin** patents the kinescope, or the picture tube, which will make television as we know it possible.

1926 **Robert H. Goddard** launches the first liquid-propellant rocket.

1926 **Ivan Pavlov** publishes his masterwork, *Conditioned Reflexes.*

1927 **William Augustus Hinton** develops a test that becomes the standard for diagnosing syphilis.

1928 **Alexander Fleming** discovers penicillin.

1928 **Margaret Mead** publishes *Coming of Age in Samoa.*

1929 **Edwin Hubble** initiates the theory of an expanding universe.

1930s–40s **B. F. Skinner** conducts experiments that convince him that behavior can be controlled through the environment.

c. 1932 **Ruth Patrick** begins studying the presence of diatoms in various marine ecosystems.

1935 **Subrahmanyan Chandrasekhar** rocks the astronomical community with his radical theories on the evolution of white dwarf stars.

1935 **Percy L. Julian** synthesizes physostigmine, a chemical used in the treatment of glaucoma.

1935 **Charles F. Richter** develops the Richter scale to measure earthquake intensity.

1935 **Robert Watson-Watt** develops radar.

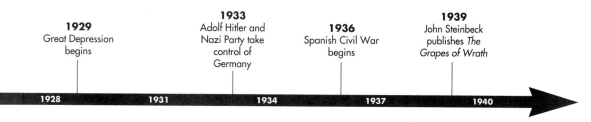

1929
Great Depression begins

1933
Adolf Hitler and Nazi Party take control of Germany

1936
Spanish Civil War begins

1939
John Steinbeck publishes *The Grapes of Wrath*

1928   1931   1934   1937   1940

Scientific Breakthroughs

c. 1935 **Berta Scharrer** and her husband Ernst begin their pioneering work in neuroendocrinology.

1935–38 **Konrad Lorenz** spends his "goose summers" confirming his many hypotheses on animal behavior patterns.

1938 **Lise Meitner,** with Otto Robert Frisch, develops the theory that explains nuclear fission.

c. 1938 **Katharine Burr Blodgett** invents nonreflecting glass.

1939 **Charles Richard Drew** develops a method to process and preserve blood plasma through dehydration.

1939 **Lloyd A. Hall** cofounds the Institute of Food Technologies.

1939 **Ernest Everett Just** publishes his findings on the role protoplasm plays in a cell.

1939 **Linus Pauling** publishes the landmark *Nature of the Chemical Bond and the Structure of Molecules and Crystals.*

1942 **Enrico Fermi** produces the first self-sustaining nuclear chain reaction.

1942 The World Health Organization adopts **Florence Seibert**'s skin test as the standard tool for diagnosing tuberculosis.

1944 **Norman Borlaug** shares agricultural advances with the Mexican government, thus starting the Green Revolution.

1944 **George H. Hitchings** and **Gertrude Belle Elion** begin their twenty-five-year collaboration developing "rational" drugs.

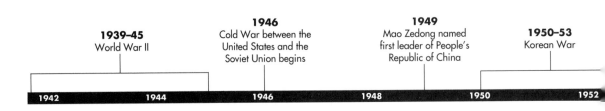

1939–45
World War II

1946
Cold War between the United States and the Soviet Union begins

1949
Mao Zedong named first leader of People's Republic of China

1950–53
Korean War

1942   1944   1946   1948   1950   1952

1944 **Barbara McClintock** begins her studies that will lead to her discovery of "jumping genes."

1944 **Vivien Thomas** perfects the surgical technique that will save thousands of "blue babies."

1945 **J. Robert Oppenheimer** sees the culmination of his work as director of the Manhattan Project: two atomic bombs are dropped on Japan to end World War II.

1947 **Carl Ferdinand Cori** and **Gerty T. Cori** share the Nobel Prize for their studies on sugar metabolism, begun in the early 1920s.

1947 **Thor Heyerdahl** crosses the Pacific on the balsa raft *Kon-Tiki.*

1947 **Edwin H. Land** introduces the instant camera.

1947 **William Shockley** and his research team develop the transistor.

1948 **Dorothy Hodgkin** begins using X-ray crystallography to determine the structure of vitamin B^{12}.

1948 **Norbert Wiener** publishes *Cybernetics,* detailing his theories on control and communication in humans and machines.

c. 1948 **Albert Baez,** with Paul Kirkpatrick, builds the first X-ray microscope.

1949 **Maria Goeppert-Mayer** publishes her hypothesis for the structure of atomic nuclei.

1951 **R. Buckminster Fuller** patents the geodesic dome.

1951–52 **Jacques Cousteau,** with the *Calypso,* undertakes his first extensive expedition.

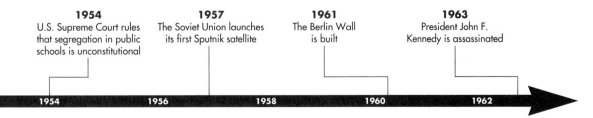

1954
U.S. Supreme Court rules that segregation in public schools is unconstitutional

1957
The Soviet Union launches its first Sputnik satellite

1961
The Berlin Wall is built

1963
President John F. Kennedy is assassinated

1954　　1956　　1958　　1960　　1962

1952   Through X-ray diffraction, **Rosalind Franklin** makes a preliminary determination of the structure of DNA.

1952   **Dorothy Horstmann** concludes that the virus that causes polio travels through the bloodstream to reach the nervous system.

1953   **Auguste Piccard** and **Jacques Piccard** set a depth record of almost two miles in their bathyscaphe *Trieste*.

1953   **James D. Watson** and **Francis Crick** unravel the mystery of the structure of DNA.

1954   **Angeles Alvariño** begins groundbreaking studies of marine zooplankton.

1955   **Jonas Salk**'s polio vaccine is pronounced effective, potent, and safe.

1955   **An Wang** patents techniques for developing magnetic core memories in computers.

1956   **Charlotte Friend** isolates the virus responsible for leukemia in mice, thereby pointing the way for future cancer research.

1956   **Chen Ning Yang** and **Tsung-Dao Lee** theorize that the unusual behavior of K-mesons violates the law of conservation of parity.

c. 1956   **Rosalyn Sussman Yalow** codevelops the diagnostic tool radioimmunoassay (RIA).

1957   **Albert Sabin** begins administering his oral polio vaccine to millions of Russian children.

1957   **Chien-Shiung Wu** conducts beta decay experiments that confirm the violation of the conservation of parity.

1958   **James Van Allen** discovers bands of high-level radiation surrounding Earth.

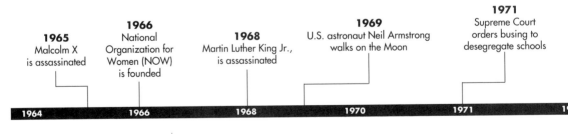

1965
Malcolm X
is assassinated

1966
National
Organization for
Women (NOW)
is founded

1968
Martin Luther King Jr.,
is assassinated

1969
U.S. astronaut Neil Armstrong
walks on the Moon

1971
Supreme Court
orders busing to
desegregate schools

1964   1966   1968   1970   1971   1972

c. 1958   **Meredith Gourdine** develops the formula for electrogasdynamics.

1959   **Luis Alvarez** develops a 72-inch bubble chamber to better study subatomic particles.

1959   **Mary Leakey** finds the 1.75 million-year-old fossilized skull of a hominid that **Louis S. B. Leakey** names "East Africa man."

1959   **Marvin Minsky** cofounds the Artificial Intelligence Project at the Massachusetts Institute of Technology (MIT).

1959   **Robert Noyce** invents the integrated circuit, or microchip, revolutionizing twentieth-century technology.

1960   **George Bass** undertakes the first excavation of an underwater shipwreck site.

1960   **Jane Goodall** establishes a camp in the Gombe Stream Reserve, beginning her long-term studies of chimpanzee behavior.

1960   **Theodore Maiman** constructs the first working laser.

1960s   **Tetsuya Theodore Fujita** develops the F Scale, used to measure the strength of tornadoes.

1962   **Rachel Carson** publishes *Silent Spring,* sparking the beginning of the environmental movement.

1966   **Keiiti Aki** develops the seismic moment, a new method of measuring the magnitude of earthquakes.

1967   **E. Margaret Burbidge** and **Geoffrey Burbidge** publish *Quasi-Stellar Objects,* one of the first surveys of quasars.

1967   **Jocelyn Bell Burnell** discovers pulsars.

1968   **James E. Lovelock** publishes his controversial Gaia theory about Earth's regulation of her ecosystems.

1973
Americans pull out of Vietnam

1974
Richard M. Nixon resigns the presidency of the United States

1976
America celebrates its bicentennial

1977
U.S. president Jimmy Carter unveils policy designed to reduce energy consumption

1973   1974   1975   1976   1977

1968   **Abdus Salam** announces his theory of the electroweak force.

1968   **Edward O. Wilson** confirms his theory of species equilibrium in a study of insect life on six islands off the Florida keys.

1970   **Bruce N. Ames** develops test for measuring the cancer-causing potential of chemicals.

1970   **Sylvia A. Earle** spends two weeks in an underwater chamber to study marine habitats.

1970   **Paul R. Ehrlich** helps found Zero Population Growth, a group that aims to educate people on the environmental dangers caused by overpopulation.

1971   **Fred Begay** begins his research into harnessing the clean, safe power of nuclear fusion.

1971   **Helen Caldicott** first organizes opposition to nuclear weapons, prompting the French government to cease atmospheric testing for a time.

1971   **Geoffrey Hounsfield** tests the first CAT scan machine.

1972   **Stephen Jay Gould** introduces the concept of punctuated equilibrium, contradicting a central tenet of the Darwinian theory of evolution.

1972   **Richard Leakey** unearths a 1.9-million-year-old *Homo habilis* skull, the oldest *H. habilis* specimen discovered so far.

1973   **Shirley Ann Jackson** is the first African American woman to earn a doctorate from MIT.

1974   **Paul Berg** publishes the "Berg letter," warning of the dangers of genetic engineering, a field he pioneered in the late 1960s and 1970s.

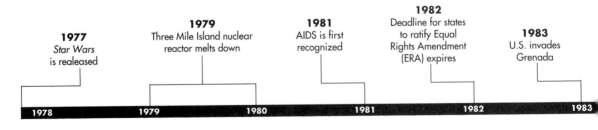

1977
Star Wars is realeased

1979
Three Mile Island nuclear reactor melts down

1981
AIDS is first recognized

1982
Deadline for states to ratify Equal Rights Amendment (ERA) expires

1983
U.S. invades Grenada

1978   1979   1980   1981   1982   1983

1974   **Donald Johanson** finds Lucy, the oldest fossilized remains of a hominid ever unearthed.

c. 1974   **Stephen Hawking** discovers that black holes emit radiation.

1975   **Sandra Faber,** with Robert Jackson, formulates the first galactic sealing law, used to help calculate distances between galaxies.

1975   **Bill Gates** begins his career as a software designer and entrepreneur when he cofounds Microsoft.

1976   **Maxine Singer** helps formulate guidelines for responsible biochemical genetics research.

c. 1976   **James S. Williamson** supervises the design of the first solar-powered electricity-generating plant in the United States.

1977   **Steven Jobs** and Stephen Wozniak introduce the Apple II computer, touching off the personal computer revolution.

1977   **Louis Keith** and his twin brother found the Center for the Study of Multiple Births.

1978   **Elizabeth H. Blackburn** begins groundbreaking work that leads to the discovery of the enzyme telomerase.

1978   **Patrick Steptoe** produces the first test-tube baby.

1980   **Lynn Conway** publishes *Introduction to VLSI Systems,* which simplifies the way computer chips are produced.

1980   **Levi Watkins Jr.,** performs the first implantation of the automatic heart defibrillator.

1982   **Robert K. Jarvik** implants the Jarvik-7 artificial heart into Barney Clark.

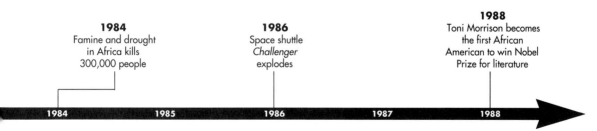

1984
Famine and drought
in Africa kills
300,000 people

1986
Space shuttle
Challenger
explodes

1988
Toni Morrison becomes
the first African
American to win Nobel
Prize for literature

1984   1985   1986   1987   1988

| Scientific Breakthroughs

1983   **Irene Diggs** publishes *Black Chronology,* focusing on the accomplishments of people of African descent.

1984   **Helene D. Gayle** begins research on the effects of AIDS on children throughout the world.

1984   **Jaron Lanier** founds VPL Research Inc., to provide virtual reality software to the general computer user.

1985   Using technology he calls telepresence, **Robert D. Ballard** discovers the remains of the sunken *Titanic.*

1986   **Sally Fox** opens a mail-order business to sell the naturally colored cotton fibers she developed.

1986   **Margaret Geller** reports finding a "Great Wall" of galaxies, forcing some cosmologists to rethink existing theories of the beginning of the universe.

c. 1986   **Francisco Dallmeier** begins biodiversity research and education programs in several countries.

1987   **Anthony S. Fauci**'s research team discovers how the AIDS virus is transmitted.

1987   **Oliver Wolf Sacks**'s 1973 book *Awakenings,* about his treatment of patients with sleeping sickness, is made into a popular film.

1990   **Walter Gilbert** starts the human genome project to compile a genetic map of the entire human being.

1993   **Mark Plotkin** publishes *Tales of a Shaman's Apprentice,* discussing his excursions into the Amazon rain forest in search of medicinal plants and traditions.

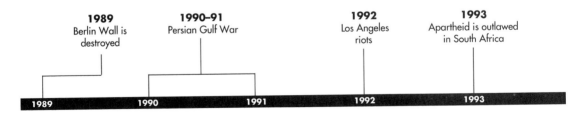

1989
Berlin Wall is destroyed

1990–91
Persian Gulf War

1992
Los Angeles riots

1993
Apartheid is outlawed in South Africa

1989   1990   1991   1992   1993

Words to Know

Meredith Gourdine

A

Absolute zero: the theoretical point at which a substance has no heat and motion ceases; equivalent to -276°C or -459.67°F.

Algae: a diverse group of plant or plantlike organisms that grow mainly in water.

Alpha particle: a positively charged nuclear particle that consists of two protons and two electrons; it is ejected at a high speed from disintegrating radioactive materials.

Alternating current: the flow of electrons first in one direction and then in the other at regular intervals.

Amino acids: organic acids that are the chief components of proteins.

Anatomy: the study of the structure and form of biological organisms.

Anthropology: the science that deals with the study of human beings, especially their origin, development, divisions, and customs.

Archaeology: the scientific study of material remains, such as fossils and relics, of past societies.

Artificial intelligence: the branch of science concerned with the development of machines having the ability to perform tasks normally thought to require human intelligence, such as problem solving, discriminating among single objects, and response to spoken commands.

Asteroid: one of thousands of small planets located in a belt between the orbits of Mars and Jupiter.

Astronomy: the study of the physical and chemical properties of objects and matter outside Earth's atmosphere.

Astrophysics: the branch of physics involving the study of the physical and chemical nature of celestial objects and events.

Atomic bomb: a weapon of mass destruction that derives its explosive energy from nuclear fission.

B

Bacteria: a large, diverse group of mostly single-celled organisms that play a key role in the decay of organic matter and the cycling of nutrients.

Bacteriology: the scientific study of bacteria, their characteristics, and their activities as related to medicine, industry, and agriculture.

Bacteriophage: a virus that infects bacteria.

Behaviorism: the school of psychology that holds that human and animal behavior is based not on independent will nor motivation but rather on response to reward and punishment.

Beta decay: process by which a neutron in an atomic nucleus breaks apart into a proton and an electron.

Big bang: in astronomy, the theory that the universe resulted from a cosmic explosion that occurred billions of years ago and then expanded over time.

Biochemistry: the study of chemical compounds and processes occurring in living organisms.

Biodiversity: the number of different species of plants and animals in a specified region.

Biology: the scientific study of living organisms.

Biophysics: the branch of biology in which the methods and principles of physics are applied to the study of living things.

Biotechnology: use of biological organisms, systems, or processes to make or modify products.

Botany: the branch of biology involving the study of plant life.

C

Carcinogen: a cancer-causing agent, such as a chemical or a virus.

Cathode: a negatively charged electrode.

Cathode rays: electrons emitted by a cathode when heated.

Chemistry: the science of the nature, composition, and properties of material substances and their transformations.

Chromosome: threadlike structure in the nucleus of a cell that carries thousands of genes.

Circuit: the complete path of an electric current including the source of electric energy; an assemblage of electronic elements.

Climatology: the scientific study of climates and their phenomena.

Combustion: a rapid chemical process that produces heat and light.

Conductor: a substance able to carry an electrical current.

Conservation biology: the branch of biology that involves conserving rapidly vanishing wild animals, plants, and places.

Conservation laws: laws of physics that state that a particular property, mass, energy, momentum, or electrical charge is not lost during any change.

Cosmic rays: charged particles, mainly the nuclei of hydrogen and other atoms, that bombard Earth's upper atmosphere at velocities close to that of light.

Cosmology: the study of the structure and evolution of the universe.

Cross-fertilization: a method of fertilization in which the gametes (mature male or female cells) are produced by separate individuals or sometimes by individuals of different kinds.

Cryogenics: the branch of physics that involves the production and effects of very low temperatures.

Crystallography: the science that deals with the forms and structures of crystals.

Cytology: the branch of biology concerned with the study of cells.

D

Diffraction: the spreading and bending of light waves as they pass through a hole or slit.

Direct current: a regular flow of electrons, always in the same direction.

DNA (deoxyribonucleic acid): a long molecule composed of two chains of nucleotides (organic chemicals) that contain the genetic information carried from one generation to another.

E

Earthquake: an unpredictable event in which masses of rock shift below Earth's surface, releasing enormous amounts of energy and sending out shockwaves that sometimes cause the ground to shake dramatically.

Ecology: the branch of science dealing with the interrelationship of organisms and their environments.

Ecosystem: community of plants and animals and the physical environment with which they interact.

Electrochemistry: the branch of physical chemistry involving the relation of electricity to chemical changes.

Electrodes: conductors used to establish electrical contact with a nonmetallic part of a circuit.

Electromagnetism: the study of electric and magnetic fields and their interaction with electric charges and currents.

Electron: a negatively charged particle that orbits the nucleus of an atom.

Entomology: the branch of zoology dealing with the study of insects.

Environmentalism: the movement to preserve and improve the natural environment, and particularly to control pollution.

Enzyme: any of numerous complex proteins that are produced by living cells and spark specific biochemical reactions.

Epidemiology: the study of the causes, distribution, and control of disease in populations.

Ethnobotany: the plant lore of a race of people.

Ethnology: science that deals with the division of human beings into races and their origin, distribution, relations, and characteristics.

Ethology: the scientific and objective study of the behavior of animals in the wild rather than in captivity.

Evolution: in the struggle for survival, the process by which successive generations of a species pass on to their offspring the characteristics that enable the species to survive.

Extinction: the total disappearance of a species or the disappearance of a species from a given area.

F

Fossils: the remains, traces, or impressions of living organisms that inhabited Earth more than ten thousand years ago.

G

Gamma rays: short electromagnetic wavelengths that come from the nuclei of atoms during radioactive decay.

Gene: in classical genetics, a unit of hereditary information that is carried on chromosomes and determines observable characteristics; in molecular genetics, a special sequence of DNA or RNA located on the chromosome.

Genetic code: the means by which genetic information is translated into the chromosomes that make up living organisms.

Genetics: the study of inheritance in living organisms.

Genome: genetic material of a human being; the complete genetic structure of a species.

Geochemistry: the study of the chemistry of Earth (and other planets).

Geology: the study of the origin, history, and structure of Earth.

Geophysics: the physics of Earth, including studies of the atmosphere, earthquakes, volcanism, and oceans.

Global warming: the rise in Earth's temperature that is attributed to the buildup of carbon dioxide and other pollutants in the atmosphere.

Greenhouse effect: warming of Earth's atmosphere due to the absorption of heat by molecules of water vapor, carbon dioxide, methane, ozone, nitrous oxide, and chlorofluorocarbons.

H

Herpetology: the branch of zoology that deals with reptiles and amphibians.

Hominids: humanlike creatures.

Hormones: chemical messengers produced in living organisms that play significant roles in the body, such as affecting growth, metabolism, and digestion.

Horticulture: the science of growing fruits, vegetables, and ornamental plants.

Hybridization: cross-pollination of plants of different varieties to produce seed.

I

Immunology: the branch of medicine concerned with the body's ability to protect itself from disease.

Imprinting: the rapid learning process that takes place early in the life of a social animal and establishes a behavioral pattern, such as a recognition of and attraction to its own kind or a substitute.

In vitro fertilization: fertilization of eggs outside of the body.

Infrared radiation: electromagnetic rays released by hot objects; also known as a heat radiation.

Infertility: the inability to produce offspring for any reason.

Invertebrates: animals lacking a spinal column.

Ion: an atom or groups of atoms that carries an electrical charge-either positive or negative-as a result of losing or gaining one or more electrons.

Isotopes: atoms of a chemical element that contain the same number of protons but a different number of neutrons.

L

Laser: acronym for light amplification by stimulated emission of radiation; a device that produces intense light with a precisely defined wavelength.

Light-year: in astronomy, the distance light travels in one year, about six trillion miles.

Limnology: the branch of biology concerning freshwater plants.

Logic: the science of the formal principles of reasoning.

M

Magnetic field: the space around an electric current or a magnet in which a magnetic force can be observed.

Maser: acronym for microwave amplification of stimulated emission of radiation; a device that produces radiation in short wavelengths.

Metabolism: the process by which living cells break down organic compounds to produce energy.

Metallurgy: the science and technology of metals.

Meteorology: the science that deals with the atmosphere and its phenomena and with weather and weather forecasting.

Microbiology: branch of biology dealing with microscopic forms of life.

Microwaves: electromagnetic radiation waves between one millimeter and one centimeter in length.

Molecular biology: the study of the structure and function of molecules that make up living organisms.

Molecule: the smallest particle of a substance that retains all the properties of the substance and is composed of one or more atoms.

Mutation: any permanent change in hereditary material, involving either a physical change in chromosome relations or a biochemical change in genes.

N

Natural selection: the natural process by which groups best adjusted to their environment survive and reproduce, thereby passing on to their offspring genetic qualities best suited to that environment.

Nervous system: the bodily system that in vertebrates is made up of the brain and spinal cord, nerves, ganglia, and other organs and that receives and interprets stimuli and transmits impulses to targeted organs.

Neurology: the scientific study of the nervous system, especially its structure, functions, and abnormalities.

Neurosecretion: the process of producing a secretion by nerve cells.

Neurosis: any emotional or mental disorder that affects only part of the personality, such as anxiety or mild depression, as a result of stress.

Neutron: an uncharged particle found in atomic nuclei.

Neutron star: a hypothetical dense celestial object that consists primarily of closely packed neutrons that results from the collapse of a much larger celestial body.

Nova: a star that suddenly increases in light output and then fades away to its former obscure state within a few months or years.

Nuclear fallout: the drifting of radioactive particles into the atmosphere as the result of nuclear explosions.

Nuclear fission: the process in which an atomic nucleus is split, resulting in the release of large amounts of energy.

O

Oceanography: the science that deals with the study of oceans and seas.

Optics: the study of light and vision.

Organic: of, relating to, or arising in a bodily organ

Ozone layer: the atmospheric layer of approximately twenty to thirty miles above Earth's surface that protects the lower atmosphere from harmful solar radiation.

P

Paleoanthropology: the branch of anthropology dealing with the study of mammal fossils.

Paleontology: the study of the life of past geological periods as known from fossil remains.

Particle physics: the branch of physics concerned with the study of the constitution, properties, and interactions of elementary particles.

Particles: the smallest building blocks of energy and matter.

Pathology: the study of the essential nature of diseases, especially the structural and functional changes produced by them.

Periodic table: a table of the elements in order of atomic number, arranged in rows and columns to show periodic similarities and trends in physical and chemical properties.

Pharmacology: the science dealing with the properties, reactions, and therapeutic values of drugs.

Physics: the science that explores the physical properties and composition of objects and the forces that affect them.

Physiology: the branch of biology that deals with the functions and actions of life or of living matter, such as organs, tissues, and cells.

Plankton: floating animal and plant life.

Plasma physics: the branch of physics involving the study of electrically charged, extremely hot gases.

Primate: any order of mammals composed of humans, apes, or monkeys.

Protein: large molecules found in all living organisms that are essential to the structure and functioning of all living cells.

Proton: a positively charged particle found in atomic nuclei.

Psychiatry: the branch of medicine that deals with mental, emotional, and behavioral disorders.

Psychoanalysis: the method of analyzing psychic phenomenon and treating emotional disorders that involves treatment sessions during which the patient is encouraged to talk freely about personal experiences, especially about early childhood and dreams.

Psychology: the study of human and animal behavior.

Psychotic: a person with severe emotional or mental disorders that cause a loss of contact with reality.

Q

Quantum: any of the very small increments or parcels into which many forms of energy are subdivided.

Quasar: celestial object more distant than stars that emits excessive amounts of radiation.

R

Radar: acronym for radio detection and ranging; the process of using radio waves to detect objects.

Radiation: energy emitted in the form of waves or particles.

Radio waves: electromagnetic radiation.

Radioactive fallout: the radioactive particles resulting from a nuclear explosion.

Radioactivity: the property possessed by some elements (as uranium) or isotopes (as carbon 14) of spontaneously emitting energetic particles (as electrons or alpha particles) by disintegration of their atomic nuclei.

Radiology: the branch of medicine that uses X rays and radium (an intensely radioactive metallic element) to diagnose and treat disease.

Redshift: the increase in the wavelength of all light received from a celestial object (or wave source), usually because the object is moving away from the observer.

RNA (ribonucleic acid): any of various nucleic acids that are associated with the control of cellular chemical activities.

S

Scientific method: collecting evidence meticulously and theorizing from it.

Seismograph: a device that records vibrations of the ground and within Earth.

Seismology: the study and measurement of earthquakes.

Semiconductor: substances whose ability to carry electrical current is lower than that of a conductor (like metal) and higher than that of insulators (like rubber).

Shortwave: a radio wave having a wavelength between ten and one hundred meters.

Sociobiology: the systematic study of the biological basis for all social behavior.

Solid state: using semiconductor devices rather than electron tubes.

Spectrum: the range of colors produced by individual elements within a light source.

Steady-state theory: a theory that proposes that the universe has neither a beginning nor an end.

Stellar spectra: the distinctive mix of radiation emitted by every star.

Stellar spectroscopy: the process that breaks a star's light into component colors so that the various elements of the star can be observed.

Sterilization: boiling or heating of instruments and food to prevent proliferation of microorganisms.

Supernova: a catastrophic explosion in which a large portion of a star's mass is blown out into space, or the star is entirely destroyed.

T

Theorem: in mathematics, a formula, proposition, or statement.

Thermodynamics: the branch of physics that deals with the mechanical action or relations of heat.

Trace element: a chemical element present in minute quantities.

Transistor: a solid-state electronic device that is used to control the flow of electricity in electronic equipment and consists of a small block of semiconductor with at least three electrodes.

V

Vaccine: a preparation administered to increase immunity to polio.

Vacuum tube: an electric tube from which all matter has been removed.

Variable stars: stars whose light output varies because of internal fluctuations or because they are eclipsed by another star.

Variation: in genetics, differences in traits of a particular species.

Vertebrate: an animal that has a spinal column.

Virology: the study of viruses.

Virtual reality: an artificial computer-created environment that seeks to mimic reality.

Virus: a microscopic agent of infection.

W

Wavelength: the distance between one peak of a wave of light, heat, or energy and the next corresponding peak.

X

X ray: a form of electromagnetic radiation with an extremely short wavelength that is produced by bombarding a metallic target with electrons in a vacuum.

Z

Zoology: the branch of biology concerned with the study of animal life.

Zooplankton: small drifting animal life in the ocean.

SCIENTISTS:

The Lives and
Works of
150 Scientists

Bill Gates

Born October 28, 1955
Seattle, Washington

Bill Gates is an American entrepreneur who designed and developed innovative software for the personal computer (PC). Cofounder of the Microsoft Corporation, one of the most successful companies in history, he created such popular software products as MS-DOS and Windows. He has also been instrumental in popularizing and promoting CD-ROM technology. As a major figure in the computer revolution of the 1980s and 1990s, Gates has helped make the PC a common and accessible household item.

"Our success is based on only one thing: good products. It's not very complicated."

Meets future business partner

William Henry Gates III was born on October 28, 1955, in Seattle, Washington, the second child and only son of William Henry Gates Jr., a prominent Seattle attorney, and Mary Maxwell Gates, a schoolteacher. Although his parents wanted him to go into law, Gates developed an early interest in computer science. He began studying computers in the sev-

Bill Gates's supreme accomplishment was to design and develop innovative software for the personal computer (PC). He helped make PCs the universally popular machines they are today. Communicating with computers is a matter of "translating" a person's native language into the codes that a computer understands. The easier this translation is to make, the easier it is to work with the computer and the more accessible and widely used the computer becomes. Gates's gift for designing "user-friendly" software—along with his superior business skills—has made Microsoft a multibillion-dollar empire that sets the standards for the computer industry.

enth grade at Lakeside School in Seattle, where he met childhood pal Paul Allen. Allen, who was two years older than Gates and shared his interest in technology, would eventually become the budding entrepreneur's business partner.

Begins career debugging and hacking

Gates's early experiences with computers included debugging (or eliminating errors from) programs for the Computer Center Corporation's PDP-10. Soon after Gates enrolled at Lakeside, the school bought a teletype machine that, for a fee, could be hooked up to the PDP-10, which was located in downtown Seattle. The teletype machine was basically a printer and keyboard that allowed the user to communicate with the PDP-10 over a telephone line. After visiting Lakeside's computer room with his math class, Gates was immediately fascinated. Computers quickly became the focus of his life.

Along with debugging, Gates and his friend Allen also spent a great deal of time hacking (programming and solving problems with a computer). A large part of figuring out what a computer could do meant learning to understand programs (the sets of instructions that a computer uses to operate). Gates and Allen both picked up quickly on the programming of software (the set of programs, procedures, and related documentation associated with a computer). Soon Gates was hacking, or creating, game programs of his own. The first was a simple tic-tac-toe game. Then he wrote a lunar lander game, in which the player had to land a spaceship on the Moon before running out of fuel.

By his mid-teens Gates was as interested in making money as he was in computer programs. In 1971, as a high school junior at Lakeside, he formed a business with Allen, then a freshman at Washington State University in Pullman. Calling their venture Traf-O-Data, they helped Seattle-area cities control traffic by using a computer to analyze traffic patterns. This small company earned Gates and Allen $20,000 in fees for their services.

Reprimanded for creating a virus

While working with the PDP-10, Gates was responsible for what was probably the first computer virus (a program that copies itself into other programs and ruins data). Discovering that the machine was hooked up to a national network of computers known as Cybernet, Gates invaded the network and installed a program on the main computer that sent itself to the rest of the computers on the network. Cybernet crashed. When Gates was found out, he was severely reprimanded and kept away from computers for his entire junior year at Lakeside. Without the lure of computers, Gates made plans for college and law school. The next year, however, he was back helping Allen write a class-scheduling program for the high school's computer.

Invents a BASIC language

Gates entered Harvard University in 1973 and pursued his studies for the next year and a half. But his life changed in January 1975. One day Allen showed him the latest issue of *Popular Electronics* magazine. The cover photo featured a small metal box with several switches and lights on it. Called the Altair, it was the first personal computer. It cost $397, came in kit form, and had to be put together. Allen and Gates saw that, however primitive, the Altair was a huge step forward. It was also, they believed, the beginning of a revolution — one that might someday end with computers in virtually every American home.

But Altair inventor Ed Roberts needed a "language" that would enable his computer to run programs. Without a language, the Altair would be next to useless. Gates and Allen told Roberts that they had written a BASIC interpreter for the Altair. ("BASIC" was a simplified language designed in the 1960s for programming computers; "interpreter" is a program that executes a source program by reading it one line at a time and performing operations immediately.) They lied. The computer duo had not even started designing the operating-system language when they offered to sell it to Roberts.

When Roberts accepted, Gates and Allen promised delivery within a few weeks. They now had to keep their word—but they did not even have an Altair to work with. Allen had to figure out how to make the PDP-10 at Harvard work like an Altair. Gates's job was to write the language itself, to make a BASIC that would fit in the Altair's small memory. It took eight weeks of nearly constant work (after a month, a friend named Monte Davidoff pitched in); following a series of seemingly endless all-nighters, they were done. Allen then flew to Albuquerque to meet with Roberts and test their version of BASIC. It worked. Roberts began offering the Altair for sale, and the orders flooded in. Gates and Allen would receive money for each machine sold with their BASIC.

Starts Microsoft

Before receiving money from sales of their BASIC, Gates and Allen had to create a formal business partnership. In the summer of 1975, after Gates dropped out of Harvard, they created Micro-Soft. The name Micro-Soft is short for micro-computer software. Soon they dropped the hyphen, making it just Microsoft. Thus began Gates's career as a software designer and entrepreneur.

Gates and Allen set up Microsoft in Albuquerque, close to Roberts's company, MITS, which produced the Altair. They hired a few employees, young computer enthusiasts like themselves who could write entertaining programs for use on the Altair. Writing programs for the early Apple and Commodore machines, they expanded their BASIC to run on microcomputers other than the Altair.

Eckert and Mauchly

Presper Eckert and John William Mauchly, American Computer Engineers

Early computer industry pioneers J. Presper Eckert (1913–) and John William Mauchly (1907–1980) made significant contributions to computer technology. In the late 1930s they produced the ENIAC (Electronic Numerical Integrator and Computer), an enormous, power hungry, and slow—compared to the average personal computer of today—computer with a calculating speed one thousand times faster than any mechanical calculator built up to that time. After World War II Eckert and Mauchly developed the UNIVAC (Universal Automatic Computer) and the BINAC (Binary Automatic Computer), the first computers to employ magnetic tape drives for data storage.

The UNIVAC proved its value in the 1952 presidential election between Dwight Eisenhower and Adlai Stevenson, when, less than an hour after the polls closed, it accurately predicted that Eisenhower would be the next president of the United States. Eckert and Mauchly's patent on the ENIAC was eventually challenged in a lawsuit. In 1973 the court invalidated the ENIAC patent and asserted that Iowa State University professor John Vincent Atanasoff (1903–) was the true inventor of the digital computer. In the late 1930s, while teaching in Iowa, Atanasoff had designed and built an electronic computing machine with one of his graduate students, Clifford Berry. The Atanasoff-Berry Computer (ABC) was probably the first machine to use vacuum tubes to perform calculations.

After a while Microsoft employed several more young programmers, a few of them former Lakeside students whom Gates and Allen had recruited. From the beginning the atmosphere in the workplace was informal. Even now rock music blares out of employees' offices; dress codes and phony administrative bureaucracy are virtually nonexistent. But employees are held to the highest quality and productivity standards and often have to put in sixty- to eighty-hour workweeks.

Creates MS-DOS

Gates's big opportunity arrived in 1980, when he was approached by IBM to help design the operating system for its personal computer project, code-named Project Chess. Gates developed the Microsoft Disk Operating System, or MS-DOS as it is popularly known. Not only did he sell IBM on the new operating system, he also convinced the computer giant to shed the veil of secrecy surrounding the specifications of its PC so that others could write software for the machine. The result was that licenses for MS-DOS quickly multiplied as software developers moved to make their products compatible with IBM.

Over two million copies of MS-DOS were sold by 1984. Because IBM's PC architecture was opened up by Gates, MS-DOS and its related applications can run on almost any IBM-compatible PC (commonly referred to as IBM clones). By the early 1990s Microsoft had sold more than 100 million copies of MS-DOS, making the operating system the all-time leader in software sales. For his achievements in science and technology, Gates was presented the Howard Vollum Award in 1984 by Reed College in Portland, Oregon.

Creates Windows

Gates next focused on the area dominated by the Apple Corporation's popular Macintosh computers. Apple founder **Steven Jobs** (see entry) took a different approach to computer operations. Instead of having the PC user type in special coded commands (as required on IBM-type systems), Macintosh screens have easy-to-use pictures (called icons) that can be selected to give the commands; the icon then opens a "window" on the screen. This system proved very popular, especially among those who had little or no experience with computers. Apple computers quickly became known for being "user friendly." In 1985, when Gates introduced Windows, his own version of so-called "user-friendly" software for the PC, it also became popular.

Promotes CD-ROM

In 1987 Gates entered the world of computer-driven multimedia when he began promoting CD-ROM (compact disc read-only memory) technology. With a high capacity for picture storage and easy connection to a PC, a CD-ROM disc can contain encyclopedias, feature films, and complex interactive games. Hoping to expand his business by combining PCs with the information reservoirs provided by CD-ROM, Gates was soon marketing a number of multimedia products.

Gates's competitive drive and fierce desire to win has made him a powerful force in business, but it has also consumed much of his personal life. For instance, during the six years between 1978 and 1984, he reportedly took a total of only two weeks' vacation. In 1985 a popular magazine included him on a list of most eligible bachelors. His status did not change until New Year's Day 1994, when he married Melinda French, a Microsoft manager, on the Hawaiian island of Lanai. A daughter would be born in April 1996. Gates's fortune at the time of the wedding was estimated at close to $7 billion. Gates and his wife are building a uniquely designed home near Seattle. Constructed partly underground, the house will feature wall-size, high-resolution computer screens throughout.

Introduces new projects

In a highly publicized international advertising campaign in August 1995, Gates introduced Windows 95, a new operating-system software for personal computers. Two months later he announced that he had purchased the Bettmann Archive, a collection of seventeen million photographs and other images. Gates is developing a software program that will combine the archive with digitized artworks from several prominent museums for use on home computers. Gates also published *The Road Ahead,* a book in which he discusses the Information Superhighway (a continually developing interconnection of computers with seemingly limitless potential for global communication), the future of the computer industry, and the impact of technology on our lives.

Further Reading

"Bill Gates's Carnival," *New York Times,* August 26, 1995, p. 18.

Business Week, February 24, 1992; March 1, 1993.

Gates, Bill, with Nathan Myhrvold and Peter Rinearson, *The Road Ahead,* Viking, 1995.

Ichbiah, David, and Susan L. Knepper, *The Making of Microsoft,* Prima, 1991.

Manes, Stephen, and Paul Andrews, *Gates,* Doubleday, 1993.

Newsweek, November 30, 1992; November 27, 1995, pp. 54–74.

New Yorker, January 10, 1994, pp. 48–61.

New York Times, January 3, 1994.

Rothstein, Edward, "Bill Gates Is Imitating Art," *New York Times,* October 15, 1995.

Wallace, James, and Jim Erickson, *Hard Drive,* Wiley, 1992.

Karl Friedrich Gauss

Born April 30, 1777
Brunswick, Germany
Died February 23, 1855
Göttingen, Germany

A true child prodigy, Karl Friedrich Gauss was as eccentric as he was brilliant. Although he is known primarily for his work in mathematics, he also made contributions in physics, astronomy, and magnetism. He devised the statistical method of least squares and calculated the orbit of the asteroid Ceres, enabling astronomers to rediscover it after it had been lost. Later his theories of perturbations between the planets led to the discovery of the planet Neptune. Working in the field of geometry, Gauss constructed an equilateral polygon of seventeen sides and established a non-Euclidean geometry. He was hailed by his contemporaries as one of the greatest mathematicians who ever lived.

Makes important discoveries as a teenager

Gauss was born into an extremely poor family in Brunswick, Germany, on April 30, 1777. He amazed his par-

German mathematician Karl Friedrich Gauss is best known for his important achievements in physics, astronomy, and magnetism.

When Karl Friedrich Gauss demonstrated that only polygons with certain numbers of sides could be constructed with a ruler and compass, he showed that some mathematical constructions were impossible. This discovery ultimately led to the important work of the twentieth-century Austrian-born American mathematician Kurt Gödel, who argued that proof must often be found outside systems based on logic. Gödel's work in turn had an impact on the current theory of artificial intelligence (the capability of a machine to imitate intelligent human behavior).

ents by learning to add numbers and make calculations before he was able to talk. By the age of three he was correcting his father's addition, and he even taught himself to read. When Gauss was fourteen years old he received a stipend from Duke Ferdinand of Brunswick to study science. He eventually entered the University of Göttingen in 1795, obtaining his doctorate degree in 1799.

While Gauss was still in his teens he made numerous mathematical discoveries. He advanced the work of French mathematician Adrien-Marie Legendre by working out the method of least squares. (The method of least squares involves fitting a curve to a set of points representing statistical data in such a way that the sum of the squares of the distances of the points from the curve is a minimum.) Moving beyond the work of the ancient Greeks in geometry, in 1796 Gauss showed how to construct a polygon (closed plane figure made up of straight lines) with seventeen sides of equal length by using just a ruler and compass. In addition, he demonstrated that only polygons with certain numbers of sides could be constructed with those two tools. This discovery, which meant that some mathematical constructions were impossible, would have a profound impact on modern mathematical theory.

Becomes one of world's greatest mathematicians

In 1801, at the age of only twenty-four, Gauss calculated an orbit for Ceres, the first known asteroid (one of the very small planets whose orbit is located between Mars and Jupiter). Found and named by Italian astronomer Giuseppe Piazzi that same year, Ceres was lost as it passed behind the Sun. When the asteroid was recovered exactly where Gauss predicted it would be, his remarkable calculation established his reputation. Gauss also calculated theories of perturbations between the larger planets. (A perturbation is a disturbance of the regular elliptical motion of a celestial body, produced by an outside force.) His theories led to the independent location of the planet Neptune in 1845 by English astronomer John Couch Adams and French astronomer Jean Urbain Leverrier. Neptune was discovered and named by German astronomer Johann Gottfried Galle in 1846.

Eventually, Gauss came to be recognized as one of the greatest mathematicians of all time. He went on to work out a non-Euclidean geometry that was based on axioms different from those of Euclid (see box), the ancient Greek mathematician whose work served as the foundation for geometry until the nineteenth century. Unfortunately, Gauss tended to keep some of the results of his work secret for a while, and two other mathematicians received credit for the discovery by publishing their findings first. In 1799 Gauss proved that every algebraic equation has a root of the form $a + bi$, which is one of the fundamental theorems of algebra.

Invents heliotrope

In 1807 Gauss was appointed director of the Göttingen Observatory, a position he held for the rest of his life. During his work at the observatory he became interested in geodesy, the branch of applied mathematics concerned with measuring and surveying large areas of Earth. Geodesy was necessary to pinpoint the exact location of the observatory and led him to create a new, improved method of surveying. In 1821 he invented a device called the heliotrope, an instrument that could reflect sunlight over long distances. With the heliotrope parallel rays of light could be used to mark straight lines on the curved Earth, allowing for precise trigonometric calculations. Next Gauss became involved in magnetism and established the first observatory to specialize in that field. Working with colleague Wilhelm Weber, Gauss began making a worldwide magnetic survey, the results of which allowed the accurate determination of Earth's magnetic poles.

Euclid, Greek Mathematician

Karl Friedrich Gauss's work was significantly influenced by the scholarship of Euclid, the ancient Greek mathematician who flourished in the fourth century B.C. Euclid studied and analyzed the entire body of mathematical knowledge that had accumulated in the world up to his time. He synthesized the results and compiled them in a treatise titled *The Elements*. The work is divided into thirteen smaller books on such subjects as plane geometry, number theory, irrational numbers, and solid geometry. The theorems and axioms of *The Elements* are arrived at through rigorous logic devoid of any unnecessary reasoning. The clear and concise style of the treatise became the world standard for scientific discourse over the next two thousand years. Euclid is probably best remembered as the principal codifier of plane (flat) geometry, or what became known as Euclidian geometry. The principles of Euclidian geometry were presented so powerfully that for thousands of years people assumed that the workings of the entire universe could be attributed to them.

Works on telegraph device

Gauss and Weber then moved from magnetism to experiments in electromagnetism (the study of electric and magnetic fields, and their interaction with electric charges and currents). Using magnetic induction, which was discovered by **Michael Faraday** (see entry) in 1831, they invented a telegraph. Their version differed from the device developed by American physicist Joseph Henry, who was in the process of inventing his own telegraph at the same time. Henry's receiver used a metal arm that clicked up and down; Gauss's version consisted of a large coil positioned over a magnet to create the current that deflected (turned aside) a magnetic needle at the receiver.

Attempting to test their device, in 1833 Gauss and Weber ran a telegraph wire across the city of Göttingen from their physics laboratory to the observatory. They were forced to abandon their project, however, when they were unable to gain support for additional development. Ironically, in 1837 Charles Wheatstone patented his telegraph in England, and in 1840 Samuel Morse received a patent in the United States.

Metric unit and asteroid named for him

After 1840 Gauss's scientific work slowly began to decline. On February 23, 1855, he died at Göttingen. Gauss has been honored twice by the scientific community. The standard unit of magnetic influence was named the *gauss,* although it has since been replaced in the metric system with the *tesla* in honor of another eccentric genius, **Nikola Tesla** (see entry). A more lasting tribute remains in asteroid number 1001, which is known as Gaussia.

Further Reading

Burke, James, "Show Time!" *Scientific American,* February 1996, p. 132.

Helene D. Gayle

Born August 16, 1955
Buffalo, New York

"I don't regret having placed a high priority on a career that enables me to make a contribution to mankind."

H elene D. Gayle is a noted epidemiologist, one who studies the distribution, causes, and potential control measures of disease in a given population. She specializes in the epidemiology of acquired immunodeficiency syndrome (AIDS) and the human immunodeficiency virus (HIV) in children and teenagers. As coordinator of the AIDS Agency and chief of the HIV/AIDS Division at the U.S. Agency for International Development in the early 1990s, Gayle traveled to Africa and Asia to investigate the ways AIDS affects different societies and to help coordinate international efforts to study the disease. In September 1995 Gayle was chosen to head the newly created Centers for Disease Control and Prevention's office for the prevention of AIDS and other sexually transmitted diseases.

Influenced by parents' commitment

Helene Doris Gayle was born on August 16, 1955, in Buffalo, New York, the third of five children of Jacob Gayle

Sr., an entrepreneur, and Marietta Gayle, a psychiatric social worker. From an early age Gayle was influenced by her parents, who impressed upon their children the importance of working for the betterment of the world. Also moved by the civil rights movement as she was growing up during the 1960s, Gayle served as head of the black student union in her high school.

Studies medicine

Gayle received a bachelor of arts degree in psychology in 1976 from Barnard College in New York City, then in 1981 she earned a medical degree from the University of Pennsylvania in Philadelphia. She told Renee D. Turner in an *Ebony* magazine profile that medical school opened the door to the "social and political aspects of medicine." Having heard a noted researcher speak on the pioneering efforts to eradicate (wipe out) the deadly smallpox virus throughout the world, Gayle decided to seek a master's degree in public health at Johns Hopkins University in Baltimore, Maryland. Upon graduating that same year she began an internship and residency in pediatrics (the study of childhood diseases) at Children's Hospital Medical Center in Washington, D.C., where she worked for three years.

Specializes in AIDS

In 1984 Gayle was accepted into the epidemiology training program at the Centers for Disease Control and Prevention (CDC) in Atlanta, Georgia. During her training she focused on the alarming spread of the AIDS virus. (The disease was first recognized in 1981.) Gayle held various positions at the CDC, concentrating her efforts on the effects of AIDS on American

≹IMPACT≸

As former coordinator of the AIDS Agency and chief of the HIV/AIDS Division at the U.S. Agency for International Development, and as director of the Centers for Disease Control and Prevention's office for the prevention of AIDS and other sexually transmitted diseases, Helene D. Gayle has made a great impact on AIDS awareness worldwide. In her posts she has studied how different societies are affected by AIDS as well as the risk factors that contribute to the transmission of HIV/AIDS. She has written numerous articles on such topics as mother-to-child transmission of HIV and the prevalence of HIV among university students.

A model of the HIV virus.

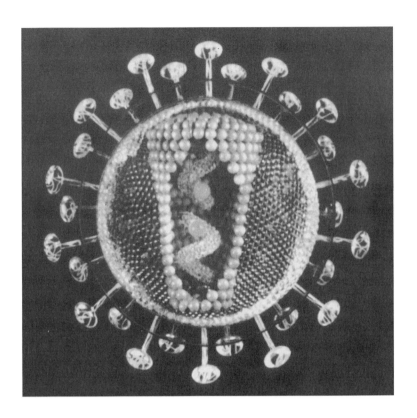

children, adolescents, and their families, then expanding her studies worldwide. (Recent statistics show that 90 percent of HIV-infected people live in developing [third world] countries.) She discovered that the African American community, especially its women, is at particularly high risk of contracting the fatal disease. The CDC estimated that in the mid-1990s, 1 in 98 African American women aged twenty-seven to thirty-nine were infected with HIV.

Promotes AIDS education

An advocate of education as an important tool in the prevention of HIV/AIDS, Gayle feels that learning more about the spread of the disease will also help combat it. In her position with the HIV/AIDS Division at the U.S. Agency for International Development, she traveled extensively, studying the risk factors that contribute to the transmission of HIV/AIDS. In September 1995 Secretary of Health and Human Services

Signs of Hope in the AIDS Battle

After the discovery of the AIDS virus in 1981, medical researchers and pharmaceutical companies sought to develop drugs to combat the disease. In 1987 the U.S. Food and Drug Administration approved the use of azidothymidine (AZT) as an AIDS treatment. (See **Anthony S. Fauci** entry.) AZT prevents the action of an enzyme known as reverse transcriptase that the AIDS virus uses to transform its genetic code so it can be readily accepted into an infected cell. As the AIDS virus reproduces in the body, however, it often mutates (changes) into forms that are resistant to reverse transcriptase inhibitors like AZT.

By the mid-1990s researchers had developed new drugs to overcome this problem. Called protease inhibitors, these new drugs prevent the work of protease, an enzyme that AIDS uses in a later stage of its reproduction cycle. Used in combination with older drugs like AZT, protease inhibitors reduce the amount of AIDS virus in a patient's blood. While not a cure, the new and old drugs together give people infected with the AIDS virus a chance to survive longer.

Donna Shalala appointed Gayle director of the Centers for Disease Control and Prevention's office for the prevention of AIDS and other sexually transmitted diseases, as well as tuberculosis.

The author of many articles and studies on HIV/AIDS risk factors, Gayle has received numerous awards, including the Henrietta and Jacob Lowenburg Prize, the Joel Gordon Miller Award, and the U.S. Public Health Service achievement medal. She has taught at various universities and is on the editorial board of the *Annual Review of Public Health.*

Further Reading

Black Enterprise, October 1988.

New England Journal of Medicine, November 29, 1990.

New York Times, July 5, 1996, pp. A1, C6; July 7, 1996, pp. A1, A6.

Turner, Renee D., "The Global AIDS Warrior," *Ebony,* November 1991.

Margaret Geller

Born December 8, 1947
Ithaca, New York

"There is something fundamentally missing from our understanding of the way things work."

Margaret Geller is an astronomer who helped discover a system of thousands of galaxies in space known as the Great Wall. This structure, the largest ever seen in the universe, stretches at least 500 million light-years. The existence of such a phenomenon has caused some scientists to question existing theories of the early universe.

Wide range of experience as an astronomer

Margaret Joan Geller was born in Ithaca, New York, on December 8, 1947, to Seymour and Sarah Levine Geller. After receiving a bachelor's degree from the University of California at Berkeley in 1970, she spent three years as a National Science Foundation fellow. She earned a master's degree in 1972 and a doctorate in 1975, both from New Jersey's prestigious Princeton University. After a six-year stint at the Harvard-Smithsonian Center for Astrophysics, she served as an assistant professor at Harvard University from 1980 to 1983. Geller became an astrophysicist with the Smithsonian Astrophysical Observatory in 1983 and a full professor of astronomy at Harvard in 1988.

Maps galaxies

Since 1980 Geller has collaborated with astronomer John P. Huchra on a large-scale survey of galaxies. Cosmologists (scientists who study the origin and nature of the universe) have long predicted that galaxies are uniformly distributed in space, despite recent evidence of irregularities. Geller and Huchra hypothesized that a three-dimensional mapping of galaxies — targeted beyond a certain brightness on the visible light spectrum and over a large enough distance (500 million light-years) — would confirm the predictions of uniformity. A light-year is the distance light travels in a vacuum in one real year — 365 days, 6 hours, 9 minutes, 4.1 seconds — or about 6 trillion miles.

The visible light spectrum consists of electromagnetic radiation (light) that appears to the human eye as different colors. Shorter wavelengths form the blue end of the spectrum, and longer wavelengths form the red end. Geller and Huchra used redshifts — or shifts toward the red end of the visible light spectrum — to measure the distance of galaxies. A redshift is caused by an increase in the wavelength of an object, usually because the object (or wave source) is moving farther away from the observer. Astronomers usually determine a redshift ratio by comparing the distance between the wavelength of a specific line on the spectrum made by a star or galaxy and the laboratory wavelength of the line. In some cases, however, the redshift is calculated by determining the ratio between the speed at which an object is moving away and the speed of light.

IMPACT

Margaret Geller's discovery of the Great Wall, a structure composed of thousands of galaxies across the universe, was a significant advancement in the field of astronomy. Research and discourse on the Great Wall have prompted astronomers to question existing astronomical ideas, such as the theory of the big bang and concepts about how the universe works.

Discovers Great Wall

In January 1986 Geller and Huchra published their first results. Instead of the expected galactic distribution, their "slice" of the cosmos (135 degrees wide by 6 degrees thick) showed sheets of galaxies appearing to line the walls of bubble-like spaces. The two scientists called this system of thousands of galaxies arranged across the universe the Great Wall. They could not determine the full width of the wall, which contains about five times the average density of galaxies, because it fell off the edges of their survey map.

Large structures like the Great Wall pose a problem for astronomers. They seem too large to have formed as a result of gravitational pull exerted since the "big bang" (the theory that the universe resulted from a cosmic explosion and then expanded over time), unless a significant amount of "clumpiness" were present at the origin of the cosmos.

The "clumpiness" theory is contradicted, though, by the smoothness of the cosmic microwave background, or "echo" of the big bang. An alternative explanation of the Great Wall's origin is that it is made up of dark matter—invisible particles left over from the big bang. These particles are believed to constitute about 90 percent of the mass of the universe. But even dark matter may not be capable of producing so large an object as the Great Wall. Between January 1986 and November 1989, Geller and Huchra published four maps, and in each they found the same line of galaxies. Their survey will eventually plot about fifteen thousand galaxies.

Receives "genius award"

In 1990 Geller won a MacArthur fellowship, also known as a "genius award," for her research. That same year she received the Newcomb-Cleveland Prize of the American Academy of Arts and Sciences. In addition to galactic distribution, Geller is interested in the origin and evolution of galaxies and the burgeoning field of X-ray astronomy (the satellite-aided study of electromagnetic radiation from cosmic sources). She is a member of the International Astronomical Union, the American Astronomical Society, and the American Association for the Advancement of Science.

Further Reading

Bartusiak, Marcia, "Mapping the Universe," *Discover,* August 1990, pp. 60–63.

Powell, Corey S., "Up Against the Wall," *Scientific American,* February 1990, pp. 18–19.

Margaret Geller

Walter Gilbert

Born March 21, 1932
Cambridge, Massachusetts

Walter Gilbert is a molecular biologist who shared the 1980 Nobel Prize in chemistry for his discovery of how to sequence deoxyribonucleic acid (DNA) molecules, which contain the genetic blueprint for cells. Gilbert also identified repressor molecules, which modify or repress the activity of certain genes, and collaborated with Nobel laureate James D. Watson in his efforts to isolate messenger ribonucleic acid (mRNA). Later in his career Gilbert helped form the biotechnology firm Biogen, serving as its chief executive officer. He became a moving force in the medical research undertaking known as the human genome project.

Studies physics on his own

Walter Gilbert was born in Cambridge, Massachusetts, on March 21, 1932. His father, Richard V. Gilbert, was an economist at Harvard University, and his mother, Emma Cohen Gilbert, was a child psychologist who provided her children's early education at home. In 1939 the family moved to Washington, D.C., where Gilbert initially performed poorly in school. He did, however, show considerable interest in science. Fascinated by astronomy, he ground his own glass for telescopes at the age of twelve. During his senior year at Sidwell Friends High School, he went regularly to the Library of Congress to expand his knowledge of nuclear physics (the study of the structure of atomic nuclei).

In 1949 Gilbert entered Harvard University with a major in chemistry and physics, earning his bachelor's degree with highest honors in 1953. He remained at Harvard for a master's degree in physics, which he received the following year. Gilbert went on to Cambridge University in England for doctoral work in theoretical physics, studying under the physicist **Abdus Salam** (see entry). After receiving his Ph.D. in mathematics in 1957, Gilbert returned to Harvard on a National Science postdoctoral fellowship in physics. He was appointed assistant professor in 1959.

Moves on to study molecular biology

While at Cambridge University, Gilbert met biologists **James D. Watson** and **Francis Crick** (see entries). Only a few years earlier they had established the structure of DNA and constructed a three-dimensional model of the molecule. Their work launched a new field of science called molecular biology. When Watson moved to Harvard in 1960 and met Gilbert again, he told Gilbert about his interest in isolating messenger RNA (mRNA). This is the substance believed to be responsible for transmitting information from DNA to ribosomes (the cellular structures in which protein synthesis takes place).

Gilbert accepted Watson's invitation to work on this project. Their collaboration prompted Gilbert's move into molecular biology, where he felt he had a future. Making up for a lack of formal training in biochemistry through hard work, Gilbert was publishing articles on molecular biology within a few years. He was appointed tenured associate professor of biophysics at Harvard in 1964, then advanced to full professor of biochemistry four years later. In 1972 Harvard named him the American Cancer Society Professor of Molecular Biology.

In the mid-1960s Gilbert had begun research on how genes are activated within cells. This was a question that had been introduced by the French geneticists François Jacob and Jacques Lucien Monod. Since DNA should in theory encode proteins with genetic information continually, they wondered what made some cells specialize in certain functions. If cells contain an element that in effect represses some genes, this would partially explain how cells perform different functions even though each cell contains the same set of genetic instructions. Gilbert decided to determine whether actual "repressor" substances exist within each cell.

Finds lac repressor

Working with the *Escherichia coli* (*E. coli*) bacterium, Gilbert attempted to find what he called the lac repressor. *E. coli* manufactures the enzyme betagalactosidase when the milk sugar lactose is present. Gilbert hypothesized that the gene responsible for producing the enzyme was repressed by a substance that would detach itself from the DNA molecule only in the presence of lactose. If this hypothesis could be proven, it would confirm the existence of repressors. In 1966 Gilbert and his colleagues added radioactive lactose-like molecules to a concentration of *E. coli* as a means of tracing any potential lac repressor activity. As he had hoped, the lac repressor detached itself from the bacteria's DNA in the presence of lactose-like radioactive material, thereby setting the enzyme production process into motion. By 1970 Gilbert was able to determine the precise region of DNA (called the lac operator) to which the repressor bonds in the absence of lactose.

Discovers DNA sequencing

The next phase of Gilbert's research focused on sequencing DNA; his aim was to identify and describe chemically any strand of DNA. Working with graduate student Allan Maxam, he began to sequence parts of a DNA strand. It was already known that the molecules could be "broken" at specific chemical junctures by using certain chemical substances. A colleague introduced Gilbert and Maxam to a procedure that broke DNA molecules into fragments that were easier to describe. After breaking radioactively labeled DNA into fragments, Gilbert and Maxam worked to separate them further. They used a technique known as gel electrophoresis, in which an electric current causes the fragments to pass through a gel substance. Upon exposure to X-ray film, the fragments can be read and the chemical code of DNA can be identified. Working independently, the British scientist Frederick Sanger (see box) developed a similar sequencing technique. In recognition of both their contributions, Gilbert and Sanger were awarded half the 1980 Nobel Prize in chemistry. The other half went to the American biochemist **Paul Berg** (see entry) for his work with recombinant DNA, more commonly referred to as "gene splicing."

Embarks on business venture

With the breakthroughs being made by Gilbert, Sanger, Berg, and others, the concept of applying technological principles to biology—biotechnology—was established in the 1970s. The idea of being able to alter the genetic composition of a cell opened up such possibilities as curing or even eradicating many diseases. The potential of biotechnology intrigued not only scientists but also the business community. Here was a concept that could be both revolutionary and lucrative—a company that held the patent to a definitive cure for cancer, for example, could become a gold mine.

IMPACT

In late 1990 Walter Gilbert and other members of the biomedical community began work on a ten- to twenty-year government-financed program to map the entire genetic structure of humans. Called the human genome project, this task involves work on 100,000 genes. By 1992 scientists had plotted geographic locations on the chromosomes of about 4,000 human genes. The goal is not only to pinpoint the remaining genes but also to decode the biochemical information down to the so-called "letters" of inheritance. The letters represent the four basic constituents of all genes, called nucleotides: A (adenine), C (cytosine), G (guanine), and T (thymine). These nucleotides are linked in sequential pairs in the double helix (spiral) of DNA; a total of three billion pairs are involved in the process, but only thirty-five million have been deciphered. Gilbert, who heads the project, sees it as a way to accelerate medical research.

Business leaders approached scientists, Gilbert among them, with proposals. Most scientists were skeptical at first, but in 1978 Gilbert met with a group of venture capitalists who wanted to start a biotechnology firm. After receiving assurances that they would have considerable control over research and development, he and other scientists formed Biogen N.V., with Gilbert as the chairman of the scientific board of directors. Gilbert was so convinced of the potential of Biogen that he left Harvard in 1981 to become the company's chief executive officer.

Despite widespread belief in the company's potential, Biogen had a difficult beginning. After four years it was still unprofitable, and Gilbert became increasingly disillusioned with the business. He found the differences between the business world and the scientific community difficult to handle. The science of creating new products is significantly different from the business of bringing them to market. Scientists need to be patient because their breakthroughs might take years to achieve, but sound business practice dictates cutting one's losses when a project fails to produce after a reasonable time.

These clashing concerns—sound research versus profit —led to conflicts within Biogen. Gilbert also found the running of a company to be time-consuming and expensive (although he personally profited from the venture). In late 1984 he resigned his position at Biogen, while maintaining some involvement with the firm. The next year he was named H. H. Timken Professor of Science in the cellular and developmental biology department at Harvard. He later became chairman of the department and Carl M. Loeb University Professor.

Starts human genome project

Freed from the responsibilities of running a business, Gilbert returned to his research. But he soon became interested in an undertaking that was even bigger than Biogen: the human genome project. This project would unravel the biochemical makeup of the entire genetic material, or genome, of a human being, providing extraordinary insights into human

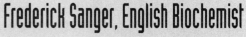

Frederick Sanger, English Biochemist

Frederick Sanger (1918–) was awarded two Nobel Prizes for his groundbreaking work in biochemistry. In 1958 he was honored for determining the arrangement of the amino acids that make up insulin, becoming the first person to identify a protein molecule. In 1980 he shared the award with Walter Gilbert and **Paul Berg** (see entry) for determining the sequences of nucleic acids in deoxyribonucleic acid (DNA) molecules. Sanger's contribution was the invention of a new sequencing technique in which a single-strand DNA molecule is allowed to replicate itself but is stopped at various stages of replication. Depending on the chemical used to stop replication, the researcher can then determine the nucleotide present at the end of the molecule. Repeated applications of this process allowed Sanger to reconstruct the sequence of nucleotides present in a DNA molecule.

biology. The plan was to create a map or library of human DNA. Such information would help researchers find cures for diseases and identify potentially harmful gene mutations.

Gilbert enthusiastically promoted the genome project and, along with many others, he encouraged the U.S. Congress to support it with federal funds. Then, frustrated by the political process and believing that the project would be damaged by the bureaucracy imposed by federal participation, he tried a different approach. In 1987 he announced plans to create his own company, Genome Corporation, which would sequence DNA, copyright the information, and sell it. Although he failed to obtain adequate backing for that project, in late 1990 he did win a $2 million annual grant from the U.S. government to conduct his work at Harvard under the auspices, or support, of the National Institutes of Health.

Sees benefits of gene mapping

In a 1992 interview with *Omni* magazine, Gilbert explained what he sees as some of the benefits of a complete genetic map of the human being: "The differences between people are what the genetic map [is] about. That knowledge will yield medicine tailored to the individual. One will first identify obvious genetic defects like cystic fibrosis. The next round of genetic mapping will show us clusters of genes for common diseases from arthritis to schizophrenia. We will be able to predict the side effects of those drugs and tailor the right dose to each person." Gilbert has estimated that the project would take at least ten to twenty years to complete.

In addition to the Nobel Prize, Gilbert shared with Sanger the Albert Lasker Basic Medical Research Award in 1979. He also won the Louisa Horwitz Gross Prize from Columbia University in 1979 and the Herbert A. Sober Memorial Award of the American Society of Biological Chemists in 1980. His memberships include the American Academy of Arts and Sciences, the National Academy of Sciences, and the British Royal Society. Gilbert has been married to Celia Stone since 1953; the couple has a son and a daughter.

Further Reading

Current Biography, H. W. Wilson, 1992, pp. 13–16.

Dorit, Robert L., Lloyd Schoenbach, and Walter Gilbert, "How Big Is the Universe of Exons?" *Science,* December 7, 1990.

Gilbert, Walter, "Towards a Paradigm Shift in Biology," *Nature,* January 10, 1991, p. 92.

Hall, Stephen S., *Invisible Frontiers,* Atlantic Monthly Press, 1987.

Kanigel, Robert, "The Genome Project," *New York Times Magazine,* December 13, 1987, p. 44.

Liversidge, Anthony, "Interview: Walter Gilbert," *Omni,* November 1992, pp. 91–101.

Rennie, John, "Down for the Count," *Scientific American,* March 1991.

Roberts, Leslie, "Large-Scale Sequencing Trials Begin," *Science,* December 7, 1990.

"Towards a Paradigm Shift in Biology," *Nature,* January 10, 1991.

Robert H. Goddard

Born in 1882
Worcester, Massachusetts

Died in 1945
Annapolis, Maryland

Robert H. Goddard was a rocket science pioneer whose innovations were crucial to the development of the U.S. space program.

American physicist Robert H. Goddard almost singlehandedly created the field of rocket science. His research was crucial to the development of the U.S. space program and provided the American military with the technology to produce a new generation of extremely powerful and precise armaments (all the weapons of war).

Dreams of space travel

Robert Hutchings Goddard was born in Worcester, Massachusetts, in 1882. When he was still young, his family moved to Boston, where his father became part-owner of a machine shop. His mother suffered from tuberculosis, a debilitating lung disease that kept her bedridden much of the time. A thin and sickly child, Goddard missed so much school because of illness that he eventually fell years behind in his education. He spent his days alone at home playing with kites, slingshots, and rifles. Thus began a lifelong interest in flying projectiles, objects that are shot into the air by force.

In 1898 the Goddard family returned to rural Worcester. Around this time Goddard became a devoted fan of the science fiction genre after reading *War of the Worlds,* the classic tale by H. G. Wells about a Martian invasion of Earth. According to biographical accounts, Goddard became fascinated with the idea of space travel one day when he was well enough to do yard work. He reportedly climbed the cherry tree behind his house to trim it. Looking out into the meadow, he starting daydreaming about spaceships and the possibility of traveling to Mars. The feeling it gave him was so powerful that he never forgot the date—October 19, 1899.

Experiments with rockets

That same year Goddard entered Worcester South High School as a sophomore at the age of nineteen. He finished at the top of his class in 1904, being the oldest graduate in the history of the school at the age of twenty-two. A few months later he enrolled at Worcester Polytechnic, a small college where he studied physics. By his senior year Goddard was experimenting with rockets in the small basement laboratory at the college.

At that time the only rockets available were powder rockets, which were little more than fireworks. Goddard devoted himself to testing the amount of energy they released, eventually deciding that manned rockets would require a different source of propulsion (a force that causes forward motion). In 1908 he graduated from Worcester Polytechnic with a bachelor's degree in physics, then became a physics instructor at the college. He also embarked on graduate studies at nearby Clark University, where he met Arthur Gordon Webster, a professor with whom he would develop the background he needed for advanced rocket research. Goddard went on to earn a doctoral degree from Clark in 1911. After suffering a near-fatal case of tuberculosis, he returned to Clark two years later to teach part-time and to conduct research.

Develops rocket

For the next few years Goddard tried various ways to improve rocket design. He changed the shape of the exhaust nozzle to a tapered cone and used a more efficient explosive powder. In 1914 he applied for his first two patents, including a design for a two-stage rocket (a rocket that would fire once to begin motion and, later, fire again to keep moving or move faster). The patented designs, the first of their kind, featured combustion chambers suited for liquid propellants, demonstrating that Goddard was already thinking of liquid fuel.

Invents bazooka

When the United States entered World War I in 1917, Goddard wrote to the Smithsonian Institution about the possible military applications of the rocket. Convinced of Goddard's vision, the Smithsonian asked the U.S. Department of War to contribute up to $50,000 —a considerable sum of money at the time—toward his research. Soon Goddard had his own well-equipped laboratory and shop at Clark, with seven men working for him full time. By the time the shop was relocated to Pasadena, California, in the summer of 1918, Goddard's team had already developed two military rocket launchers.

The following November, at the Aberdeen Proving Ground in Maryland, Goddard demonstrated the launcher, which could propel a rocket through a hand-held tube. Intended as a portable weapon for foot soldiers, the rocket launcher amazed military observers, who requested immediate production. But the weapon in question—which was the first bazooka (a light weapon that launches armor-piercing rockets and is fired from the shoulder)—was never used in combat; World War I ended five days after the demonstration.

After the war Goddard returned to Clark to teach physics and continue his research on high-altitude rockets. Meanwhile,

Wernher von Braun, German-born American Rocket Engineer

A rocketry pioneer and an early promoter of space travel, Wernher von Braun (1912–1977) directed the teams that designed the V-2, Redstone, Jupiter, and Pershing military missiles. He was also a driving force in the development of the Juno and Saturn launch vehicles that carried most of the early National Aeronautic and Space Administration (NASA) satellites and spacecraft beyond Earth's atmosphere and ultimately to the Moon. Von Braun became both a celebrity and a national hero in the Unites States despite his World War II involvement with the German military.

Von Braun first worked as a scientist in his native Germany, where he reluctantly joined the German army ordnance department to develop liquid-fueled rockets in 1932. Four years later his staff completed the V-2 rocket, which would ultimately revolutionize rocket technology. The first fully operational V-2s were fired in 1944. By the end of World War II approximately six thousand rockets had been manufactured at an underground protection site named *Mittlewerk,* using the slave labor of concentration camp inmates and prisoners of war. Although several thousand V-2s struck London, England, and Antwerp, Belgium, as well as other Allied targets, they were not strategically significant in the German war effort. Their importance lies in the technological advances they brought to the development of rocketry. This fact and von Braun's later importance in the American spaceflight effort—he surrendered to the Americans in Bavaria in 1944 and worked for the U.S. government until the early 1970s—often overshadows the issues of his ethical responsibility for the suffering and loss of life associated with the V-2.

the Smithsonian had published his paper titled "A Method of Reaching Extreme Altitude," in which he suggested the feasibility of manned space travel. But his prediction was met with ridicule in the press and by the public—some called him the

| Robert H. Goddard

"Moon Man"—causing him to be more secretive about his theories in the future.

Builds liquid rocket

In the summer of 1924 Goddard married Esther Kisk. A secretary at Clark, she became his assistant, keeping notes and photographic records of his work for the rest of his life. On March 16, 1926, Goddard launched the world's first liquid propellant rocket, which traveled 184 feet in 2.5 seconds. Because of his previous negative experience with the press, he did not immediately announce his success, waiting several months to notify even the Smithsonian Institution of his achievement.

Receives support for testing

For the next three years Goddard experimented with rockets of different sizes and shapes. He also wrote several reports that elaborated on the principles of manned space flight and lunar exploration. Among those who read Goddard's articles was the wife of philanthropist Harry F. Guggenheim. She mentioned the pioneering scientist's work to her husband, who was a friend of the aviator Charles Lindbergh. Within days Lindbergh was dazzled with a tour of Goddard's laboratory. In 1930 the Guggenheims awarded Goddard a $50,000 grant, which enabled him to begin a full-scale rocket-testing program.

Starts rocket center

Goddard later moved his laboratory to Roswell, New Mexico, which became the world center of rocket science. Hundreds of tests were performed and forty-eight launches were attempted at the desert site. Meanwhile, the rockets grew progressively larger and more sophisticated, approaching twenty-two feet in length and weighing up to a quarter ton. Goddard also invented a gyroscopic system, which permitted a rocket to "correct" its flight path as it flew. By mid-1935 his prototypes were achieving unprecedented speeds and altitudes with gyroscopically controlled rockets. In March 1936 he reported his

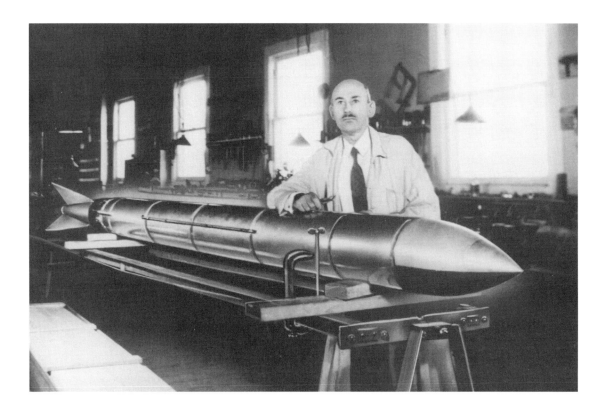

spectacular results in "Liquid-Propellant Rocket Development," which was published by the Smithsonian Institution.

Lacks military backing

In 1937 Goddard heard rumors that the Germans were working on secret military rockets. He had been frustrated by the refusal of the U.S. military to fund further research in rockets, which the navy had misguidedly dismissed as impractical and expensive. Toward the end of World War II Germany would in fact unleash its V-2 rockets on Europe; German engineers who developed the V-2 later openly credited Goddard as the source of their inspiration.

Goddard stayed at the New Mexico testing center until the United States entered the war. He then relocated to the Naval Engineering Experimental Station at Annapolis, Maryland, where he worked until dying of cancer in 1945.

Further Reading

Pursell, C., ed., *Technology in America: A History of Individuals and Ideas,* MIT Press, 1981.

Stoiko, Michael, *Pioneers of Rocketry,* Hawthorn Books, 1974.

Streissguth, Thomas, *Rocket Man: The Story of Robert Goddard,* Carolrhoda Books, 1995.

Yost, Edna, *Modern Americans in Science and Technology,* Dodd, Mead, 1962.

Maria Goeppert-Mayer

*Born July 28, 1906
Kattowitz, Germany
(now Katowice, Poland)
Died February 20, 1972
San Diego, California*

Maria Goeppert-Mayer was a groundbreaking German-born American physicist. She is remembered for her work on the Manhattan Project—a secret operation sponsored by the U.S. government to develop the first nuclear weapons during World War II—though she later renounced her involvement in the project. Through her work with nuclear physicists **Enrico Fermi** (see entry) and Edward Teller, Goeppert-Mayer developed a model for the structure of atomic nuclei. In 1963 she became the first woman awarded the Nobel Prize for theoretical physics, sharing the honor with German physicist J. Hans D. Jensen. Because of her likening of the structure of the atom to the layers of an onion, Goeppert-Mayer was nicknamed "Madonna of the Onion."

Codeveloper of the atomic fission bomb, Maria Goeppert-Mayer was the first woman to be awarded the Nobel Prize for theoretical physics.

Passes university entrance exam

An only child, Goeppert-Mayer was born Maria Gertrude Göppert on July 28, 1906, in the German city of Kattowitz in

399

Upper Silesia (now Katowice, Poland). Her mother, Maria Wolff Göppert, was a former teacher of piano and French. Her father, Dr. Friedrich Göppert, was professor of pediatrics at the University at Göttingen in Germany. Goeppert-Mayer idolized her father and treasured her long country walks with him, collecting fossils and learning the names of plants.

When Goeppert-Mayer was eight, World War I interrupted her family's idyllic life with harsh wartime deprivation. She attended a small private school run by female suffragists (activists who supported women's voting rights) to prepare young girls for university studies. When the school went bankrupt, she had completed only two of the customary three years of preparatory school. Nonetheless, she took and passed her university entrance exam.

Embarks on a rigorous course of study

Goeppert-Mayer entered the University of Göttingen in 1924; it was fast becoming the center for the study of quantum mechanics (the mathematical study of the behavior of atomic particles). Many well-known physicists visited the university, including **Niels Bohr** (see entry), a Danish physicist who developed a model of the atom. Noted physicist Max Born joined the Göttingen faculty and became a close friend of Goeppert-Mayer's family. Goeppert-Mayer began attending Born's physics seminars and decided to study physics instead of mathematics.

In 1927 Goeppert-Mayer's father died. Despite the loss she continued with her studies, determined to finish her doctorate in physics. She spent a semester in Cambridge, England, where she learned English and met **Ernest Rutherford** (see entry), the discoverer of the electron. Upon her return to Göttingen, her mother began taking student boarders into their home. One was an American physical chemistry student from California, Joseph E. Mayer, who was studying at Göttingen on a grant. Goeppert-Mayer married Mayer in 1930 and adopted a hyphenated form of their names. (When they later moved to the United States, the spelling of her family name was anglicized to "Goeppert.") Soon after the marriage, she completed her doctorate.

Immigrates to the United States

After Mayer finished his studies the young scientists moved to Baltimore, Maryland, where he had been offered a job at Johns Hopkins University. Stifled by the gender bias that was so prominent in the United States in the 1930s, Goeppert-Mayer found it difficult to adjust. Despite her impeccable credentials, she could work at Johns Hopkins only as a volunteer associate. Nonetheless, her position did allow her to conduct research on energy transfer on solid surfaces with physicist Karl Herzfeld. Later she turned her attention to the quantum mechanics (subatomic energy levels) of benzene (a highly flammable liquid hydrocarbon) and some dyes. During summers Goeppert-Mayer returned to Göttingen, where she wrote several papers with Born on beta ray decay (the emissions of high-speed electrons given off by radioactive nuclei).

These summers of physics research were cut short as Germany again prepared for war. After returning to the United States, Goeppert-Mayer met Edward Teller, a Hungarian refugee who would play a key role in the development of the hydrogen bomb. When Goeppert-Mayer's husband unexpectedly lost his position at Johns Hopkins, she went with him to Columbia University in New York City. There they collaborated on *Statistical Mechanics,* which became a classic text in the field.

Works on atom bomb

In New York Goeppert-Mayer made the acquaintance of Enrico Fermi, who had won the Nobel Prize in physics for his work on radioactivity. Fermi had recently migrated from Italy and was at Columbia on a grant researching nuclear fission. Nuclear fission (splitting an atom, thereby releasing energy) had been discovered by German scientists Otto Hahn, Fritz Strassmann, and **Lise Meitner** (see entry). They had bombarded uranium nuclei with neutrons, resulting in a break in the nuclei and an accompanying release of energy. Because Germany was building its arsenal for war, Fermi and other scientists urged the U.S. government to institute a nuclear program of its own to defend the Allies against Nazi leader Adolf Hitler. Goeppert-Mayer joined Fermi's team of researchers, although once again the arrangement was informal and without pay.

Becomes part of the Manhattan Project

In 1941 the United States entered World War II. Goeppert-Mayer was offered her first teaching job at Sarah Lawrence College in Bronxville, New York. A few months later she was invited by Harold Urey to join a research group he was assembling at Columbia University. The group's task was to separate uranium-235, which is capable of nuclear fission, from the more abundant isotope uranium-238, which is not. Working in secret, the group was given the code name SAM (Substitute Alloy Metals). The researchers were part of the Manhattan Project, which had been established by the U.S. government to develop a nuclear fission bomb.

Mixed feelings about the bomb

Like many scientists, Goeppert-Mayer had reservations about working on the development of an atomic bomb. (Her friend Born, for instance, had refused to work on the project.) To her relief the war in Europe ended early in 1945—before the bomb was ready. However, at Los Alamos Laboratory in New Mexico the atom bomb was still being developed. Teller invited Goeppert-Mayer to visit Los Alamos, but by that time she was no longer an active participant in the project. When the bombs were dropped on the Japanese cities of Hiroshima and Nagasaki in August 1945, Goeppert-Mayer's uncertainty about the nuclear weapons program had grown even stronger.

Nicknamed the "Madonna of the Onion"

In 1946 Goeppert-Mayer's husband took a job at the Institute of Nuclear Studies, established by the University of Chicago, where Fermi, Teller, and Urey were also working. She was again offered an unpaid post as a voluntary associate professor. Instead, she accepted a position as senior physicist at the nearby Argonne National Laboratory, where a nuclear reactor was under construction.

Teller asked Goeppert-Mayer to work on his theory of the origin of the elements. As she charted the number of protons and neutrons in various atomic nuclei, she noticed seven numbers—2, 8, 20, 28, 50, 82, and 126—appearing over and over again. Eventually Goeppert-Mayer called these her "magic numbers." Any element that had one of these numbers of protons or neutrons was very stable. She began to think of a shell model for the nucleus, similar to the orbital model of electrons spinning around the nucleus. Perhaps the nucleus of an atom was something like an onion, she thought, with layers of protons and neutrons revolving around each other. When Goeppert-Mayer made the comparison between the nucleus and an onion, Austrian-born American physicist Wolfgang Pauli nicknamed her the "Madonna of the Onion."

IMPACT

Maria Goeppert-Mayer won the 1963 Nobel Prize for her theory of nuclear shells. An atomic nucleus is composed of protons and neutrons, though not necessarily in equal numbers. Scientists had long known that certain isotopes (atoms of the same element with the same number of protons but different numbers of neutrons in the nucleus) appear to be unusually stable. These isotopes all had 2, 8, 20, 28, 50, 82, or 126 protons or neutrons, leading Goeppert-Mayer to develop the concept of "magic numbers" of subnuclear particles. She set forth a more sophisticated model of nuclear shells than had previously been available to physicists.

Receives Nobel Prize

Goeppert-Mayer published her "magic numbers" hypothesis in 1949. A month before her work appeared in print, a similar paper was published by Jensen in Germany. Goeppert-Mayer and Jensen began corresponding and eventually decided to collaborate on *Elementary Theory of Nuclear Shell Structure,* a book that soon gained widespread acceptance. In November 1963 Goeppert-Mayer received word that she and Jensen were to share the Nobel Prize for physics with Eugene Paul Wigner, a colleague studying quantum mechanics who had once been skeptical of her "magic numbers." After winning the Nobel Prize, Goeppert-Mayer was inducted into the National Academy of Sciences; she also received several honorary doctorates. In 1971 Goeppert-Mayer suffered a heart attack that left her comatose until her death on February 20, 1972.

Further Reading

Dash, Joan, *The Triumph of Discovery: Women Scientists Who Won the Nobel Prize,* Messner, 1991.

Opfell, Olga S., *The Lady Laureates: Women Who Have Won the Nobel Prize,* Scarecrow, 1978, pp. 194–208.

Sach, Robert G., *Maria Goeppert-Mayer, 1906–1972: A Biographical Memoir,* National Academy of Science of the United States, 1979.

Jane Goodall

Born April 3, 1934
London, England

Jane Goodall, an English ethologist (a specialist in animal behavior) and animal rights activist, is famous for her studies of the chimpanzees of the Gombe Stream Reserve in Tanzania, Africa. She is credited with the first recorded observation of chimps eating meat and using and making tools. As a result of her studies, Goodall concluded that chimpanzees are an advanced species closely related to humans. Her observations have forced scientists to redefine the characteristics once considered as solely human traits.

Goodall has also become an advocate for the ethical treatment of animals. In an effort to educate the public on the subject, she has appeared on American and British television and published five major works. Her first book, *In the Shadow of Man,* presents her observations of chimpanzees acting as an advanced species. *The Chimpanzee Family Book,* a 1989 publication written specifically for children, conveys a new, more humane view of wildlife. The book received the 1989 UNICEF/UNESCO Children's Book of the Year award.

"The more we learn of the true nature of non-human animals, especially those with complex brains and corresponding complex social behavior, the more ethical concerns are raised regarding their use in the service of man."

Jane Goodall's observations have provided convincing evidence for her assertion that chimpanzees are an advanced species. Scientists may agree with this assertion to a point, but they have been reluctant to view chimps as our distant cousins. Often they accuse scientists like Goodall of attempting to anthropomorphize (place human values and judgments upon) chimps. In the course of her research, Goodall became so emotionally attached to some of the chimps that scientists have questioned the validity and objectivity of her deductions. Despite this criticism Goodall maintains that chimpanzees are an extremely advanced—almost humanlike—species.

Reads about zoology and ethology

Goodall was born in London, England, on April 3, 1934, to Mortimer Herbert Goodall, a businessman and motor-racing enthusiast, and the former Margaret Myfanwe Joseph, who wrote novels under the name Vanne Morris Goodall. Along with her sister, Judy, Goodall was raised in London and Bournemouth, England. Her fascination with animals began in early childhood. In her free time she observed native birds and animals, keeping notes and sketches and reading many books about zoology (the scientific study of animals) and ethology (the scientific and objective study of animals under natural conditions). From an early age she dreamed of traveling to Africa to observe exotic animals in their natural habitats.

Meets Louis Leakey

Goodall attended the Uplands private school, receiving her school certificate in 1950 and a higher certificate in 1952. At age eighteen she left school to work as a secretary at England's Oxford University. In her spare time she worked at a documentary film company in London to finance a long-anticipated trip to Africa. Then she was invited by a childhood friend to visit South Kinangop, Kenya. Through other friends, she soon met the famed anthropologist **Louis S. B. Leakey** (see entry), then curator of the Coryndon Museum in Nairobi. Leakey hired her as a secretary and invited her to participate in an anthropological dig at the now famous Olduvai Gorge in Tanzania, a site rich in fossilized prehistoric remains of early ancestors of humans.

Leakey believed that a long-term study of the behavior of higher primates would provide important scientific information about evolution. He had a particular interest in the chimpanzee, which is generally said to be the second most intelligent primate. Few studies of chimpanzees had been successful; either the size of the safari frightened the chimps, causing them to act unnaturally, or the observers spent too little time in the field to gain comprehensive knowledge of their lifestyle. Leakey believed that Goodall had the proper temperament to endure long-term isolation in the wild. At his prompting, she agreed to attempt such a study. Many experts objected to Leakey's selection of Goodall because she had no formal scientific education and lacked even a college degree.

Observes first group of chimpanzees

While Leakey searched for financial support for the proposed Gombe Reserve project, Goodall returned to England to work on an animal documentary for Granada Television. On July 16, 1960, accompanied by her mother and an African cook, she returned to Africa and established a camp on the shore of Lake Tanganyika in the Gombe Stream Reserve. Her first attempts at close observation of a group of chimpanzees failed; she could not get any closer than five hundred yards before the chimps fled. After finding another suitable group of chimpanzees to follow, she established a nonthreatening pattern of observation, appearing at the same time every morning on the high ground near a feeding area along the Kakaombe Stream valley. The chimpanzees soon tolerated her presence and, within a year, allowed her to move as close as thirty feet to their feeding area. After two years of seeing her every day, they showed no fear and often came to her in search of bananas.

Starts the "banana club"

Goodall used her newfound acceptance to establish what she called the "banana club," a daily systematic feeding method she used to gain trust and to obtain a more thorough understanding of everyday chimpanzee behavior. Using this method, she became closely acquainted with more than half of the one hundred or more chimpanzees on the reserve. She imitated their behaviors, spent time in the trees, and ate their foods.

Dian Fossey, American Primatologist

American primatologist and wildlife conservation activist Dian Fossey (1932–1985) began her career in Africa with a visit to Jane Goodall in Tanzania to learn the best methods for studying primates. In 1967 Fossey established a camp, which she called the Karisoke Research Center, on the slopes of the Virunga Mountains in the tiny country of Rwanda. Fossey focused her studies on fifty-one gorillas in four families. Each group was dominated by a mature silverback, named for the characteristic gray hair on its back. Younger bachelor males served as guards for the silverback's harem and their juvenile offspring. One day in early 1970 Fossey made history when a gorilla she had named Peanuts reached out and touched her hand.

Throughout the nearly twenty years she spent studying mountain gorillas in central Africa, Fossey tenaciously fought poachers and bounty hunters who threatened to wipe out the endangered primates. She published an account of her struggle in her book *Gorillas in the Mist,* published in 1983. She was brutally murdered—many believe by a vengeful poacher—at her research center in 1985. Three years later *Gorillas in the Mist,* a film version of Fossey's story, was released.

By remaining in almost constant contact with the chimps, Goodall discovered a number of previously unobserved behaviors. She noted that chimps have a complex social system, complete with ritualized behaviors and primitive but discernible communication methods, including a "language" system containing more than twenty individual sounds. Goodall is credited with making the first recorded observations of chimpanzees eating meat and using and making tools. Prior to her discovery toolmaking was thought to be an exclusively human trait—one that distinguished man from animals.

Goodall also noted that chimpanzees throw stones as weapons, use touch and embraces to comfort one another, and develop long-term familial bonds. The male plays no active role in family life but is part of the group's social stratification. The chimpanzee "caste" system (social divisions) places the dominant males at the top. The lower castes often act subservient in their presence, trying to ingratiate themselves to avoid possible harm. The male's rank is often related to the intensity of his entrance performance at feedings and other gatherings.

Ethologists had long believed that chimps were exclusively vegetarian. Goodall witnessed chimps stalking, killing, and eating large insects, birds, and some larger animals, including baby baboons and bushbacks (small antelopes). On one occasion, she recorded acts of cannibalism. In another instance, she observed chimps inserting blades of grass or leaves into termite hills to lure worker or soldier termites onto the blade. Sometimes, in true toolmaker fashion, they modified the grass to achieve a better fit. Then they used the grass as a long-handled spoon to eat the termites.

Appears on television and writes books

In 1962 Baron Hugo van Lawick, a Dutch wildlife photographer, was sent to Africa by the National Geographic Society to film Goodall at work. The assignment ran longer than anticipated; Goodall and van Lawick were married on March 28, 1964. Their European honeymoon marked one of the rare occasions on which Goodall was absent from the Gombe Stream region. Her other trips abroad were necessary to finish her studies in Cambridge University, at Cambridge, England, where she received a Ph.D. in ethology in 1965. She was only the eighth person in the university's long history who received a doctorate without first earning a baccalaureate degree. Her doctoral thesis, "Behavior of the Free-Ranging Chimpanzee," detailed her first five years of study at the Gombe Reserve.

Delia Owens and Mark Owens, American Conservation Biologists

Inspired by the plight of endangered animals in Africa, American biologists Delia Owens (c. 1949–) and Mark Owens (c. 1944–) moved to Botswana in 1973 to study the habits of desert carnivores such as lions, hyenas, cheetahs, leopards, wild dogs, and jackals. They wrote a 1984 bestseller, *Cry of the Kalahari,* chronicling their work. After the Owenses were ousted from Botswana for their politically unpopular recommendations to protect the environment, they returned to the United States. But soon they launched another Africa project, rehabilitation of the North Luangwa Park in Zambia. Their second book, *The Eye of the Elephant: An Epic Adventure in the African Wilderness,* published in 1992, describes their attempts to eliminate poaching of endangered species, improve the Zambian economy, and publicize the benefits of wildlife conservation. The Owenses serve as roving contributing editors for *International Wildlife* magazine, and they and their work were the subject of a colorful National Geographic television special, *An African Odyssey,* which aired on PBS in 1988.

Van Lawick's film, *Miss Goodall and the Wild Chimpanzees,* was first broadcast on American television on December 22, 1965. The film introduced the shy, attractive, unimposing yet determined Goodall to a wide audience. Goodall, van Lawick (along with their son, Hugo, born in 1967), and the chimpanzees began to appear regularly on American and British public television. Through these programs, Goodall challenged scientists to redefine the long-held "differences" between humans and other primates.

Goodall's fieldwork led to the publication of numerous articles and five major books. She was known and respected first in the scientific world and then, through the media, became a minor celebrity. *In the Shadow of Man,* her first major text, appeared in 1971. The book, a field study of chimpanzees, blends elements of science and intrigue. Goodall's prose brings the chimps to life, although her tendency to make the animals seem like humans struck some critics as being manipulative. Her writings reveal an animal world that is very

Gombe Chimps on CD-ROM

Jane Goodall's Gombe chimps can now been viewed in action on CD-ROM. Gary Seaman, a professor of anthropology at the University of Southern California, is creating two hundred CD-ROMs that feature highly descriptive texts, maps, and other materials gleaned from Goodall's field research. Field biologists and anthropologists alike are enthusiastic about the project, and some are using the technique to even store observations of humans. They say the interactive computer discs will be an incomparable resource for students as well as researchers, who have long depended on note-taking, audio recordings, and somewhat subjective observations.

much like our world, where there are good times and bad, and where individuals interact and sometimes disagree.

Becomes an activist

From 1970 to 1975 Goodall held a visiting professorship in psychiatry at Stanford University. In 1973 she was appointed honorary visiting professor of zoology at the University of Dar es Salaam in Tanzania, a position she still holds. Until recently, Goodall's life has revolved around Gombe Stream. But after attending a 1986 conference in Chicago that focused on the ethical treatment of chimpanzees, she began directing her energies toward educating the public about the wild chimpanzee's endangered habitat and about the unethical treatment of chimpanzees that are used for scientific research.

To preserve the wild chimpanzee's environment, Goodall encourages African nations to develop nature-friendly tourism programs, a measure that calls attention to wildlife as a profitable resource. She actively works with business and local governments to promote ecological responsibility. Her efforts on behalf of captive chimpanzees have taken her around the world on a number of lecture tours.

Goodall outlined her positions strongly in her 1990 book *Through a Window:* "The more we learn of the true nature of

Jane Goodall with a curious chimpanzee at the Gombe Stream Reserve in Tanzania in 1972.

non-human animals, especially those with complex brains and corresponding complex social behavior, the more ethical concerns are raised regarding their use in the service of man—whether this be in entertainment, as 'pets,' for food, in research laboratories, or any of the other uses to which we subject them." Goodall contends that scientists must try harder to find alternatives to the use of animals in research. However, she has openly declared her opposition to militant animal rights groups who engage in violent or destructive demonstrations. Extremists on both sides of the issue, she believes, divide into factions (closed-minded groups) and make constructive dialogue nearly impossible. While she is reluctantly resigned to the continuation of animal research, she feels that young scientists must be educated to treat animals more compassionately. "By and large," she has written, "students are taught that it is ethically acceptable to perpetrate, in the name of science, what, from the point of view of animals, would certainly qualify as torture."

Receives numerous awards and honors

In recognition of her achievements, Goodall has received numerous honors and awards, including the Gold Medal of Conservation from the San Diego Zoological Society in 1974, the J. Paul Getty Wildlife Conservation Prize in 1984, the Schweitzer Medal of the Animal Welfare Institute in 1987, the National Geographic Society Centennial Award in 1988, and the Kyoto Prize in Basic Sciences in 1990. Many of Goodall's endeavors are conducted under the auspices of the Jane Goodall Institute for Wildlife Research, Education, and Conservation, a nonprofit organization located in Ridgefield, Connecticut.

Further Reading

Birmbaum, Bette, *Jane Goodall and the Wild Chimpanzees,* Raintree Publishers, 1989.

Brody, Jane E., "Gombe Chimps Archived on Video and CD-ROM," *New York Times,* February 20, 1996, p. B5.

Fromer, Julie, *Jane Goodall, Living With the Chimps,* Twenty-first Century Books, 1992.

Goodall, Jane, *The Chimpanzee Family Book,* Picture Studio Book, 1989.

Goodall, Jane, *Through a Window,* Houghton-Mifflin, 1990.

Montgomery, Sy, *Walking With the Great Apes: Jane Goodall, Dian Fossey, Biruté Galdikas,* Houghton Mifflin, 1991.

Senn, J. A., *Jane Goodall: Naturalist,* Blackbirch Press, 1994.

Stephen Jay Gould

Born September 10, 1941
New York, New York

Evolutionary biologist Stephen Jay Gould is a Harvard University professor of geology, biology, and the history of science. He is also a prolific writer of informative, entertaining books on scientific topics for the general reader. In the scientific community Gould is recognized as an international authority on the small, tropical Cerion snail and as a theorist of evolution. He has been awarded literary and academic honors, including a National Book Award and a MacArthur Prize.

"In my youth, I was very much into this macho idea of science as rigid, hard, quantifiable. Now I'm more interested in the beautiful and quirky contingencies that nature often takes."

Inspired by dinosaurs and evolutionary theory

Stephen Jay Gould was born on September 10, 1941, in New York City, the son of Leonard Gould and Eleanor (Rosenberg) Gould. He grew up in a lower-middle-class home in Queens, New York, with his younger brother Peter. Leonard Gould was a court stenographer in the Queens County Supreme Court and an amateur naturalist (a student of natural history). Stephen Gould recalls that during a trip with his father to the

415

American Museum of Natural History in Manhattan when he was five years old, he saw a reconstruction of the dinosaur *Tyrannosaurus rex* for the first time. That day he made the decision to devote his life to the study of geological periods.

At the age of eleven Gould read George Gaylord Simpson's book *Meaning of Evolution,* in which Simpson urged his fellow paleontologists (scientists who study fossils and ancient forms of life) to accept the theory of evolution by natural selection developed by **Charles Darwin** (see entry). According to Darwin's theory, only the organisms best suited to their environment tend to survive and pass on their genetic characteristics to their offspring. Over millions of years, species may change dramatically. Disappointed with the treatment of evolution in his biology textbooks when he was still in high school, Gould started reading Darwin.

Becomes paleontologist and teacher

After graduating from high school Gould attended the University of Colorado for the summer, then entered Antioch College in Yellow Springs, Ohio, where he received a bachelor's degree in 1963. Inspired by the fossil collection of an Antioch professor, Gould began an investigation of fossil land snails in Bermuda when he enrolled for his doctoral studies at Columbia University in New York City. In 1966 he returned to Antioch to teach geology (the science that studies the origin, history, and structure of the earth).

Having earned his Ph.D. in paleontology from Columbia in 1967, Gould left Antioch to become assistant professor of geology at Harvard University, where he advanced to associate professor in 1971 and to full professor in 1973. He also became curator of invertebrate paleontology at the Museum of Comparative Zoology at Harvard. While teaching biology and geology, he expanded his study of land snails to the West Indies and other parts of the world. His courses at Harvard became popular because of his lively and stimulating teaching style and enthusiasm for his subject.

Develops punctuated equilibrium theory

In the early 1970s Gould introduced his most noted contribution to evolutionary theory, the concept of punctuated equilibrium, which he developed with fellow paleontologist Niles Eldredge. The theory contradicts a central idea of Darwinian evolution commonly known as phyletic gradualism. According to Darwin's theory, adaptations (changes) in species are the result of a continuous, gradual process. Eldredge and Gould theorized that evolution is not quite so orderly as Darwin implied, but rather characterized by somewhat lengthy, stable periods that are punctuated (marked) by "moments" of massive change. During these periods of great change species evolve abruptly and new adaptations appear. Gould proposed that such unpredictable events alter the course of natural history.

Gould and Eldredge first published their theory in 1972 in a paper titled "Punctuated Equilibria: An Alternative to Phyletic Gradualism," which appeared in *Models in Paleobiology*. Gould developed the theory in subsequent papers, and his work was recognized in 1975 with the Schuchert Award, presented by the Paleontological Society for excellence in research by a paleontologist under the age of forty.

IMPACT

Stephen Jay Gould has a gift for making scientific information understandable to readers who are not scientists. Esteemed for his insightful analogies, Gould is a master of establishing connections between seemingly unrelated subjects and communicating the excitement of scientific discovery. Among his most popular books—some of which have been bestsellers—are *The Panda's Thumb* (1980), *Hen's Teeth and Horse's Toes* (1983), *The Flamingo's Smile* (1985), *Wonderful Life* (1989), and *Eight Little Piggies* (1993). In 1996 Gould published his seventh collection of essays, mostly from his *Natural History* monthly columns, titled *Dinosaur in a Haystack: Reflections in Natural History.*

Writes for educated nonscientists

In 1974 Gould began writing a monthly column titled "This View of Life" in the magazine *Natural History.* Addressing educated readers who are not themselves scientists, Gould clarified evolution in ordinary terms without simplifying concepts. "The problem is that in this country the notion of writing for the public got somehow [associated with]

Carl Sagan, American Physicist and Astronomer

Although some of his over-simplified explanations of complex scientific principles make his colleagues cringe, astronomer and physicist Carl Sagan (1934–) has popularized a number of areas of science, particularly astronomy. He is best known for his wildly popular television series *Cosmos*, which explained secrets of space to millions of nonscientists. Sagan published his first book intended for nonscientists, *The Cosmic Connection*, in 1973. The book was a great success, and Sagan was invited by television talk-show host Johnny Carson to appear on his program. Sagan impressed the audience and Carson (himself an astronomy buff) enough to be invited back many times. In the late 1970s Sagan began producing the thirteen-week television series *Cosmos*. It became one of the most popular broadcasts in PBS history, and Sagan later wrote the companion volume to the series. In 1978 he discussed the evolution of the human brain in *The Dragon of Eden*, which won a Pulitzer Prize, and seven years later he tried his hand at a novel, producing *Contact*, a fictional account of the search for extraterrestrial civilizations.

the notion of cheapening, simplifying, adulterating," Gould said in an interview in *Rolling Stone* magazine. "There's no reason why it should." In 1977 he published the first collection of his essays in book form under the title *Ever Since Darwin: Reflections in Natural History.*

Becomes popular writer

During the early 1980s Gould became an increasingly popular writer by making science accessible to general readers as well as scholars. His next book, *The Panda's Thumb,* won the 1981 American Book Award in science. In this work he concentrated on an oddity of nature: the peculiar, enlarged wrist bone of the panda, which functions as a thumb and enables the animal to strip leaves from bamboo shoots. Although the mutation in the wrist may have been minor, Gould asserts, the eventual result was a significant genetic change that transformed the panda from a meat-eating bear like others in its species to a primarily plant-eating animal.

The following year Gould's *The Mismeasure of Man* won the National Book Critics Circle Award for essays and criticism. The book features an explanation of the misuse of intelligence testing to assign value to human beings and to promote stereotyping and prejudice. Gould concedes that human intelligence can be located in a specific area of the brain and can even be measured by a standard number score. However, he argues against any efforts to label particular groups as being inferior or superior in intelligence because of brain structure. Gould regards this as a misuse of scientific data and a violation of the scientific process.

Appears as star witness

In 1981 Gould served as an expert witness in a trial in Little Rock, Arkansas, that challenged a state law mandating the teaching of "creation science" (the belief that a higher being created the earth) in conjunction with evolutionary theory. Arguing in favor of evolution, Gould questioned the literal interpretation of Biblical scriptures. For example, he discounted the view that Noah's flood (prompted by a rain of forty days and nights) could account for fossil remains found throughout the world. Gould argued that the theories of creation science are contradicted by all available scientific evidence and therefore do not deserve scientific status. As a result of Gould's testimony, the court recognized creationism as religion and not science. That same year, he received a grant—often referred to as the "genius" award—from the MacArthur Foundation, which annually recognizes the work of people who have made significant contributions in their fields.

Illness leads to a shift in interests

In 1982 Gould was diagnosed as having mesothelioma, a particularly deadly form of cancer. After recovering from the illness and the treatment, he continued his work with a renewed sense of urgency. Gould further explored the misuse of standardized testing to label social groups, which he had addressed in *The Mismeasure of Man.* He also began writing essays about an increasingly wide range of topics, including the black widow spider, the "Hottentot Venus" (an African woman who was caged and publicly displayed in nineteenth-century Europe), and the disappearance of .400 hitters in baseball. He won popular recognition for these essays, which were collected in *The Flamingo's Smile* in 1985.

Writes first bestseller

In 1989 Gould wrote *Wonderful Life: The Burgess Shale and the Nature of History,* which became a bestseller and won the Rhône-Poulenc Prize, a prestigious literary award. The Burgess Shale is a slab of exposed rock located in Yoho National Park in western Canada. Spawned by a catastrophic event (a violent and sudden change in a feature of Earth) that occurred half a billion years ago, the Burgess Shale unveils some of the strangest animal fossils in existence. According to Gould, the Burgess fossils show the random aspects of the development of life and demonstrate that the evolution of living beings is neither orderly nor progressive. Arguing that evolution does not necessarily mean progress, Gould questions the belief that life moves forward, toward a perfected state.

Continues work on evolution

In 1965 Gould married artist and writer Deborah Lee, whom he met at Antioch College and who now teaches. Before their marriage ended they lived in Cambridge, Massachusetts, with their sons, Jesse and Ethan. Gould's future projects include the composition of a major work that modifies Charles Darwin's theory of evolution. "I could not dent the richness in a hundred lifetimes," Gould wrote in *The Flamingo's Smile,* "but I simply must have a look at a few more of those pretty pebbles."

Further Reading

Angier, Natalie, "An Evolving Celebrity," *New York Times,* February 11, 1993, p. C1.

Goode, Stephen, "A Giant Totters: Can Darwin Survive?" *Insight,* December 21, 1992, pp. 6–11, 32.

Horgan, John, "Profile: Stephen Jay Gould," *Scientific American,* August 1995, pp. 37–41.

Levy, Daniel S., "Evolution, Extinction, and the Movies," *Time,* May 14, 1990.

Natural History, various issues, 1974–.

New York Times Book Review, January 21, 1996.

Tierney, John, "Stephen Jay Gould," *Rolling Stone,* January 15, 1987, pp. 38–41, 58–61.

Meredith Gourdine

Born September 26, 1929
Newark, New Jersey

Meredith Charles Gourdine pioneered electrogasdynamics technology, an energy conversion system that affects the daily lives of people throughout the world.

Meredith Gourdine is a pioneer in electrogasdynamics (EGD) technology, an energy conversion process that produces high voltage electricity. The holder of more than seventy patents, Gourdine is president and chief executive officer (CEO) of Energy Innovations, a Houston-based firm devoted to overseeing and improving his many technological innovations. The many practical applications of Gourdine's research and development in energy conversion systems have affected the daily lives of people throughout the world.

Shows intense motivation

One of four children, Meredith Charles Gourdine was born in Newark, New Jersey, on September 26, 1929. Although his father had won a scholarship to Temple University, he decided not to attend and worked instead at various maintenance jobs. Gourdine's mother was a teletype operator who was also interested in mathematics. In 1936 the family moved to the Harlem district of New York City, where Gourdine was inspired by a math teacher at his elementary school. Gourdine went on to attend the highly competitive Brooklyn Tech High School, where he combined schoolwork with swimming and track and excelled as a quarter-mile runner. He also worked long hours for a radio and telegraph company, a job that provided him with funds to finance his first semester of college at Cornell University. Entering Cornell in 1948, Gourdine soon distinguished himself as a student and was awarded a scholarship.

At Cornell Gourdine became interested in physics as a more practical application of mathematics, a discipline he felt was too abstract. Because his high school grades were not good enough Gourdine was not allowed to take classes in engineering physics, which was considered the most demanding and selective course at the university. Fueled by his desire and his newly found love of physics, Gourdine worked hard to score high grades in chemistry, engineering, physics, and calculus. Seeing his dedication and ability, the school allowed him to transfer after his first term from electrical engineering to engineering physics.

Becomes star athlete

Gourdine balanced his studies at Cornell with a developing career as a star athlete. In 1952 he earned a place on the United States Olympic track team and won a silver medal in the broad jump competition at Helsinki, Finland, missing the gold by four centimeters. Graduating in 1953 with a bachelor's degree in engineering physics, Gourdine married June Cave, whom he had met during his sophomore year (they would have four children together and later divorce). He then joined the navy for two years as a former Naval Reserve Officers' Training Corps student, but found the work undemanding. Turning his attention back to math and physics, Gourdine applied for fellowships at Princeton and Cornell Universities, as well as the California Institute of Technology (Cal Tech).

IMPACT

Meredith Gourdine's career as a researcher and inventor spans over thirty years. Some of his energy-saving and cost-efficient applications include a battery for electric cars, a system for clearing fog at airports, a method of extracting oil from oil shale, a procedure for repairing potholes by recovering rubber from old car tires and combining it with asphalt, and the means for producing better refrigerators and air conditioners.

Discovers formula for electrogasdynamics

Gourdine decided to accept a Guggenheim Fellowship to Cal Tech. During his graduate school years, he also received the Ramo-Woolridge Fellowship and developed the formula for electrogasdynamics while working at Jet Propulsion Labs. Electrogasdynamics involves the interaction between an electrical field and charged particles suspended in gas, an event that produces high voltage electricity. The phenomenon of EGD had been known since the eighteenth century, but its uses were limited until Gourdine figured out how to employ the principle to produce enough electricity for practical applications in the modern world. Although Gourdine was put off by Jet Propulsion Lab's lack of interest in his research, he was not yet ready to take on the responsibility of his own company.

By 1960 Gourdine had earned a Ph.D. in engineering science, an interdisciplinary field based on a comprehensive understanding of all branches of physics. From 1960 to 1962 he was laboratory director of Plasmadyne Corporation, where he continued his research into magnetohydrodynamics (MHD), another conversion method that generates power through the interaction between magnetic fields and gases. Once again he found he had no corporate support, so he moved on. Within two years, while serving as chief scientist of Curtiss-Wright Corporation's Aero Division, Gourdine decided to work independently.

Founds his own business

As the president and chairman of the board for Gourdine Systems, based in Livingston, New Jersey, Gourdine worked on patenting practical applications of EGD, MHD, and plasma physics (the study of electrically charged, extremely hot gases). From 1964 to 1973 Gourdine received nearly seventy patents

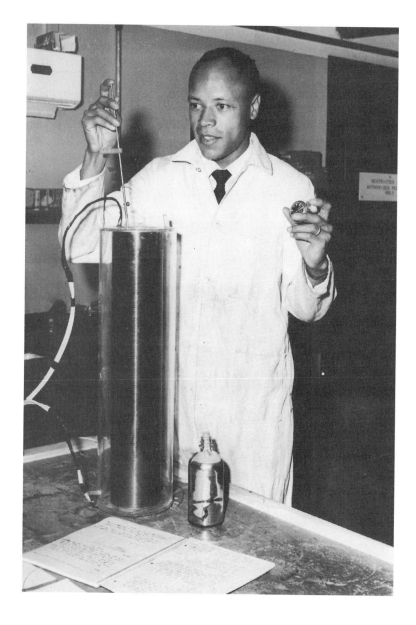

for his inventions. Knowing his own limitations, both personal and financial, he decided not to manufacture or sell his inventions. Instead, he licensed the patents to other companies.

One of Gourdine's inventions was the Electradyne Spray Gun, which used electrogasdynamics to atomize (reduce to small particles) and electrify any kind of paint, allowing for the easy spray-painting of irregularly shaped objects, such as bicycles. He also invented the Incineraid, a device to reduce air pollution emitted by apartment building incinerators. In 1970 Gourdine Systems became a publicly owned company and decided to do its own manufacturing and selling of products, although it soon fell prey to bad timing and poor business strategies. For example, Gourdine Systems spent more money marketing the spray gun than it made, and when incinerators were outlawed in New York City, Incineraid became unsalable.

Establishes new company

Despite these setbacks, Gourdine held fast to his goal of inventing and licensing practical applications for the highly specialized technologies of EGD, MHD, and other direct energy conversion methods such as thermovoltaics, which involves the conversion of chemical and thermal energy into electricity. In 1974 Gourdine founded a new company, Energy Innovations, based in Houston, Texas.

In 1986 Gourdine lost his eyesight due to diabetic retinopathy (a disease of the retina). After he first developed diabetes during his time in the navy, his eyesight gradually deteriorated over the years. This disability, however, did not prevent him from running Energy Innovations. Although Gourdine cannot read Braille (the diabetes has reduced sensation in his fingertips), he continues to produce new applications for his technologies and license them to other companies with the help of his son and second wife, Carolina. His many honors include election to the National Academy of Engineering and a citation for service as a member of the United States Army Science Board. He is a member of the Black Inventors Hall of Fame and in 1987 was honored for outstanding contributions as a scientist by North Carolina State University. Known for his vigor and positive attitude, Gourdine practices yoga and meditation, swims, and enjoys spectator sports.

Further Reading

Field, Alan M., "Father of Invention," *Houston Metropolitan,* February 1991, pp. 43–45, 53–54.

Van Sertima, Ivan, ed., *Blacks in Science: Ancient and Modern,* Transaction Books, 1983, pp. 226–27.

Lloyd A. Hall

Born June 20, 1894
Elgin, Illinois
Died January 2, 1971
Altadena, California

Chemist Lloyd A. Hall is best known for his work in the field of food technology, where he developed processes to cure and preserve meat, prevent rancidity (spoilage) in fats, and sterilize spices. In 1939 he cofounded the Institute of Food Technologists, establishing a new branch of industrial chemistry.

Encounters racism

Lloyd Augustus Hall was born in Elgin, Illinois, on June 20, 1894. His father, Augustus Hall, was a Baptist minister and son of the first pastor of the Quinn Chapel A.M.E. Church, the first African American church in Chicago. His mother, Isabel, was a high-school graduate whose mother was a runaway slave who had fled to Illinois via the Underground Railroad at the age of sixteen. Hall became interested in chemistry while attending East Side High School in Aurora, Illinois, where he was active in extracurricular activities such as debate, track,

A pioneer in the field of food technology, Lloyd A. Hall developed processes to preserve and sterilize foods.

427

football, and baseball. During his first four years at the school he was one of only five African American students.

When he graduated near the top of his class, Hall was offered scholarships to four Illinois universities. He chose to attend Northwestern University, working his way through school while he studied chemistry. During this time he met Carroll L. Griffith, a fellow chemistry student, who would later play a part in his career. Hall graduated from Northwestern in 1916 with a bachelor of science degree in chemistry, then continued his studies in graduate classes at the University of Chicago.

During World War I Hall served as a lieutenant in the Ordnance Department, inspecting explosives at a plant in Wisconsin. However, he was subjected to such prejudice and discriminatory treatment that he asked to be transferred. The discrimination was also apparent in the civilian world: at one point, he was hired over the telephone by the Western Electric Company. When he arrived for work, he was told no jobs were available.

Starts long career in food chemistry

In 1916 Hall was able to find a position in the Chicago Department of Health Laboratories. Within a year he became a senior chemist, and for the next six years he worked at several industrial laboratories. By 1921 he was chief chemist at Boyer Chemical Laboratory in Chicago, where he began his involvement in the developing field of food chemistry. The following year he was named president and chemical director of the Chemical Products Corporation, a consulting laboratory in Chicago.

In 1924 one of Hall's clients, Griffith Laboratories (the company of his old lab partner Carroll L. Griffith) offered him a space where he could work while continuing his consulting practice. By 1925 he had become chief chemist and director of research at Griffith; in 1929 he gave up his consulting practice to work full time for Griffith. His career would last for the next thirty years.

Develops "flash-drying" method

When Hall started at Griffith, current meat-curing and preservation methods were very poor. It was known that sodium chloride (common table salt) preserved meat, while chemicals containing nitrogen, called nitrates and nitrites, were used for curing. However, not much was known about how these chemicals worked, and food could not be preserved for an extended period of time. By conducting experiments Hall discovered that nitrites and nitrates penetrated the meat more quickly than the sodium chloride, causing the salt to disintegrate before the meat could be preserved. The problem was to get the salt to penetrate the meat first, thereby preserving the meat before curing it. He solved the problem through "flash-drying," a quick method of evaporating a solution of all three salts, so that crystals of sodium chloride enclosing the nitrite and nitrate were formed. Thus, when the crystals dissolved, the sodium chloride would penetrate the meat first.

Discovers how to sterilize spices

Hall's next accomplishment was in the area of spices. Although meat could now be preserved and cured effectively, the natural spices that were used to enhance and preserve it often contained contaminants. Spices such as allspice, cloves, cinnamon, and paprika, as well as dried vegetable products like onion powder, contained yeasts, molds, and bacteria. Hall's task was to find a way to sterilize the spices and dried vegetables without destroying their original flavor and appearance. Heating the foods above 240°F would sterilize them, but it would also destroy their taste and color. Hall discovered that ethylene oxide, a gas used to kill insects, would also kill the germs in the spices. He used a vacuum chamber to remove the moisture from the spices so that the gas could permeate and sterilize them when introduced into the chamber. The times and temperatures varied according to the type of bacteria, mold, or yeast being destroyed.

Researches effects of antioxidants on fats

In his work at Griffith, Hall also discovered the use of antioxidants, substances that inhibit the spoiling of foods containing fats and oils. Rancidity (spoiling) is caused by oxidation when components of fats react with oxygen. By experimenting with various antioxidants, Hall found that certain chemicals in crude vegetable oil worked as antioxidants. Mixing some of these chemicals with salt, he produced an antioxidant salt mixture that protected foods containing fats and oils from spoiling.

Makes important contributions to food industry

During his thirty-five years at Griffith Laboratories, Hall worked in several areas of food chemistry, including seasoning, spice extracts, and enzymes. In 1951 he and an associate developed a way to reduce the time for curing bacon from between six and fifteen days to a few hours. The quality of the bacon was also improved, both in appearance and stability. He was also very interested in vitamins and the development of yeast foods. By 1959 Hall held more than 105 patents in the United States and abroad and had published numerous papers on food technology.

Hall also served as an adviser or was seated on various committees. During World War II he was a member of the Committee on Food Research of the Scientific Advisory Board of the War Department's Quartermaster Corps. From 1943 to 1948, in that position, he advised the military on the preservation of food supplies. In 1944 he joined the Illinois State Food Commission of the State Department of Agriculture, serving until 1949.

As a further sign of the establishment of food chemistry as a field of science, the Institute of Food Technologists was founded in 1939, with Hall being a charter member. He also edited its magazine, *The Vitalizer,* and served on the executive board for four years. In 1954 Hall became chairman of the Chicago chapter of the American Institute of Chemists. The following year he was elected a member of the national board of directors, becoming the first African American man to hold that position in the Institute's thirty-two-year history.

Expands role during retirement

Upon his retirement from Griffith in 1959, Hall continued to serve as a consultant to various state and federal organizations. He also continued to work, and in 1961 he spent six months in Indonesia advising the Food and Agricultural Organization of the United Nations. From 1962 to 1964 he was a member of the American Food for Peace Council, an appointment made by President John F. Kennedy. After retiring, Hall and his wife, Myrrhene, moved to Altadena, California, where Hall remained active in community affairs until his death on January 2, 1971.

Further Reading

"Dr. Lloyd A. Hall," *Jet,* June 26, 1995, p. 27.

Sammons, Vivian Ovelton, *Blacks in Science and Medicine,* Hemisphere Publishing, 1990, pp. 109–10.

Stephen Hawking

Born January 8, 1942
Oxford, England

"I simply can't manage very complicated equations, so I have developed geometrical ways of thinking, instead."

The most brilliant theoretical physicist since Albert Einstein, Stephen Hawking has spent his career studying the origin and fate of the universe. Concentrating on the puzzling cosmic bodies called black holes, he extends his interest to such specialized fields as particle physics, supersymmetry, and quantum gravity. Although few people are able to understand these subjects in depth, Hawking has gained a worldwide following among other scientists and the general public alike for his brilliant theories as well as for his being able to present the basic concepts behind them in terms even nonscientists can understand.

Shows little promise as a child

Stephen William Hawking was born on January 8, 1942, in Oxford, England. He often refers to the fact that his birth date coincided with the three-hundredth anniversary of the death of Galileo Galilei, the great Italian mathematician and astronomer. Hawking was the eldest child of an intellectual and accomplished family. His father, Frank Hawking, was a physician and research biologist who specialized in tropical diseases. His mother, Isobel, a well-read, lively woman, was active for many years in the British Liberal Party. After Hawking was born his parents had two daughters, Mary and Philippa, and adopted another son, Edward.

Hawking spent his early years in Highgate, a London suburb. In 1950, when he was eight, the family moved to St. Albans, a cathedral town about twenty miles northwest of London. Two years later his family enrolled him in St. Albans School, a private institution affiliated with the cathedral. As Michael White and John Gribbin describe the young school-boy in *Stephen Hawking: A Life in Science,* "He was eccentric and awkward, skinny and puny. His school uniform always looked a mess and, according to friends, he jabbered rather than talked clearly, having inherited a slight lisp from his father." Hawking's abilities made little impact on his teachers or fellow students. But he already knew he wanted to be a scientist, and by the time he reached his middle teens, he had decided to pursue the study of physics or mathematics.

Pioneers study of black holes

Gangly and unathletic, Hawking formed close friendships with a small group of other precocious boys at school. He became intrigued by subjects that focused on measurable quantities and objective reasoning, showing increasing skill at mathematics. Soon he was outdistancing his peers with high grades while spending very little time on homework. In 1958 Hawking and his friends built a primitive computer that actually worked. In Spring 1959 he won an open scholarship in natural sciences to University College at Oxford University, his father's old college. At Oxford Hawking's unusual abilities began to become more obvious. His ease at handling difficult problems made it seem to others that he did not need to study. In 1962, after receiving a first-class honors degree from Oxford, Hawking set off for Cambridge University to begin studying for a Ph.D. in cosmology (the study of the nature of the universe).

Ranked with Galileo Galilei, Sir Isaac Newton, and Albert Einstein as one of the world's greatest thinkers, Stephen Hawking has performed work in theoretical physics that has led him to the brink of discoveries that may well explain the universe. His book *A Brief History of Time: From the Big Bang to Black Holes* introduced millions to the theories of the nature of the universe.

Hawking was beginning to think about questions that would preoccupy him throughout his life. One was the inadequately understood matter of black holes. As scientists were later to realize, a black hole is a cosmic body that by its very nature can never be seen. One type of black hole is thought to be the remnant of a collapsed star, which possesses such intense gravity that nothing can escape from it, not even light. Hawking was also intrigued by "space-time singularities." (A "singularity" is an infinitely dense point with no dimensions where all scientific laws governing space and time are distorted by immense gravitational forces.) In attempting to understand a black hole and the space-time singularity at its center, Hawking made pioneering studies using formulas developed more than half a century earlier by **Albert Einstein** (see entry).

Formulates Hawking radiation theory

After earning a Ph.D. in 1965, Hawking obtained a fellowship in theoretical physics at Gonville and Caius College at Cambridge University. He continued his work on black holes, frequently collaborating with Roger Penrose (see box), a mathematician who was also deeply interested in theories of space-time.

Although he was still in his twenties, Hawking was beginning to acquire quite a reputation. He would often attend conferences where he shocked people by questioning the findings of eminent scientists much older than himself. He joined the staff of the Institute of Astronomy in Cambridge in 1968. He and Penrose began using complex mathematics to apply the laws of thermodynamics to black holes. (Thermodynamics is the branch of physics that deals with the mechanical action or relations of heat.) He traveled to the United States, the former Soviet Union, and other countries. In 1973 he published a highly technical book, *The Large Scale Structure of Space-Time,* which he wrote with G. F. R. Ellis. Not long afterward Hawking challenged the conventional notion that nothing can escape a black hole. He proved that mini-black holes emit particles and radiation (energy in the form of waves), gradually evaporate, and then explode. His theory has since been accepted by most physicists, and Hawking radiation is the term used to describe emissions from black holes.

Seeks origin of the universe

In 1974, at the unusually young age of thirty-two, Hawking was named a fellow of the Royal Society. Soon afterward he spent a year as Fairchild Distinguished Scholar at the California Institute of Technology in Pasadena. Upon returning to England he continued to work toward a theory of the origin of the universe. In this endeavor he made progress toward resolving apparent contradictions between the two major theories of modern physics: general relativity (which states that gravity controls the universe and does so in a predictable manner) and quantum mechanics (which states that matter behaves randomly at the level of the atom and below). Long sought by researchers as the explanation of everything in the universe, the linking of these theories is called the Grand Unification Theory.

In 1978 Hawking received the Albert Einstein Award of the Lewis and Rose Strauss Memorial Fund, the most prestigious award in theoretical physics. The following year he edited a book with Werner Israel, titled *General Relativity: An Einstein Centenary Survey.* Hawking was also named Lucasian Professor of Mathematics at Cambridge, a position held three centuries earlier by Sir Isaac Newton, the British physicist and mathematician who formulated the theory of gravity.

During the 1980s Hawking's work was beginning to lead him to question the big bang theory, which most other scientists were accepting as the probable explanation of the origin of the universe. Hawking asked whether there really had ever

Roger Penrose, English Mathematical Physicist

Roger Penrose (1931–) and Stephen Hawking extended our understanding of black holes and the big bang theory with the assistance of Penrose's invention of the "twistor." The twistor is a mathematical tool used for describing physical objects and space that incorporates energy, momentum, and spin—the three properties possessed by all objects moving through space-time. A twistor has either six or eight dimensions, each of which involves either movement or change in size.

Another of Penrose's areas of interest is tiling, which involves completely covering a flat surface with a regular pattern of tiles. Expanding on Penrose's work, other scientists extended the tiling concept to three dimensions, devising solid polyhedrons (geometric figures formed by plane faces) to fill space without any gaps. Penrose discusses his theories on a variety of subjects in his 1989 book *The Emperor's New Mind: Concerning Computers, Minds, and the Laws of Physics.*

been a beginning to space-time (a big bang), or whether one universe simply gave birth to another without beginning or end. Hawking suggested that new universes might be born frequently through little-understood irregularities in space-time. He also investigated string theory and exploding black holes, and showed mathematically that numerous miniature black holes may have formed early in the history of the universe.

Publishes popular book on the cosmos

Always interested in ways to make his work accessible to those who have no background in science, Hawking wrote a book that he hoped would accomplish that goal. Published in 1988, *A Brief History of Time: From the Big Bang to Black Holes* surveys centuries of thought on the nature of the universe, from Aristotle through Einstein and Hawking himself. Hawking's readable and often humorous treatment of such a complex topic was phenomenally successful, and he became an immediate celebrity, appearing on television programs and being featured in magazine articles. Many reviewers attribute

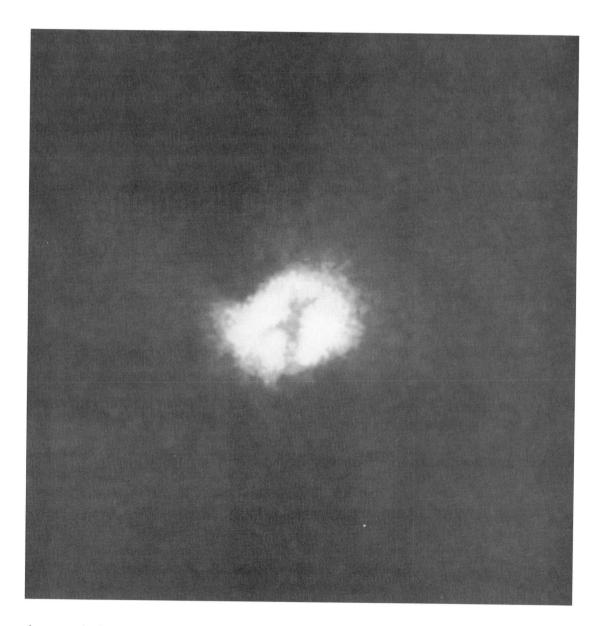

the appeal of the book to the spiritual overtones of Hawking's quest to understand the moment of creation and thus "know the mind of God."

Triumphs over debilitating disease

In 1992 a documentary film, *A Brief History of Time*, was made about Hawking's life and work. Through interviews with

This photo, taken by the Hubble Space Telescope on December 20, 1991, shows a black hole silhouetted against the nucleus of the nearby galaxy M51.

George F. Smoot, American Astrophysicist

American astrophysicist George F. Smoot (1945–) made a major advance in the big bang theory in 1992. He and his team at the Lawrence Berkeley Laboratory in Berkeley, California, detected minute ripples in cosmic microwave radiation (short-wave energy dispersed from its source in the form of waves and particles) thought to be the afterglow of the big bang. The ripples, a key missing link to the big bang theory, were detected in data sent to Earth by the Cosmic Background Explorer (COBE) satellite, which Smoot helped design. Smoot's announcement was greeted with excitement throughout the world's scientific community. Stephen Hawking called the finding "the discovery of the century—if not of all time."

Although Smoot says he is not religious, he sees cosmology as the place where "science and religion meet." He serves on a committee at the University of California that is designed to "give better public appreciation of science and show how scientists are real people." The astrophysicist believes his findings will help people understand how the universe evolved and will ultimately enrich human life.

his family, friends, and colleagues as well as illustrative techniques, the film makes Hawking's complex theories understandable to the general audience. A major focus, however, is Hawking's long battle with amyotrophic lateral sclerosis (ALS). Also called Lou Gehrig's disease, ALS confines him to a wheelchair and requires him to use a computer and voice synthesizer to speak—in fact, he narrates the film with the computer-synthesized voice.

Hawking was twenty-one years old when doctors determined that he had ALS, a degenerative condition affecting the spinal cord, which causes weakness throughout the body. Death usually comes two or three years after the initial diagnosis, when the chest muscles weaken to the point where the patient can no longer breathe. Hawking, however, has prevailed over the disease for more than thirty years. He credited marriage and family as well as his work with giving him purpose. In 1965 he married Jane Wilde, a language student at Cambridge; they later had two sons and a daughter. The couple divorced in 1995, and Hawking married his former nurse, Elaine Mason. Today he is able to move only a few fingers of one hand, enough to get around in his motorized wheelchair and to talk through the voice synthesizer. Nurses, family members, and colleagues attend to his other needs. Yet, as one observer commented, while his body has withered and wasted away, his mind is "capable of somersaulting through space and time."

Continues to think and write

After the publication of *A Brief History of Time,* Hawking turned down requests to write another book, saying he had "a lot of science" he wanted to do first. Then he changed his mind and published, in 1993, *Black Holes and Baby Universes and Other Essays,* which became a bestseller like his previous book. That same year he also made his television drama debut, portraying himself on an episode of the television series *Star Trek: The Next Generation.* When Hawking is not traveling around the world lecturing and presenting papers, he works in his office at Cambridge.

Hawking has received honorary degrees from several institutions, among them the University of Chicago, Princeton University, and the University of Notre Dame. His numerous awards include the Eddington Medal of the Royal Astronomical Society (1975), the Pius XI Gold Medal (1975), the Maxwell Medal of the Institute of Physics (1976), the Franklin Medal of the Franklin Institute (1981), the Gold Medal of the Royal Society (1985), the Paul Dirac Medal and Prize (1987), and the Britannica Award (1989).

Further Reading

Begley, Sharon, with Jennifer Foote, "Why Past Is Past," *Newsweek,* December 28, 1992, pp. 52–53.

Boslough, John, *Stephen Hawking's Universe,* Quill/William Morrow, 1985.

"A Brief History of a Brief History," *Popular Science,* August 1989, pp. 70–72.

Hawking, Stephen, *Black Holes and Baby Universes and Other Essays,* Bantam, 1993.

Hawking, Stephen, *A Brief History of Time: From the Big Bang to Black Holes,* Bantam, 1988.

Lipton, Michael A., "Trek Stop," *People Weekly,* June 28, 1993, pp. 81–82.

Lubow, Arthur, "Heart and Mind: 'A Brief History of Time' Is Made Into a Motion Picture," *Vanity Fair,* June 1993.

Raymond, Chet, "Stephen Hawking and the Mind of God," *Commonweal,* April 6, 1990, pp. 218–20.

Sampson, Russ, "Two Hours with Stephen Hawking," *Astronomy,* March 1993, pp. 13–16.

White, Michael, and John Gribbin, *Stephen Hawking: A Life in Science,* Plume/Penguin, 1992.

William Herschel

Born November 15, 1738
Hanover, Germany
Died August 25, 1822
Slough, England

German-born English astronomer William Herschel discovered the planet Uranus as well as twenty-five hundred star clusters and nebulae and eight hundred double stars. He is also credited with the discovery of infrared radiation (energy dispersed from its source in the form of waves or particles). Finding that the astronomical instruments of his day weren't of high enough quality to support his research, Herschel ground his own telescope lenses and designed his own instruments to aid in his work. His forty-foot reflector was the largest telescope in England until 1969.

William Herschel's discovery of Uranus effectively doubled the previously accepted size of the solar system.

Inspired by Newton

Friedrich Wilhelm Herschel, known by his Anglicized name William Herschel, was born in Hanover, Germany, at a time when the city belonged to England under the rule of George II. Herschel's father was a musician in the Hanoverian army, and Herschel himself was trained in music in order to

441

William Herschel made pioneering discoveries in nearly every branch of astronomy. He classified star clusters and nebulae (clouds of gas or dust), proposing an evolutionary pattern for their classes. His method for calculating the size of stars led to the field of quantitative stellar photometry (the study of the intensity of stars' light), and he deduced that infrared rays did exist. One of Herschel's most important achievements was his discovery of the planet Uranus and its two satellites. He also identified satellites of the planet Jupiter.

enter the same profession. The Seven Years War, however, made military life an unattractive option, so in 1757 Herschel moved to England. After several years of hardship, in 1766 he began working as an organist and music teacher in Bath. Through his interest in the theory of music and the scientific basis for musical sounds, Herschel learned about astronomy, which led him to mathematics and then optics (the study of light).

Herschel was inspired to study the stars by a treatise on optics written by the seventeenth-century English mathematician and physicist Isaac Newton. Unable to find an affordable telescope of a high enough resolution (the capability of distinguishing sources of light), Herschel decided to grind his own lenses and to design his own instruments. He was helped by his sister Caroline (see box), who came to England in 1772. The first telescope he built, in 1773 and 1774, was a six-foot reflector, one of the best of its kind, which he used to conduct a systematic survey of the stars and planets. (In a reflector telescope light passes down an open tube, then hits a curved mirror at the lower end that reflects the light back up. The light is then directed onto a smaller mirror called a diagonal that again reflects the light into the eyepiece.) Throughout his life Herschel built numerous telescopes, each more sophisticated and more powerful than the last.

Finds new planet

Herschel's first major discovery occurred in 1781 during his second survey of the sky, when he announced the existence of a new planet located in the constellation of Taurus. His name for the planet was *Georgium Sidus,* George's star, in honor of King George III of England. Eventually it came to be known as Uranus, after the mythical father of Saturn. The dis-

Although William Herschel did not work directly with the theories of Ptolemy (c. 100–170), he and other astronomers were indebted to the ancient Greek astronomer. Ptolemy's chief contribution to science is a series of books in which he compiled the knowledge of the ancient Greeks, his primary source being Hipparchus. Because most of Hipparchus's writings have not survived from antiquity, many of the ideas he espoused about the universe have become known as the Ptolemaic system.

Ptolemy's system places Earth directly at the center of the universe. The Sun, Moon, and all planets orbit around Earth. Such a scheme did not match the observed motion of planets, however, and, to make a better fit, Ptolemy added small orbits to planets called epicycles and introduced other mathematical devices. Despite its errors and complications, the Ptolemaic system was adequate enough to make predictions of planetary positions, and it influenced thinking for fourteen centuries. It was not until 1543 that Polish astronomer Nicolaus Copernicus published his book refuting the Ptolemaic system.

covery of Uranus, which effectively doubled the previously accepted size of the solar system, caused a popular and scientific sensation. In recognition of this achievement, George III appointed Herschel to the position of Royal Astronomer while providing him with a small yearly allowance that enabled him to pursue astronomy full time. In 1789 he completed a forty-foot reflector, which until 1969 was the largest telescope ever used in England.

Makes major contributions to astronomy

Herschel made his most significant achievements in the area of sidereal astronomy (pronounced sie-DEER-ee-awl; the study of stars or constellations), to which he contributed the first systematic body of evidence on the order and nature of the stars and the planets. Whereas several theories had been proposed by prominent philosophers of the time on the systems that might govern the universe, none were supported by

Nicolaus Copernicus, Polish Mathematician and Astronomer

William Herschel used astronomical methods developed by the Italian astronomer Galileo Galilei (1564–1642), who was himself influenced by Polish astronomer Nicolaus Copernicus (1473–1543). When Copernicus began studying Earth's solar system in 1496, the tables of planetary positions, based on the Ptolemaic system, were complex and inaccurate. For instance, predicting the positions of the planets over long periods of time was haphazard at best, and the seasons were out of synch with the position of the Sun. Copernicus realized planetary positions could be calculated more easily and accurately if he made the assumption that the Sun, not Earth, was the center of the solar system and that the planets, including Earth, orbited the Sun. He first proposed this theory in 1507.

Copernicus not only wished to refute Ptolemy's view of the universe, he also claimed that Earth itself was very small and unimportant compared to the vast vault of the stars. He was reluctant to make his ideas public, realizing his theory contradicted the Greek scientists and went against the teachings of the Roman Catholic Church. In 1530 he allowed a summary of his ideas to circulate among scholars, who received it with great enthusiasm. His entire book, titled *Revolution of the Heavenly Spheres,* was not published until shortly after his death in 1543.

scientific data. In 1783 Herschel began to search for nebulae (clouds of gas or dust) in the sky, raising their known total from a little more than one hundred to twenty-five hundred.

During the eighteenth century astronomers set out to determine stellar distance (the distances between stars). Trigonometrical calculations (involving measurements of triangles and arcs) based on the apparent annual movement of stars, however, had failed. As a better method of calculating stellar distance, the seventeenth-century Italian astronomer Galileo Galilei (see box) had proposed the study of the positions of double stars (pairs of stars located very close together). The fainter member of the pair, being far away, could represent a fixed point from which the annual movement of its brighter companion could be measured. Applying this method in his second survey, Herschel searched for double stars. Over the next forty years he produced three catalogs that listed 848 examples.

Proposes cosmogony for the universe

Another astronomer who had seen Herschel's work later discovered that these double stars were in fact companions. The star pairs were held together in space by gravitational forces and were therefore equidistant from Earth. Assuming that companions in space would have been of equal brightness, Herschel had discounted this possibility. Nonetheless, he produced evidence for the powers of attraction between stars. In three papers he delivered between 1784 and 1789, he proposed a cosmogony (a theory of origin or creation) for the universe. According to Herschel's theory stars were initially randomly scattered throughout the universe, then they clustered together over time around the regions from which they had originally developed.

Studies Milky Way

Herschel was the first to embark upon a scientific study of the Milky Way, and half of his work, though less influential, focused upon the solar system. Studying the Sun, he observed that what we see is not the Sun itself but the clouds of gases that cover its surface. He also examined the nature of the infrared section of the spectrum (outside the visible light spec-

Galileo Galilei, Italian Mathematician and Astronomer

Nicolaus Copernicus's theories about the Sun being the center of the solar system were validated seventy years after his death by Italian astronomer Galileo Galilei (1564–1642), who is credited with establishing the modern experimental method. In 1613 Galileo published a book that for the first time openly defended the model of the solar system proposed by Copernicus. While there was some support, even among church authorities, for Galileo's proof of the Copernican theory, the Roman Catholic hierarchy ultimately determined that a revision of the long-held astronomical doctrines of the church (based on the Ptolemaic system) was unnecessary. Thus in 1616 the church issued a decree declaring the Copernican system "false and erroneous," and Galileo was forbidden to support it.

With the permission of Pope Urban III, Galileo published in 1632 his *Dialogue Concerning the Two Chief World Systems—Ptolemaic and Copernican.* Despite his agreement not to favor the Copernican view, in his *Dialogue* Galileo made church objections sound unconvincing and even ridiculous. Summoned to Rome to stand before the Inquisition (religious court), he was accused of violating the 1616 order forbidding him to promote the Copernican theory. Put on trial for heresy (holding opinions counter to the teachings of the church), he was found guilty and ordered to recant his errors. At some point during this ordeal Galileo is supposed to have made his famous statement: "And yet it moves," referring to the Copernican doctrine of Earth's rotation on its axis.

trum at the red end) by which some of the Sun's heat is transmitted, and calculated the height of lunar mountains. Herschel studied the other known planets—Mercury, Venus, Mars, Jupiter, and Saturn—determining their rotation period. He also checked the inclination of their axes, their shape, and the nature of their atmospheres. Herschel closely examined Saturn and its rings, arguing at one point that the rings were solid, but later conceding they were in fact composed of floating particles.

Changes perception of the solar system

Herschel's work on nebulae led him to conclude that they might well be other solar systems seen only as a luminous

Caroline Herschel, German Astronomer

William Herschel received invaluable assistance in his astronomical work from his sister, Caroline Lucretia Herschel (1750–1848), who had moved from Germany to live with him in 1772. She helped him grind and polish mirrors for his telescope and copied astronomical catalogs and tables for his reference. As she became more proficient with her own telescope, she made a name for herself in a largely male domain. In 1783 she discovered three new nebulae, and from 1786 to 1797 she discovered eight comets. King George III awarded her a salary as well, a rare gesture at the time. Caroline Herschel then took on a formidable task: a thorough index of the star catalog created by John Flamsteed (1646–1719), the first Royal Astronomer. Following her brother's death she returned to Hanover, Germany, but remained in close contact with his son, astronomer John Herschel (1792–1871), for whom she compiled a new catalog of nebulae. Along with Scottish scientific writer Mary Somerville, Herschel became the first woman to be awarded an honorary membership in the prestigious Royal Society.

cluster of stars around a brighter one. As a result, he saw the Milky Way galaxy and Earth as only one rather insignificant part of the universe. In this sense he changed the way the solar system was viewed as part of the universe. Herschel's contribution was comparable to that of the sixteenth-century Polish astronomer Nicolaus Copernicus (see box), who revolutionized man's understanding of Earth when he showed that the planets revolved around the Sun rather than around Earth.

Herschel married a wealthy widow in 1788; their only son, John Frederick, also became an astronomer. Herschel was knighted in 1816. He died in Slough, England, on August 25, 1822.

Further Reading

Armitage, Angus, *William Herschel,* Doubleday, 1963.

Hoffman, Paul, "On the Spot," *Discover,* November 1989.

Mullaney, James, "Exploring the Herschel Catalogue," *Sky and Telescope,* September 1992.

Thor Heyerdahl

Born October 6, 1914
Larvik, Norway

"Man is man wherever you find him; I feel he cannot be divided or united according to height, color, or pencil lines on a map."

Norwegian explorer and anthropologist Thor Heyerdahl launched a daring journey across the Pacific in 1947 that thrilled the public and rocked the scientific world. Setting sail from Peru in a primitive balsa-wood craft called the *Kon-Tiki*, he and his five-man crew traveled 4,300 miles before crashing against a reef east of Tahiti. Until that day, most anthropologists had insisted that the various Polynesian islands in the eastern-central Pacific Ocean had been settled exclusively by Asians because prehistoric South Americans would not have been able to make the ocean journey. Although the successful trip made by the *Kon-Tiki* did not prove that such a migration actually occurred, it nevertheless demonstrated the real possibility of South Americans landing on the islands. Since then, Heyerdahl has gathered a wealth of evidence to support his view that prehistoric travel by sea was quite common. In addition, he believes strongly that the inter-relatedness of all human beings overshadows any regional, racial, or religious differences that might separate peoples.

Becomes interested in Polynesia

Heyerdahl was born in Larvik, Norway, on October 6, 1914. His father was president of a brewery and mineral water plant, while his mother headed a local museum. Heyerdahl grew up with a love of the outdoors and an interest in anthropology (the study of the ways people live). He was also very interested in the Polynesian island group. When he entered the University of Oslo, he began studying biology, zoology, and geography. However, in 1936, he left school to do research on the island of Fatu Hiva in the Marquesas, a group of islands in French Polynesia.

Studies the culture of Fatu Hiva

Over the course of the next year Heyerdahl immersed himself in the culture of Fatu Hiva, scrutinizing language, artifacts, and myths, especially the legend of the sun god Tiki, who was similar to a pre-Incan South American hero called Kon-Tiki. He also studied the winds and currents and noted that they moved east to west, from South America *toward* Polynesia—not the direction one would expect, given the accepted theory that Asians had drifted eastward by sea and come upon Polynesia. By the end of his stay Heyerdahl had abandoned his study of biology and zoology. He began to explore the possibility that ancient inhabitants of South America had constructed vessels using native woods and reeds that were capable of crossing the Pacific.

Develops theory of Pacific crossing

To gather evidence that would back his theory, Heyerdahl spent the rest of the 1930s and early 1940s learning all he could about ancient civilizations in both North and South America and Polynesia. He discovered rock carvings and massive stone statues that existed in remarkably similar forms on both sides of the Pacific. He also examined the legend of Kon-Tiki, which tells of a race of white people who fled pre-Inca Peru and sailed west across the Pacific to avoid being massacred by native tribes. He compared it to Polynesian myths that describe the arrival of whites from across the sea. But the scientific community ridiculed his efforts and refused to take him seriously.

Proves his theory

Heyerdahl finally decided to prove the plausibility of his theory by making the Pacific crossing himself in a type of boat prehistoric Indians might have used. In April 1947 he and five other Scandinavians left Peru aboard the *Kon-Tiki*, a forty-five-foot-long balsa raft outfitted with a sail. Skeptics had predicted that the raft was not seaworthy, that it would become waterlogged and sink within a few days. However, contrary to their predictions, 101 days and 4,300 miles later, the *Kon-Tiki* smashed into a coral reef off the Polynesian island chain of Tuamotu. The triumphant Heyerdahl and his crew waded ashore.

Faces more skepticism

The daring voyage brought Heyerdahl worldwide renown; his riveting written account of his adventure, *Kon-Tiki: Across the Pacific by Raft* (later published as *The Kon-Tiki Expedition*), was an international bestseller. His documentary film on the journey won an Academy Award. Yet many scientists dismissed the entire event as a publicity stunt and continued to reject Heyerdahl's theory on the basis that the Galápagos Islands, a chain much closer to South America than Polynesia, had never been settled.

The Galápagos became Heyerdahl's next stop. In 1953 he and two archaeologists (scientists who study material remains) conducted the first thorough study of the islands. Pottery fragments and other evidence they unearthed indicated that prehistoric South Americans had indeed visited the Galápagos many times but established no permanent settlements due to an inadequate supply of drinking water.

Turns attention to Easter Island

After completing additional research in several South American countries, Heyerdahl turned his attention to Easter Island. Located 2,300 miles west of Chile, it is the Polynesian island closest to South America. Teaming up with five archaeologists to examine ancient artifacts, Heyerdahl was able to prove with carbon-dating techniques that humans had been there around A.D. 380 (one thousand years earlier than previously thought) and that three different waves of migration had occurred. These migratory waves included a white race whose members were apparently responsible for carving the island's famous stone statues (similar to those found in Peru) and for introducing several plants native to South America.

Becomes interested in Egypt and Peru

Throughout the late 1950s and early 1960s Heyerdahl spent much of his time writing, researching, lecturing, and

The Kon-Tiki under sail in the Pacific Ocean.

presenting his findings to fellow scientists, some of whom gradually came to accept the idea that Polynesia was settled not only by Asians but by significant numbers of South Americans as well. By that time, however, Heyerdahl was already contemplating another possible path of migration—this one from ancient Egypt to Peru. Anthropologists had long noted many striking similarities between the two cultures: stepped pyramids and giant stone statues, hieroglyphic (picture or symbol) writing, sophisticated calendars based on astronomical observations, and customs among royalty involving marriage, mummification, and burial. Heyerdahl himself was intrigued by Egyptian tomb paintings of ships made from papyrus (a tall, grasslike water plant) that closely resemble vessels depicted on ancient Inca pottery. (Smaller and more simplified versions of those boats still sail the waters of Lake Titicaca between Bolivia and Peru.) But no one believed that a ship made of papyrus was capable of crossing the Atlantic.

Embarks on a new mission

Heyerdahl again decided to challenge the skeptics and prove that such a journey was possible. In May 1969 he and a crew of six left Morocco in a fifty-foot-long papyrus raft bound for the Caribbean. Named the *Ra* in honor of the Egyptian sun god and the Polynesian word for sun, it was a replica of the type of vessel ancient Egyptians had sailed around the Mediterranean. The *Ra* traveled 2,700 miles across the Atlantic in eight weeks before heavy seas forced the crew to abandon ship about 600 miles from Barbados. Ten months later, Heyerdahl and a seven-man crew tried again with a slightly shorter, lighter, and stronger version of the original *Ra*. Named *Ra II,* it completed the 3,200-mile trip from Morocco to Barbados in fifty-seven days, once again demonstrating that ancient civilizations were not necessarily cut off from one another by the oceans.

Continues his work

Since the *Ra* expeditions, Heyerdahl has continued to pursue his theories regarding prehistoric travel by sea. In 1977, for example, he suggested that the Mesopotamians (ancient peoples who lived in the region between the Tigris and Euphrates rivers—modern-day Turkey and Iraq—and founded the first known urban civilization) may have spread their culture as far away as India. To prove his point Heyerdahl sailed a sixty-foot reed boat called the *Tigris* from the mouth of the Shatt-al-Arab River into the Persian Gulf and from there crossed the Indian Ocean to Pakistan. He has also conducted additional archaeological research on land, including explorations of the Maldives (a chain of islands in the Indian Ocean) that suggest they were a popular stopover for prehistoric traders who sailed between China, India, and Africa. More recently Heyerdahl has supervised an ambitious project to study a remote area of Peru where twenty-six pre-Incan pyramids—the largest such complex in the Americas—have been left virtually undisturbed for over a thousand years.

Further Reading

Architectural Digest, February 1987, pp. 102–09.

Heyerdahl, Thor, *Aku-Aku: Paaskeoeyas Hemmelighet,* Gyldenal, 1957, translation published as *Aku-Aku: The Secret of Easter Island,* Rand McNally, 1958, reprinted, Ballantine, 1974.

Heyerdahl, Thor, *Kon-Tiki Ekspedisjonen,* Gyldenal, 1948, translation published as *Kon-Tiki: Across the Pacific by Raft,* Rand McNally, 1950, new edition printed as *The Kon-Tiki Expedition,* 1968.

Heyerdahl, Thor, *Ra,* Gyldenal, 1970, translation published as *The Ra Expeditions,* Doubleday, 1970.

Heyerdahl, Thor, with Christopher Ralling, *Kon-Tiki Man: An Illustrated Biography of Thor Heyerdahl,* Chronicle, 1991.

National Geographic, January 1971, pp. 44–70.

People, December 11, 1989, pp. 181–88.

U.S. News and World Report, April 2, 1990, pp. 55–60.

Westman, Paul, *Thor Heyerdahl, Across the Seas of Time,* Dillon Press, 1982.

David Hilbert

*Born January 23, 1862
Wehlau, East Prussia
Died February 14, 1943*

*German
mathematician
David Hilbert
conducted important
research on
invariant theory.*

When David Hilbert retired from his position as chairperson of the University of Göttingen mathematics department, he was the best-known and most influential mathematician in the world. His contributions had a profound impact not only on mathematics but on other fields as well. Yet his career ended in disappointment: he had led one of the great centers for mathematical research and teaching, but after his retirement he watched it be destroyed by the Nazi government under Adolph Hitler. Nevertheless, Hilbert's legacy, in the form of theoretical contributions and the students he trained, has outlasted the disruptions of World War II.

Progresses rapidly in academe

David Hilbert was born in Wehlau, near Königsberg, East Prussia (a former German state), on January 23, 1862. His family was staunchly Protestant, although Hilbert himself later left the church in which he was baptized. His father, Otto

Hilbert, was a prominent lawyer in the Königsberg area, and his mother's family name was Erdtmann. The name David ran in the family, a fact Hilbert subsequently had to verify to the staunchly anti-Semitic Nazi regime, which suspected that anyone with the name David was of Jewish ancestry.

After obtaining his early education in Königsberg, Hilbert entered the University of Königsberg in 1880. He received his Ph.D. from the university five years later and took a teaching position in 1886. By 1892 he had been appointed the equivalent of assistant professor at Königsberg and had risen to the rank of full professor the following year. In 1895 he moved to the University of Göttingen as chairperson of the mathematics department, which had become renowned as the world's greatest mathematical center.

Summarizes state of number theory

Hilbert's closest friend in the mathematics community was Hermann Minkowski, who was two years younger than Hilbert but had become well-known at an earlier age. At first Hilbert's family did not approve of their friendship because Minkowski was the son of a Jewish rag merchant. Hilbert nonetheless kept in touch with his friend, who had won a prize from the French Academy while he was still in his teens. Hilbert eventually managed to bring Minkowski to Göttingen.

In 1893 the German Mathematical Association gave Hilbert and Minkowski the project of summarizing the current state of the theory of numbers. Number theory was the oldest branch of mathematics, as it dealt with the properties of whole numbers. Extensive new work had been done by **Karl Friedrich Gauss** (see entry), and throughout the second half of the nineteenth century further progress had been made. Minkowski eventually withdrew from the project, and in 1897 Hilbert submitted a report titled *Der Zahlbericht* ("Number Report"). His work advanced number theory to a more technical level, which has been maintained throughout the twentieth century. Many of the results still bear Hilbert's name, a tribute to the importance of his influence.

avid Hilbert made his mathematical reputation through his research in invariant theory. The concept of an invariant had been created in the nineteenth century as an expression of something that remains the same even though it undergoes various transformations. For example, if all the coefficients (constant factors) in an equation are doubled, the solutions of the equation remain the same. When Hilbert began his research, considerable work had already been done in classifying invariants and in trying to prove the kinds of invariants that existed. The results were massive calculations, and books on invariant theory consisted of pages completely filled with symbols. Hilbert made most of this work obsolete by taking a path that did not require fully expressed calculation. Practitioners of invariant theory were alarmed by his daring attitude. Invariant theory quickly disappeared from the center of mathematical interest because Hilbert's work required some time to be absorbed. Only much later was the field reopened, when invariant theorists were at last ready to proceed from his calculations.

Examines Euclidean geometry

Hilbert next pursued an unexpected direction in his research. After working with algebra he turned to the foundations of geometry. The ancient Greek mathematician Euclid had already laid the foundations more than two thousand years before, but detailed analysis of some of Euclid's proofs revealed gaps in his presentation. He had made assumptions that were neither clearly stated nor justified by his earlier proofs. In addition to problems posed by the gaps, non-euclidean geometries had discovered new approaches during the nineteenth century.

While these systems shared some axioms (statements accepted as true) with Euclidean geometry, they differed in many respects. For example, in Euclidean geometry the sum of the angles of a triangle is equal to 180 degrees, while in non-euclidean geometries the sum could be greater or less than 180. One of the reasons it had taken so long to develop non-euclidean theories was a disagreement over what was true about geometrical objects. Hilbert felt the only way to make progress was to state each proof completely and not to rely on unspoken assumptions.

According to Hilbert, the safest way to avoid unclear assumptions is to regard the terms of the subject as being defined only by the axioms they use. For instance, mathematicians might think they know what a "line" means and may be tempted to use this mental image in trying to prove a fact about lines. But the mental image might easily add something to the concept of a line beyond what is actually given in an axiom. The axiom could therefore be considered a definition of the terms used within it. As Hilbert noted, theorems (formulas, propositions, or statements) that follow from axioms should remain unchanged if the terms of the subject—such as point, line, or plane—are replaced by other words. The form of the axiom, not the result, is the important consideration. Hilbert's idea caused a controversy about the philosophy of mathematics that has lasted throughout most of the twentieth century. Nevertheless, his theories helped mathematicians better understand the foundations of geometry.

Makes permanent contributions to mathematical theory

One of the highlights of Hilbert's career came in 1900, when he was invited to address the International Congress of Mathematicians in Paris, France. In his talk he presented twenty-three problems for mathematicians to solve during the twentieth century. Although all of the problems have not proved to be of equal importance, Hilbert created an agenda that has been followed by many prominent theorists. The first problem addressed the question of how many real numbers (numbers that have no imaginary parts, the rational and irrational numbers) there are, compared to the total of whole numbers (nonnegative integers). The problem was not resolved until 1963, when the answer was shown to depend on which axioms are selected as the basis for the theory of sets. (A set is a collection of mathematical elements.)

Hilbert's seventh problem dealt with the irrationality of real numbers. (A rational number can be multiplied, divided, added, and subtracted only a finite number of times.) According to Hilbert, a number is rational if it is the ratio of two whole numbers. Conversely, a number is irrational if it cannot be expressed as the ratio of two whole numbers. Finally, a number is transcendental if it is not the solution to a polynomial equation (consisting of one or more algebraic terms) with whole number coefficients (constants). Although Hilbert was not the first to prove the numbers "e" and "pi" are transcendental, he simplified the proofs considerably. ("E" is the base of a

Pythagoras, Greek Philosopher and Mathematician

Modern mathematical theorists such as David Hilbert have built on foundations established by ancient thinkers such as Pythagoras (c. 580–c. 500 B.C.). During Pythagoras's lifetime, the Greeks found a way of dealing with pure numbers by themselves, rather than thinking of numbers as merely representing other things, like pieces of land. Pythagoras has been given credit for this discovery. Once numbers were freed from the purely physical realm and allowed to exist on their own, mathematical ideas could be applied to new areas of thought. Today, mathematics helps us understand many aspects of the world, from the orbits of the planets to the behavior of atoms. Mathematics, in fact, is the language of modern science. Thus we must trace much scientific achievement directly to the theories of Pythagoras. Pythagoreans held that numbers lie behind everything—that mathematical ideas can be used to explain the world. For Pythagoras, numbers exerted an unseen, yet total control over the universe, and mathematics bore a very close connection to religion.

natural logarithm, or the power to which a number must be raised to produce a given number. "Pi" is the ratio of the circumference of a circle to its diameter.) A mathematician named A. O. Gelfond solved the seventh problem by establishing that a whole class of numbers is transcendental. Hilbert's tenth problem, on the solubility of certain equations, required considerable progress in mathematical logic before it could be solved. In fact, entire books and conferences have since been devoted to solutions to Hilbert's problems.

Hilbert next turned to the study of mathematical analysis. The previous generation of mathematicians had found defects in one of the standard principles from earlier in the nineteenth century. Hilbert showed that the principle could be preserved, proceeding from there to make progress in the study of integral equations. (An integral equation contains one or more mathematical numbers, the negatives of these numbers, or zero; it is regarded as a complete entity.) Although mathematicians performed more work in this area after Hilbert, he has been credited with the creation of foundational analysis.

Fights the establishment

In 1910 Hilbert received the Bolyai Prize, which confirmed his stature as a great mathematician. By this time he had become an important and colorful international figure. His distinctive appearance, from his Panama hat to his bearded chin and sharp voice, set the tone for mathematicians in Germany and throughout the world. During World War I he refused to sign the "Declaration to the Cultural World," a document that claimed Germany was innocent of alleged war crimes. He also demonstrated his commitment to placing mathematics above nationality by including an obituary of a French mathematician in the journal *Mathematische Annalen,* which was a showpiece of German pride at the time. These acts made him unpopular with German nationalists.

Similarly, Hilbert took pleasure in fighting the academic establishment. For instance, he supported the cause of fellow mathematician Emmy Noether, a Jewish woman who was prohibited from teaching at Göttingen because of her gender and ethnic origins. Hilbert was able to arrange for her to teach by announcing a class in mathematics under his name and then letting her lecture in his place. She was later hired as a lecturer and given a small salary. He also encouraged women to study mathematics: several of the sixty-nine students who wrote their theses under Hilbert were women.

Andrew J. Wiles, English-born American Mathematician

Recently Andrew J. Wiles (1953–), a professor of mathematics at Princeton University, may have solved Fermat's Last Theorem, a puzzle that has frustrated mathematicians for centuries. In 1627 French lawyer and number theorist Pierre Fermat scrawled a general math equation in the margin of his copy of Diophantus's *Arithmetic,* along with a bold statement declaring that the equation $X^n + Y^n = Z^n$ can never be true when the exponent n is greater than two. Fermat provided no proof to his theorem because, he wrote, "the margin is too small to hold it." The theorem concerns an equation similar to the famous Pythagorean theorem. Pythagoras said that the square of the longest side of a triangle equals the sum of the squares of the other two sides ($a^2 + b^2 = c^2$). For example, 3 squared (9) plus 4 squared (16) equals 5 squared (25). Many other values also make this equation true, as long as the exponent is two. According to Fermat's theorem, however, an equation of the same form will never be true with any other whole number.

Many mathematicians have tested and tried to disprove or prove Fermat's Last Theorem. In 1954 Japanese mathematician Yutaka Taniyama proposed a modular form to a set of mathematical equations called elliptical curves. His proposal was called the Taniyama conjecture. (A conjecture in mathematics is a fascinating but unproved theory.) The next theory came in the 1980s from German mathematician Gerhard Frey, who suggested that an elliptical curve can be used to represent all the solutions to Fermat's equation. American Kenneth Ribet proved Frey's idea in 1986, and this changed Wiles's perception of the last theorem. Wiles believed he could prove that the elliptical curve representing the solutions to Fermat's equation could not exist and thereby prove Fermat's Last Theorem to be true. He virtually withdrew from his professional life, except to teach classes at Princeton, to pursue his quest. On June 23, 1993, Wiles announced that he had proven the Taniyama conjecture. Almost as an afterthought, he added that this meant that Fermat's Last Theorem was also proven true. His work has been submitted to a review process by other mathematicians, and if it passes, the centuries-old problem will be considered solved.

Returns to philosophy of mathematics

After working briefly in theoretical physics, Hilbert returned to questions of the philosophy of mathematics that had arisen earlier during his study of geometry. He was eager to establish a secure foundation for mathematics. While he was willing to grant importance to finite mathematics (a system that has a limited number of elements and terms), he felt infinite mathematics (a system that has an unlimited number of elements and terms) required special treatment.

Hilbert set out to prove the consistency of mathematical theory by means of a program called formalism. This enterprise put him in conflict with other philosophers of mathematics. When he expressed his views in an address titled "On the Infinite" in 1925, he was challenged by several thinkers. The incompleteness theorem of the young Austrian mathematician Kurt Gödel in particular threatened Hilbert's entire program. According to Gödel's theorem, it is impossible to create an axiom or set of axioms capable of producing complete and consistent mathematical systems. Although Hilbert's attempts at discovering a foundation for mathematics was virtually ended, some of his ideas have survived under the title of proof theory.

Witnesses Nazi destruction of intellectual community

In 1892 Hilbert had married Kathe Jerosch, who was a source of strength during his periods of disappointment. One source of unhappiness was their only child, Franz, who never lived up to his father's expectations and who probably suffered from a mental disorder. The last years of Hilbert's life were also darkened by the advent of National Socialism (Nazism) under the regime of Adolf Hitler. Hitler purged the universities of professors who did not adhere to the rigid and repressive dictates of the Nazi Party, and the effect on the German intellectual community was devastating.

Hilbert retired from Göttingen University at age sixty-eight in 1930, and three years later the Nazis came to power. It was too late for him to look for a new home. Many of his students had found academic appointments abroad, and the university could not be rebuilt in the face of anti-Semitism and anti-intellectualism practiced by the Nazis. The demoralized atmosphere at Göttingen was made evident upon Hilbert's death on February 14, 1943. No more than a dozen people attended his funeral.

Further Reading

Gillespie, C. C., ed., *Dictionary of Scientific Biography,* Volume 6, Scribner, 1970–78, pp. 388–95.

Mathematical Developments Arising From the Hilbert Problems, American Mathematical Society, 1979.

Reid, Constance, *Hilbert,* Springer-Verlag, 1970.

Tiles, Mary, *Mathematics and the Image of Reason,* Routledge, 1991.

William Augustus Hinton

Born December 15, 1883
Chicago, Illinois
Died August 8, 1959
Canton, Massachusetts

William Augustus Hinton earned an international reputation as a medical researcher with his work on the detection and treatment of sexually transmitted diseases. He was integral in developing two common diagnostic procedures for syphilis, the Hinton test and the Davies-Hinton test. Hinton was the first black professor at Harvard Medical School, where he taught preventative medicine and hygiene, as well as bacteriology (the study of microorganisms) and immunology (the branch of medicine concerned with the body's ability to protect itself from disease).

Becomes teacher

Hinton was born on December 15, 1883, in Chicago, Illinois, to August Hinton and Maria Clark, who were both former slaves. Hinton grew up in Kansas, becoming the youngest student ever to graduate from Kansas City High School. After graduation he studied at the University of Kansas, where he

"I had learned that race was not the determining factor [in contracting syphilis] but that it was, rather, the socioeconomic condition of the patient. It is a disease of the underprivileged."

463

completed the three-year premed program in two years. He did additional undergraduate work at Harvard University in Cambridge, Massachusetts, and received a bachelor's degree from Harvard in 1905.

Hinton worked for a time in a law firm, but soon found he did not enjoy the legal field. He turned instead to education, teaching science for a year at Waldo University in Tennessee before taking a position at State School in Langston, Oklahoma, in 1906. He stayed at State School until 1909, when he married Ada Hawes, who was also a teacher. They subsequently had two daughters, Ann and Jane.

Embarks on medical career

That same year Hinton entered Harvard Medical School. Although he had been offered a scholarship reserved for African American students, Hinton chose to compete for an award offered to all students. He went on to win the Wigglesworth scholarship two years in a row. By skipping the second year of school and finishing the Harvard medical program in only three years, Hinton received a medical degree in 1912.

Hinton's first job was as a serologist (a scientist who works with serums, especially their reactions and properties) at the Wassermann Laboratory of the Harvard Medical School. By 1915 he was named director of the lab, which also became the official lab for the Massachusetts State Department of Public Health. The following year he was appointed head of the laboratory department at the Boston Dispensary, where he established an innovative program to train women as lab technicians. At the time, that profession was not generally open to women.

Conducts syphilis research

From the start of his career until his retirement, Hinton concentrated his research on the diagnosis and treatment of syphilis. Spread by sexual contact, syphilis begins as a small, hard, painless swelling called a primary (or Hunter's) chancre (pronounced SHANG-ker). The disease is highly contagious in the early stages. The initial sore will usually pass away in about eight weeks, but the disease will then spread through the body and lodge in the lymph nodes. In two to four months a skin rash will appear along with fever and intense headaches. This second stage can last two to six weeks. After a latent period, which can extend for years, the disease can appear in various bodily organs and then spread to others.

While medical historians believe that syphilis has been present since ancient times, it was often mislabeled or misdiagnosed; the earliest records of the disease date from 1493 in Spain. Since that time various treatments have been discovered, including arsenic-based drugs, penicillin, and other antibiotics. The first diagnostic test was developed by German physician August von Wassermann in 1906, but the drawback was that the test would take two days to complete. In 1923 a Russian-American researcher, Reuben Leon Kahn, produced a modified syphilis test that took only a few minutes to complete.

≋IMPACT≋

William Augustus Hinton made a significant contribution to the diagnosis of syphilis with the Hinton test. More efficient and accurate as well as less expensive than previous methods, the Hinton test was adopted as a standard procedure for diagnosing syphilis. Today fluorescent antibody tests are used for detection. Although there is yet no inoculation (vaccination) for syphilis, the disease can be controlled through education, safe sexual practices, and proper medical treatment.

Perfects syphilis test

In 1927 Hinton perfected a test—subsequently known as the Hinton test—to diagnose syphilis. Because it was easier, less expensive, and more accurate than previous procedures, the Hinton test was adopted as the standard method for diagnosing syphilis. Later, with Dr. J. A. V. Davies, Hinton developed the Davies-Hinton test. In 1936 Hinton wrote *Syphilis and Its Treatment,* in which he outlined correct procedures for using laboratory tests for syphilis. Although the book at first had little support in the medical community, within twenty years it had become generally accepted and widely acclaimed. In a 1952 interview with the *Boston Daily Globe,* Hinton said

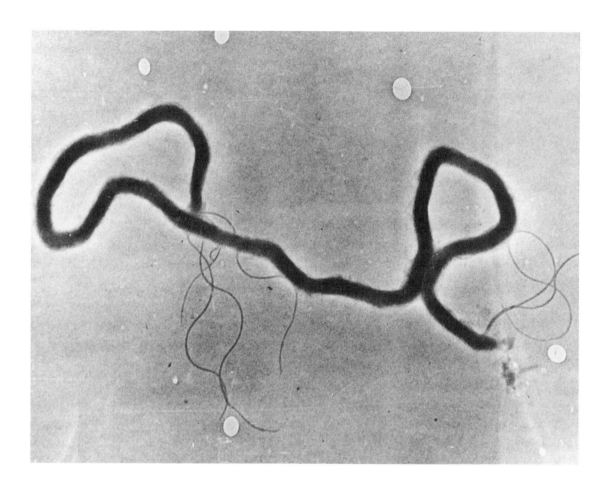

A 1944 slide from an electron microscope of Treponema pallidum, the organism that causes syphilis.

he considered the book his most important contribution because it summed up his research and the experience he gained through treating syphilis patients.

Becomes first black Harvard professor

In 1923 Hinton began his teaching career at Harvard Medical School as assistant lecturer in preventative medicine and hygiene. In addition to his teaching duties, he continued his research and served as a special consultant to the U.S. Public Health Service. In 1936 he was appointed head of laboratories at Boston Floating Hospital; he also taught at Tufts University in Medford, Massachusetts, and Simmons College in Boston, Massachusetts. Hinton lost a leg as the result of an automobile accident in 1940, but this disability did not prevent him from continuing his work. In fact, nine years later Harvard named him clinical professor of bacteriology and immunology. Hinton thus became Harvard's first black professor. After his retirement in 1950 he continued to teach without a salary. He retired from the Wassermann Laboratory in 1953, six years before his death on August 8, 1959, in Canton, Massachusetts.

Further Reading

Boston Daily Globe, September 15, 1952.

Fiftieth Anniversary Report—Harvard Class of 1905, Harvard University Printing Office, 1955.

Hinton, William Augustus, *Syphilis and Its Treatment,* Macmillan, 1936.

George H. Hitchings

Born April 18, 1905
Hoquiam, Washington

Gertrude Belle Elion

Born January 23, 1918
New York, New York

Biochemists George H. Hitchings and Gertrude Belle Elion pioneered "rational" drug design.

George H. Hitchings and Gertrude Belle Elion are biochemists best known for their study of cellular metabolism (or biochemical reactions). As collaborators at Burroughs Wellcome Company, a British pharmaceutical company with research facilities in the United States, they pioneered "rational" drug design. Their research led to the development of medications for leukemia, gout, herpes, malaria, and rejected transplanted organs. They shared the 1988 Nobel Prize for physiology or medicine.

Hitchings inspired by Pasteur

George H. Hitchings was born to George Herbert Hitchings Sr., a naval architect, and Lillian H. Belle Hitchings on April 18, 1905, in Hoquiam, Washington. Hitchings was inspired to pursue a career in medicine by his father's early death and his admiration for the scientist-philanthropist **Louis Pasteur** (see entry). He attended the University of Washington in Seattle, where he received a bachelor's degree in chemistry in 1927 and a master's degree the following year. He continued graduate work at Harvard College (now University) in Cambridge, Massachusetts, earning a Ph.D. in 1933.

Hitchings wrote his doctoral dissertation on the metabolism, or chemical change, of nucleic acids, the chemicals that make up deoxyribonucleic acid (DNA), the carrier of genetic information. He did his work before **James D. Watson** and **Francis Crick** (see entries) were given credit for discovering the structure of DNA. At the time no one was interested in nucleic acids. After receiving his doctorate Hitchings could not find a job in his field, so for nine years he worked as a teacher, first at Harvard and then at Western Reserve University in Cleveland, Ohio. In 1942 he was hired by Burroughs Wellcome in Tuckahoe, New York, where he resumed his work on nucleic acids. He became vice president of research in 1967, holding that position until 1975, when he became scientist emeritus (retired).

Elion excels academically

Gertrude Belle Elion was born on January 23, 1918, in New York City, the first of two children of Robert Elion and Bertha Cohen. Her father was a dentist who immigrated to the United States from Lithuania as a small boy, and her mother came to the United States from Russia at the age of fourteen. An excellent student, Elion was accelerated two years by her teachers and graduated from high school at the height of the Great Depression, a dark period of economic crisis in America during the 1930s.

Having witnessed the painful death of her grandfather from stomach cancer, Elion vowed to become a cancer researcher. She enrolled at Hunter College in New York City, majoring in chemistry because that seemed the best route to her goal. Elion was able to attend college only because several schools in the city, including Hunter, offered free tuition to students with good grades.

Encounters discrimination

In 1937, at the age of nineteen, Elion graduated with a bachelor of arts degree as a member of the scholastic honorary society Phi Beta Kappa. Despite her outstanding academic record, widespread discrimination against women squelched her early efforts to find a job as a chemist. She finally obtained a one-semester appointment teaching biochemistry to nurses and then took a position in a friend's laboratory. With the money she saved from these jobs, Elion began graduate school at New York University. In order to afford tuition, she lived with her parents and worked as a substitute science teacher in the New York City public school system. In 1941 she graduated with highest honors, having earned a master's degree in chemistry.

After graduation Elion again faced difficulties finding work in her field. The only position available was as a quality control chemist in the Quaker Maid Company food laboratory, checking the color of mayonnaise and the acidity of pickles. After a year and a half of searching for a more challenging job, Elion was finally offered a post as research chemist at the Johnson & Johnson Company. Six months after she arrived, however, her division closed.

The pair begins a long collaboration

The start of World War II opened a new era of opportunity for women as men left their jobs to fight in the war. Elion was thus able to find work at Hitchings's lab at Burroughs Wellcome. When they met, Elion was twenty-six years old and Hitchings was thirty-nine. Their working relationship began on June 14, 1944, and lasted for the rest of their careers. Each time Hitchings was promoted, Elion filled the spot he had just vacated. In 1967, when Hitchings retired and was named scientist emeritus, Elion was named head of the department of experimental therapy, a position she held until her own retirement sixteen years later.

Settled in her job and excited by the breakthroughs occurring in the field of biochemistry, Elion took steps to earn her doctorate. Since only one school—Brooklyn Polytechnic Institute (now Polytechnic University)—offered night classes in chemistry, she enrolled there. Attending classes required an exhausting hour-and-a-half commute each way, but Elion persevered for two years. School administrators later accused her of not being a serious student and pressed her to attend full time. Financially, however, Elion had no choice but to continue working. Abandoning her doctoral studies left Elion frustrated and distraught.

Hitchings and Elion conduct cancer cell research

Until Hitchings and Elion began working together in the 1940s, drug researchers created new drugs by modifying natural products. But the duo used a new and unusual approach to try to fight the agents of disease. By studying the biochemistry of cancer cells, harmful bacteria, and viruses, they sought to understand the differences between the metabolism of those cells and normal body cells. They were particularly interested in how disease-causing cells use nucleic acids to stay alive and grow. Hitchings and Elion reasoned that these differences could provide clues about how to selectively kill diseased tissue without harming surrounding normal tissue. Their method would come to be known as "rational" drug design.

Hitchings and Elion implemented their ideas by investigating the chemical pathways of nucleic acid synthesis (combination), which is crucial to cell metabolism. They synthesized chemical compounds similar to purines and pyrimidines, two main categories of nucleic acids that interfere with DNA synthesis. Because cancer cells divide quickly, the compounds are particularly disruptive to them, killing them as they try to divide. This effect provides the basis for a cancer treatment known as chemotherapy.

IMPACT

George H. Hitchings and Gertrude Belle Elion discovered 6-mercaptopurine (6MP), the first effective compound to be used against childhood leukemia. Studies of 6MP led to the discovery of azathioprine, which prevents rejection of transplanted human kidneys and treats rheumatoid arthritis. The duo's groundbreaking research helped lead to the 1984 discovery of AZT, the first drug approved for the treatment of AIDS.

Discovery of important drugs

In 1951 Hitchings and Elion developed 6-mercaptopurine (6MP), a compound similar to purine. Working with scientists at Sloan-Kettering Institute in New York City, they perfected the drug for use in combating childhood leukemia (a disease of the white blood cells). 6MP and thioguanine, another compound produced by Hitchings and Elion, are still used to treat acute forms of leukemia.

During the next two decades the success of 6MP prompted Hitchings, Elion, and other scientists to look for more uses for the drug. Their work led to the discovery of azathioprine, which prevents rejection of transplanted human kidneys and treats rheumatoid arthritis. Other experiments led to the discovery of allopurinol to treat gout, a disease in which excess uric acid builds up in the joints; pyrimethamine, a treatment for malaria; and trimethoprim, for urinary and respiratory tract infections. Trimethoprim is also used to treat *Pneumocystis carinii pneumonia,* the leading killer of people with acquired immunodeficiency syndrome (AIDS).

Team wins Nobel Prize

In 1968 Elion learned that a compound called adenine arabinoside showed signs of successfully fighting DNA viruses. This compound was similar in structure to 2,6-diaminopurine, a chemical created in the Wellcome lab. Although her lab was not equipped to screen antiviral compounds, she immediately began synthesizing new compounds to send to a Wellcome lab in Britain for testing. In 1969 she received notice by telegram that one of the compounds had been proven effective against the herpes simplex virus, which causes cold sores. In 1984 researchers trained by Elion and Hitchings developed azidothymidine (AZT), the first drug used to treat AIDS. Four years later Hitchings and Elion shared the Nobel Prize for physiology or medicine with Sir James Black, a British biochemist.

Pursue active retirement

Throughout his life Hitchings has supported philanthropic causes, among them the Burroughs Wellcome fund, a charitable organization for which he has served as president and director. In 1933 he married Beverly Reimer, with whom he had two children; in 1989, four years after her death, he married Joyce Shaver. In addition to winning the Nobel Prize, Hitchings has earned numerous awards, including the Gregor Mendel Medal from the Czechoslovakian Academy of Science in 1968 and the Albert Schweitzer International Prize for Medicine in 1989. The recipient of numerous honorary degrees, he has also been a member of the National Academy of Sciences since 1977.

After retiring in 1983 Elion continued as a consultant with Wellcome. In addition, she became a research professor of medicine and pharmacology at Duke University in Durham, North Carolina. Elion has served as president of the American Association for Cancer Research and as a member of the National Cancer Advisory Board. She was elected to the National Inventors' Hall of Fame, the National Academy of Sciences, and the National Women's Hall of Fame.

Further Reading

Bertsch, Sharon McGrayne, *Nobel Prize Women in Science: Their Lives, Struggles, and Momentous Discoveries,* Carol Publishing Group, 1992.

Cheng, Y.-C., ed., "Rational Design of Anticancer Drugs: Here, Imminent or Illusive?" *The Development of Target-Oriented Anticancer Drugs,* Raven Press, 1983, pp. 227–38.

McGuire, Paula, ed., *Nobel Prize Winners: 1987–1991 Supplement,* H. W. Wilson, 1992, pp. 77–78.

Dorothy Hodgkin

Born May 12, 1910
Cairo, Egypt
Died July 29, 1994
Shipston-on-Stour, England

For her contribution to determining the structure of penicillin and vitamin B^{12}, Dorothy Hodgkin was awarded the 1964 Nobel Prize for chemistry.

English chemist Dorothy Hodgkin began a new era in science by employing the technique of X-ray crystallography to determine the molecular structures of several large biochemical molecules. Hodgkin was awarded the 1964 Nobel Prize in chemistry for determining the structure of both penicillin and vitamin B^{12}.

Becomes interested in chemistry and crystals

Dorothy Crowfoot Hodgkin was born in Cairo, Egypt, on May 12, 1910, to John and Grace (Hood) Crowfoot. Her mother, although not formally educated beyond finishing school, was an expert on Coptic (Egyptian Christian) textiles and an excellent amateur botanist and nature artist. Her father, a British archaeologist and scholar, worked for the Ministry of Education in Cairo at the time of her birth. The family traveled extensively during Hodgkin's childhood. When World War I broke out in 1914, Hodgkin and her two younger sisters were sent to England for safety, where they were raised for a few years by a nanny and their paternal grandmother. Young Hodgkin saw her parents when they returned to Britain for only a few months every year. Occasionally during her youth she traveled to visit them in such distant places as Khartoum (in the Sudan) and Palestine.

Initially educated at home and in small private schools, at age eleven Hodgkin began attending the Sir John Leman School in Beccles, England, from which she graduated in 1928. After a period of intensive tutoring to prepare her for the entrance examinations, she entered Somerville College for women at Oxford University. One of her aunts paid the tuition and gave her financial support. For a time Hodgkin considered specializing in archaeology but eventually settled on chemistry and crystallography. Hodgkin's interest in chemistry and crystals had begun early in her life. The soil chemist A. F. Joseph and his colleagues had given her a tour of their laboratory and later a box of reagents (substances that cause chemical reactions) and minerals that allowed her to set up a home laboratory.

Begins studying crystallography

A combination of mathematics, physics, and chemistry, crystallography was a fledgling science at the time Hodgkin began her studies. Max von Laue, William Henry Bragg, and William Lawrence Bragg had essentially invented it in the early decades of the century (they had won Nobel Prizes in 1914 and 1915, respectively) when they discovered that the atoms in a crystal deflected X rays. The deflected X rays interacted, or interfered, with each other. If they *constructively* interfered with each other, a bright spot could be captured on photographic film. If they *destructively* interfered with each other, the brightness was canceled. The pattern of the X-ray spots—*diffraction pattern*—bore a mathematical relationship to the positions of individual atoms in the crystal. Thus, by shining X rays through a crystal, capturing the pattern on film, and doing mathematical calculations on the distances and relative positions of the spots, the molecular structure of almost

Before Dorothy Hodgkin, scientists had difficulty studying large molecules such as proteins. Proteins are more complicated than other biological molecules because they are polymers (long chains of repeating units) and they undergo their biochemical functions by folding over on themselves and taking specific three-dimensional shapes. This was not well understood at the time, however, so Hodgkin's results began a new era. X-ray crystallography could establish not only the structural layout of atoms in a molecule, even a huge one, but the overall molecular shape that contributed to biological activity.

any crystalline material could theoretically be worked out. The more complicated the structure, however, the more elaborate and difficult the calculations. Techniques for the practical application of crystallography were few, and organic chemists accustomed to chemical methods of determining molecular structure were skeptical about its usefulness.

Displays talent for X-ray studies

After Hodgkin graduated from Oxford in 1932, A. F. Joseph steered her toward Cambridge University and the crystallographic work of J. D. Borneol. Borneol already had a reputation in the field, and researchers from many countries sent him crystals for analysis. Hodgkin's first job was as Borneol's assistant. Under his guidance she began demonstrating her particular talent for X-ray studies of large molecules such as sterols (or steroid alcohols, found in fatty tissues of plants and animals) and vitamins. In 1934 Borneol took the first X-ray of pepsin (a protein crystal), and Hodgkin did the consequent analysis to obtain information about its molecular weight and structure.

Researches at Oxford

In 1934 Hodgkin returned to Oxford as a teacher at Somerville College, where she continued her research on sterols and obtained her doctorate in 1937. The crystallography and laboratory facilities there were extremely primitive, however. For instance, Hodgkin had to climb a rickety circular staircase several times a day to reach the only window with sufficient light for her to use her microscope. This was made all the more difficult because Hodgkin suffered most of her adult life from a severe case of rheumatoid arthritis, which did not respond well to treatment and badly crippled her hands and feet. And, because she was a woman, Oxford officially barred Hodgkin from research meetings of the faculty chemistry club. Fortunately her talent and quiet perseverance quickly won over students and faculty members. One of the professors helped her obtain the money to buy better equipment, and the Rockefeller Foundation awarded her a series of small grants.

One of Hodgkin's early successes at Oxford was the explanation of the molecular structure of cholesterol iodide (salt). During World War II Hodgkin and a graduate student, Barbara Low, worked out the structure of penicillin (a relatively nontoxic antibiotic acid) from some of the first crystals ever made of the vital new drug. In 1948 Hodgkin began groundbreaking work on the structure of vitamin B^{12}, which is necessary for the prevention of pernicious anemia, a chronic lack of red blood cells.

Receives Nobel Prize and Order of Merit

After the war Hodgkin helped form the International Union of Crystallography, causing American and European governments some concern because she insisted on including crystallographers from Communist countries, whose governments were seen as a threat to Western democracies. Always interested in the cause of world unity, Hodgkin was a member of several organizations that admitted Communist Party members. (A restriction on her U.S. visa was finally lifted in 1990 after the Soviet Union disbanded.)

In 1947 Hodgkin was inducted into the Royal Society, Britain's premier scientific organization. This honor brought her a dual university/college appointment with a better salary at Oxford, thus alleviating her chronic money problems. Hodgkin still had to wait until 1957 for a full professorship, however, and it was not until 1958 that she was assigned an actual chemistry laboratory at Oxford. Two years later she obtained the Wolfson Research Professorship, an endowed chair financed by the Royal Society, and in 1964 she received the Nobel Prize in chemistry. The following year she was

Kathleen Lonsdale, Irish-born English Crystallographer

Kathleen Lonsdale (1903–1971) was an early pioneer in X-ray crystallography who influenced Dorothy Crowfoot Hodgkin and others in the field. In 1929 Lonsdale proved experimentally that the hexamethylbenzene crystal, an unusual form of the aromatic compound, was both hexagonal and flat in shape. Two years later she illustrated the structure of hexachlorobenzene. In 1945 Lonsdale became one of the first women admitted as a fellow to the Royal Society. She was the first woman professor at University College of the University of London and the first woman president of both the International Union of Crystallography and the British Association for the Advancement of Science. In 1966 the lonsdaleite, a rare form of meteoric diamond, was named for her.

Lonsdale and her husband, Thomas, were also committed pacifists. In 1956 she wrote a book in reaction to extensive nuclear testing by the United States, Great Britain, and the Soviet Union. Titled *Is Peace Possible?*, the book explores the relationship between world peace and world population needs, viewed through Lonsdale's own experience as the youngest of ten children.

awarded Britain's Order of Merit, becoming only the second woman to achieve this distinction (English nurse and philanthropist Florence Nightingale was the first).

Solves the riddle of the structure of insulin

In 1969, after decades of work and waiting for computer technology to catch up with the complexity of her project,

Hodgkin unraveled the structure of insulin, a protein that is naturally secreted in the body and is used in the treatment of diabetes. She employed some sophisticated techniques in the process, such as substituting atoms in the insulin molecule and then comparing the altered crystal structure to the original.

Marries Thomas Hodgkin

Because of the job-related travel demands of her husband, African studies scholar and teacher Thomas Hodgkin, the couple maintained separate residences until he finally obtained a position teaching at Oxford. Despite this unusual arrangement they had a successful marriage—it began back in 1937—and three children. Although Hodgkin officially retired in 1977, she continued to travel widely. She also expanded her lifelong activities on behalf of world peace, working with the Pugwash Conferences on Science and World Affairs. Hodgkin died of a stroke on July 29, 1994, in Shipston-on-Stour, England.

Further Reading

Bertsch, Sharon McGrayne, *Nobel Prize Women in Science: Their Lives, Struggles, and Momentous Discoveries,* Carol Publishing Group, 1992.

Opfell, Olga S., *The Lady Laureates,* Scarecrow Press, 1986.

Dorothy Horstmann

Born July 2, 1911
Spokane, Washington

Dorothy Horstmann played a significant yet often unacknowledged role in the development of the polio vaccine.

Dorothy Horstmann is an American virologist, a scientist who studies disease-causing viruses. In the late 1940s and early 1950s, before polio immunizations were considered feasible, she proved that the virus that causes polio (a debilitating neuromuscular disease) reaches the nervous system through the bloodstream. Horstmann's conclusions were based on experiments with monkeys and chimpanzees conducted in 1952 at the Yale University School of Medicine. Even though her experiments were initially dismissed by some virologists, her conclusion was subsequently proven to be valid.

Begins career in medicine

Dorothy Millicent Horstmann was born on July 2, 1911, in Spokane, Washington, to Henry and Anna (Humold) Horstmann. She received a bachelor of arts degree in 1936 and a doctor of medicine degree in 1940, both from the University of California. After holding an internship at the San Francisco

City and County Hospital from 1939 to 1940, she completed her medical residency at Vanderbilt University in Nashville, Tennessee. In 1942 she began her long affiliation with the Yale University School of Medicine in New Haven, Connecticut.

In 1945 Horstmann was appointed associate professor of medicine at Yale, then for a year beginning in 1947 she held a National Institutes of Health postdoctoral research fellowship. By 1961 she had risen to the rank of professor of epidemiology (the branch of medical science that deals with the incidence, distribution, and control of disease) and pediatrics (medical treatment of children), and in 1969 she was named a John Rodman Paul professor of epidemiology and pediatrics. Since 1982 she has held the titles of emeritus (retired) professor and senior research scientist at Yale.

Experiments with gamma globulin

Horstmann's research was inspired by the work of William McDowell, who showed that injections of gamma globulin (an antibody-rich serum extracted from blood plasma) could produce temporary immunity to polio. From this evidence Horstmann hypothesized that the polio virus first travels through the bloodstream before finally settling in the nervous system. The discoveries she made during her experiments with monkeys and chimpanzees were initially dismissed by some virologists as inconclusive. They pointed out that no virus had been found in the blood of most patients who had developed polio.

It was subsequently confirmed, however, that by the time the symptoms of polio (muscle weakness, followed by paralysis) become evident the virus has already left the bloodstream and established itself in the nervous system. Horstmann's work and the parallel studies of David Bodian at Johns Hopkins University in Baltimore, Maryland, proved that polio is indeed an infection that can enter the nervous system through the bloodstream.

Works with polio vaccines

Throughout the 1950s and 1960s Horstmann participated in field trials to establish the effectiveness and safety of a polio vaccine (a preparation administered to increase immunity to polio). During her distinguished career Horstmann also studied maternal rubella (German measles) and the rubella syndrome in infants. She holds four honorary doctorates and has received numerous honors and awards, including the James D. Bruce Award of the American College of Physicians (1975), Denmark's Thorvold Madsen Award (1977), and the Maxwell Finland Award of the Infectious Diseases Society of America (1978). Horstmann is a member of the National Academy of Sciences, the American Society of Clinical Investigations, the American College of Physicians, and the Royal Society of Medicine.

Further Reading

Smith, Jane S., *Patenting the Sun: Polio and the Salk Vaccine,* William Morrow, 1990.

Godfrey Hounsfield

Born August 28, 1919
Newark, England

Sir Godfrey Hounsfield is an English biomedical engineer who pioneered a great leap forward in medical diagnosis: he invented computerized axial tomography, popularly known as CAT scan. Ushering in a new and sometimes controversial era of medical technology, Hounsfield's device allows a doctor to look inside a patient's body and examine a three-dimensional image far more detailed than a conventional X ray. The importance of this advance was recognized in 1979, the year Hounsfield received the Nobel Prize for physiology or medicine.

"I've always searched for original ideas; I am absolutely opposed to doing something someone else has done."

Becomes interested in technology

Godfrey Newbold Hounsfield was born on August 28, 1919, in Newark, England, the youngest of five children of an engineer-turned-farmer. Hounsfield's technical interests began when, to prevent boredom, he began figuring out how the machinery on his father's farm worked. From there he moved

483

The computerized axial tomography (CAT scan), created by Godfrey Hounsfield, was hailed by neurosurgeons as a great advance in medical technology. Before the CAT scanner, doctors wanting a detailed brain X ray had to pump chemicals or air into the patient's brain to help their equipment see through the skull. Although the scanner is very expensive (even the earliest models cost over $300,000), Hounsfield argued that, if properly used, the device actually reduces medical costs by eliminating exploratory surgery and other invasive diagnostic procedures.

on to exploring electronics, and by his teens he was building his own radio sets. After studying radio communication at City and Guilds College, he graduated in 1938. When World War II erupted, Hounsfield volunteered for the Royal Air Force, where he studied and later lectured on the new and vital technology of radar at the Royal Air Force Cranwell Radar School. Following the war he resumed his education, receiving a degree in electrical and mechanical engineering from Faraday House Electrical Engineering College in 1951. Upon graduation Hounsfield joined Thorn EMI Ltd. (EMI stands for Electrical and Musical Industries), where he has remained his entire professional life.

At Thorn EMI Hounsfield first worked on improving radar systems and then turned to computers. In 1959 a design team Hounsfield headed finished production of Britain's first large all-transistor computer, the EMIDEC 1100. Hounsfield moved on to work on high-capacity computer memory devices, in 1967 obtaining a British patent titled "Magnetic Films for Information Storage."

Creates the CAT scanner

Hounsfield's work during the mid-1960s included the problem of enabling computers to recognize patterns, thus allowing them to "read" letters and numbers. In 1967, during a long walk through the British countryside, Hounsfield's knowledge of computers, pattern recognition, and radar technology all came together in his mind. He envisioned a medical diagnostic system in which an X-ray machine would image thin "slices" through a patient's body. Then a computer would process the slices into an accurate representation that would

Allan M. Cormack, South African-born American Physicist

In 1979 Godfrey Hounsfield and Allan M. Cormack (1924–) won the Nobel Prize for physiology for their independent studies of computerized axial tomography (CAT scan). Their work is considered the most revolutionary development in the field of radiology since the discovery of the X ray by **Wilhelm Röntgen** (see entry) in 1895. Cormack was the first to analyze the possibility of such an examination of a biological system, in 1963 and 1964, and to develop the equations needed for computer-assisted X-ray reconstruction of pictures of the human brain and body.

display the tissues, organs, and other structures in much greater detail than a single X ray could produce.

Although computers available in 1967 were not sophisticated enough to make such a machine practical, Hounsfield continued to refine his idea and began working on a prototype (test model) scanner. He enlisted two radiologists, James Ambrose and Louis Kreel, who assisted him with their practical knowledge of radiology and also provided tissue samples and test animals for scans. The project attracted support from the British Department of Health and Social Services, and in 1971 a test machine was installed at Atkinson Morely's Hospital in Wimbledon.

The scanner was highly successful, and the first production model followed a year later. These original scanners were designed for imaging the brain and were hailed by neurosurgeons as a great advance. Before the invention of the CAT scanner, doctors wanting a detailed brain X ray had to help their equipment see through a patient's skull by such dangerous techniques as pumping chemicals or air into the brain.

Hounsfield, now head of EMI's Medical Systems section, continued to make improvements to the CAT scanner. He worked to lower the radiation exposure required (radiation is harmful energy emitted in the form of waves or particles), sharpen the images produced, and develop larger models that could image any part of the body, not just the head. This "whole body scanner" went on the market in 1975.

Receives Nobel Prize

The CAT scanner won Hounsfield and his company more than thirty awards, including the MacRobert Award, Britain's highest honor for engineering. In 1979 Hounsfield's collection of scientific tributes was topped off with the Nobel Prize, which he shared with Allan M. Cormack (see box), an American nuclear physicist. Hounsfield moved on to positions as chief staff scientist and then senior staff scientist for Thorn EMI. He continued to improve the CAT scanner, working on a version that could take an accurate "snapshot" of the heart between beats. He has also contributed to the next step in diagnostic technology, nuclear magnetic resonance imaging (MRI), which produces images of the content of human tissue using measurements of its molecular structure. In 1986 Hounsfield became a consultant to Thorn EMI's Central Research Laboratories in Middlesex, near his longtime home in Twickenham.

Further Reading

Current Biography Yearbook: 1979, H. W. Wilson, 1980, pp. 153–55.

Engineers and Inventors, Harper, 1986, pp. 85–86.

Edwin Hubble

Born November 20, 1889
Marshfield, Missouri
Died September 28, 1953
Mount Palomar, California

American astronomer Edwin Hubble's impact on science has been compared to the contributions of pioneering scientists such as English physicist Isaac Newton and Italian astronomer Galileo Galilei. Hubble helped change the perception of the universe in two important ways. In an era when the Milky Way was perceived as the extent of the entire universe, Hubble confirmed the existence of other galaxies through his observations from the Mount Wilson Observatory in Pasadena, California. Along with other astronomers of his time, Hubble showed that the newly discovered universe was expanding. He also developed a mathematical concept to quantify this expansion, now known as Hubble's law.

American astronomer Edwin Hubble's revolutionary work on galaxies led to the formulation of the big bang theory.

Excels as student and athlete

Edwin Powell Hubble was born on November 20, 1889, in Marshfield, Missouri, to John P. Hubble, an insurance agent, and Virginia Lee James Hubble, a descendant of the

American astronomer Edwin Hubble revolutionized the way we view our place in the universe when he discovered that there are galaxies in the universe other than our own Milky Way. He also discovered that the galaxies are moving away from each other, and hence the universe is expanding. Hubble's work later resulted in the big bang theory of the origin of the universe. Over the years scientists have made discoveries that strongly support the big bang theory; indeed, what is thought to be left-over heat from the big bang itself was detected in the early 1990s. This so-called cosmic background radiation, measured by extremely sensitive instruments, is widely viewed as final confirmation of the big bang.

American colonist Miles Standish. The third of seven children, Hubble spent his early childhood in Missouri, entering grade school in 1895. In 1898, when his father was transferred to the Chicago office of his firm, the Hubble family moved first to Evanston and then to Wheaton, Illinois, both Chicago suburbs.

Hubble attended Wheaton High School, excelling in both sports and academics. He graduated in 1906 at the age of sixteen, two years earlier than most students. For his achievement he received an academic scholarship to the University of Chicago, where he studied mathematics, physics, chemistry, and astronomy. During the summer Hubble tutored and worked to earn money for his college expenses. In his junior year he received a scholarship in physics, and by his senior year he was working as a laboratory assistant to physicist Robert A. Millikan.

Hubble graduated in 1910 with a bachelor's degree in mathematics and astronomy. In addition to pursuing an academic career, the six-foot two-inch Hubble was an amateur heavyweight boxer. According to one unconfirmed story, sports promoters urged him to become a professional boxer and fight against heavyweight champion Jack Johnson, an offer Hubble declined.

Starts out as lawyer

Upon receiving a Rhodes Scholarship in 1910, Hubble attended Queen's College at the University of Oxford in England. He studied jurisprudence (the science or philosophy of law), completing the two-year course in 1912, then began work toward a bachelor's degree in law. Eventually he changed his major to Spanish. While at Oxford Hubble also continued his athletic endeavors, excelling in the high jump, broad jump, shot put, and running. In 1913 he returned to the United States and began practicing law in Louisville, Kentucky, where his family was living. Bored with his law career within a year, Hubble returned to the University of Chicago to work toward a doctorate in astronomy at the Yerkes Observatory.

Begins life's work

At the time Hubble attended the University of Chicago, the Yerkes Observatory was a waning institution that did not actually offer formal courses in astronomy. Working under the supervision of Edwin B. Frost, the observatory's director, however, Hubble made regular observations on the Yerkes telescope and studied on his own. Hubble's work at this time was reportedly influenced by a lecture he attended at Northwestern University in Chicago. At the presentation, Lowell Observatory astronomer Vesto M. Slipher presented evidence that spiral nebulae (in that era, the term nebulae was used to describe any celestial body not obviously identifiable as a star) had high radial velocities (the velocities at which objects appear to be moving toward or away from Earth in a direct line of sight). Slipher had found spiral nebulae that were moving at much higher velocities than stars generally moved, thus suggesting that the nebulae might not be part of the Milky Way.

During his term at Yerkes, Hubble also met astronomer George E. Hale, founder of the Yerkes Observatory and then the director of Mount Wilson Observatory in Pasadena, California. In 1916 Hale invited Hubble to join the Mount Wilson staff once he received his doctorate. Hubble's acceptance of this offer was delayed by World War I, however. He joined the army in 1917, attaining the rank of major before being wounded in battle. After his discharge in 1917 he began work at Mount Wilson. The observatory had two telescopes, a 60-inch reflector and a newly operational 100-inch reflector, the largest in the world at that time. (In a reflector telescope light passes down an open tube then hits a curved mirror at the lower end that reflects the light back up the tube, directing it onto a

Johannes Kepler, German Astronomer

German astronomer Johannes Kepler (1571–1630) was instrumental in laying the groundwork for modern knowledge of the solar system. One of the first scientists to study supernovas—"Kepler's Star" blazed into view in 1604 and Kepler wrote two pamphlets about it—he also wrote about applications of optics (the scientific study of light) in astronomy and proposed a design for a telescope. After Kepler's friend Galileo Galilei (1564–1642) discovered the moons of Jupiter, Kepler used a telescope to prove to himself that the Italian astronomer's discoveries did indeed exist. He dubbed them "satellites," a name that stuck.

In 1609 Kepler published his first two laws of planetary motion. The first states that a planet orbits the Sun in an ellipse, not in a circle as Polish astronomer Nicolaus Copernicus (1473–1543) had believed. The second states that a planet moves faster when nearer the Sun and slower when farther away. (Kepler thought, incorrectly, that magnetism in the Sun was responsible for the variation.) The third law, published in 1619, determined that the square of the time it takes a planet to orbit the Sun is equal to the cube of its average distance. In other words, once it is determined how long it takes a planet to complete an orbit, its relative distance from the Sun can be calculated. In the same book in which the third law appears, Kepler devotes space to the "music of the spheres," assigning individual notes that each planet "sings." Also in 1619 he published a volume on comets. Kepler incorrectly believed them to be objects that moved in straight lines, but he had a remarkably accurate explanation of the Sun's role in producing a comet's tail.

smaller mirror that again reflects the light into the eyepiece.) Hubble would remain at Mount Wilson for his entire career.

Discovers new galaxies

Hubble's first notable achievement at Mount Wilson was the confirmation of the existence of galaxies outside the Milky Way. From observations he made in October 1923, Hubble was able to identify a type of variable star known as a Cepheid (pronounced SEF-ee-id) in the Andromeda nebula (known today as the Andromeda galaxy). (Variable stars got their name because their light output changes over time, varying between dim and bright.) By using information about the relationship between brightness, luminosity (how much light a star radiates), and the distances of Cepheid stars in Earth's galaxy, Hubble was able to estimate the distance to the Cepheid in the Andromeda nebula to be about one million light-years. (A light-year measures the distance light travels in a year, about six trillion miles).

Hubble also discovered other Cepheids, as well as other objects, and calculated the distances to them. Since scientists knew that the maximum diameter of the Milky Way was only 100,000 light-years, Hubble's figures established the existence of galaxies outside our own. Eventually he discovered nine new galaxies. Consistent with scientific terminology of his time, Hubble called the galaxies "extragalactic nebulae." The results of Hubble's work were publicly announced at the December 1924 meeting of the American Astronomical Society, settling one of the great scientific debates of that era, that galaxies other than the Milky Way did exist. In 1924 Hubble also married Grace Burke Leib.

Introduces galaxy classification system

In 1925, having proved the existence of galaxies beyond our own, Hubble introduced a system of classifying them, or breaking them down into types of galaxies. Most he divided into two main groups, regular or irregular. In addition, regular galaxies were either spiral or elliptical. Spiral galaxies, like the Milky Way, have huge arms of new stars that trail around a rotating center of older stars. The elliptical galaxies also rotate around a center of older stars, but they are shaped like saucers, lacking the new-star arms of the spiral galaxies. The system used to classify galaxies today is still based on Hubble's structure.

Uses redshifts to determine distances

Hubble continued his pioneering work on galaxies throughout the 1920s, determining distances for over twenty galaxies surrounding the Milky Way. In 1929 this work led to his most important discovery. For over a decade, scientists—including Slipher—had predicted that the light coming from some distant galaxies might indicate that the galaxies were moving apart from each other and Earth. If the galaxies were speeding fast enough away from Earth, the motion would "stretch" the light waves emitting from them. Since longer wavelengths make light take on a reddish tone, this stretching was called the "redshift."

The mathematics for predicting redshifts were based on the general theory of relativity, published in 1916 by physicist **Albert Einstein** (see entry) and extended in the 1920s by other mathematicians. General relativity held that gravity is not so much a *force* as it is *geometry*—the geometry of space. Big objects like planets bend the space around them; smaller objects simply follow the bending of space.

Formulates Hubble's law

Hubble's greatest achievement was to determine the redshifts for a large number of galaxies by measuring the wavelengths of the light coming from them. His measurements led him to two important conclusions. First, distant galaxies did seem to be moving away from Earth. Second, the farther away they were from Earth, the faster they seemed to move. This relationship, between a galaxy's distance and its speed, is now known as Hubble's law.

The Hubble Space Telescope

The Hubble Space Telescope (HST), named for Edwin Hubble, was the first optical observatory in space and the most powerful telescope in the world. Launched from the United States space shuttle *Discovery* in 1990, the telescope is orbiting 380 miles above Earth and is scheduled to remain in space for fifteen years. Weighing 12.8 tons, the HST is equipped with a high-quality mirror, a faint-object camera, and fine-guidance sensors.

Within two months after the HST was launched, however, engineers discovered major flaws in the mirror and vibration problems. Nevertheless, the HST was able to send back pictures of such quasars as the Einstein Cross and detected a white spot on Saturn. It also provided remarkable details about supernovas (exploding stars), the motion and composition of celestial objects, the formation and merging of galaxies, the activity of black holes, the composition of binary stars, and the physical processes surrounding shock waves.

In December 1993 astronauts aboard the space shuttle *Endeavour* completed repairs to the HST. A month later the spacecraft discovered a large population of aging white dwarf stars, and in May 1994 it showed evidence of a massive black hole that is swallowing up matter in a galaxy near the Milky Way. The following July the HST took hundreds of pictures as large chunks of the comet Shoemaker-Levy 9 smashed into Jupiter. These images have provided information about the composition of comets and Jupiter as well as the dynamics of celestial crashes. In September 1995 a group of astronomers reported they had used the HST to confirm earlier findings that the universe appears to be younger than some of its stars.

Facing page:
*Edwin Hubble surveys the
sky through the Schmidt
Photographic Telescope at
the Mount Palomar
observatory in June 1949.*

At first glance, this observation of the movement of galaxies relative to Earth might make it seem that Earth was somehow the center of the universe. Instead, though, the motion of the galaxies can be explained by an idea based on Einstein's theory of relativity: the expansion of space itself. It is not so much that the galaxies are moving by themselves, according to this idea; rather, they are moving along with the expanding space around them.

Arrives at proof of big bang

Thanks to Hubble's observations, scientists now had a way of starting to answer the seemingly unanswerable question of how old the universe is and how it began. If the universe were expanding, they figured, that expansion had to start somewhere. Aleksandr Friedman and Georges Lemaitre, two mathematicians who had extended Einstein's work in the 1920s, had found that relativity suggested an origin for the universe. That origin, they said, was a single point from which the universe had first expanded. From this tiny point, known as a singularity, space, time, and matter (or material substance; virtually everything in the universe is made up of matter) expanded into being.

This idea was highly controversial. Leading cosmologists argued against it. They suggested instead that the universe exists in a steady state, without beginning or end, in which expansion comes from the constant creation of new matter. Taking the position opposite the steady-staters were scientists like George Gamow, who came up with the term big bang in 1946 to describe the universe's earliest expansion.

Hubble himself stayed out of such cosmological arguments. Dignified and gentlemanly, he puffed a pipe and spoke with a slight British accent picked up in his three years at Oxford. He viewed his role as simply one of observing and reporting what he observed. For example, he described the galaxies as only *appearing* to be moving according to his measurements. He left it to others to claim that that was what they were *actually* doing.

Becomes associated with Mount Palomar

By the 1930s, Hubble had firmly established himself as America's leading astronomer. He was now in charge of the Mount Wilson Observatory, a father figure to a whole generation of astronomers who studied there. They read his books and articles, including his volume about galaxies, *The Realm of the Nebulae* (1936). Many of them imitated his way of talking and manner.

During the 1930s and 1940s, Hubble was closely involved in the planning and construction of a new 200-inch telescope at Mount Palomar, another Southern California observatory not far from Mount Wilson. It was called the Hale telescope, after Hubble's mentor at Mount Wilson, George E. Hale. During World War II Hubble worked for the army as the head of a research department, and in 1948, when the Hale telescope was completed, he was the first to use it.

Despite suffering from heart disease in the last years of his life, Hubble continued to work at Mount Wilson and Mount Palomar. He died on September 28, 1953, of a cerebral thrombosis (a type of stroke) while preparing for a four-day observation on Mount Palomar.

Further Reading

Christianson, Gale E., *Edwin Hubble: Mariner of the Nebulae,* Farrar, Straus, Giroux, 1995.

"The Hubble Space Telescope: First Light on a New Frontier," *Ad Astra,* March 1990.

Jones, Brian, "The Legacy of Edwin Hubble," *Astronomy,* December 1989, pp. 38–44.

"A Man Named Hubble," *U.S. News & World Report,* March 26, 1990, p. 61.

Osterbrock, Donald E., Ronald S. Brashear, and Joel A. Gwinn, "Edwin Hubble and the Expanding Universe," *Scientific American,* July 1993, p. 84.

Osterbrock, Donald E., Ronald S. Brashear, and Joel A. Gwinn, "Self-Made Cosmologist: The Education of Edwin

Hubble," in *Evolution of the Universe of Galaxies: Edwin Hubble Centennial Symposium,* Astronomical Society of the Pacific, 1990, pp. 1–18.

Petersen, Carolyn Collins, and John C. Brandt, *Hubble Vision: Astronomy With the Hubble Space Telescope,* Cambridge University Press, 1995.

Smith, Robert W., "Edwin P. Hubble and the Transformation of Cosmology," *Physics Today,* April 1990, p. 52.

Wilford, John Noble, "New Data: Stars Still Seem Too Old," *New York Times,* September 12, 1995, p. C5.

Shirley Ann Jackson

Born August 5, 1946
Washington, D.C.

The first black female to earn a doctorate from the Massachusetts Institute of Technology (MIT), Shirley Ann Jackson is among America's leading pysicists.

Shirley Ann Jackson is an American physicist who has spent her career researching subatomic particles. She was the first African American woman to receive a Ph.D. from the Massachusetts Institute of Technology (MIT), and she spent many years conducting research at American Telephone and Telegraph (AT&T) Bell Laboratories. She was named professor of physics at Rutgers University in 1991 and is the recipient of many honors, scholarships, and grants.

Cultivates an early interest in science

Shirley Ann Jackson was born on August 5, 1946, in Washington, D.C., to George and Beatrice Jackson. Her parents placed a high value on education, and her father fostered his daughter's interest in science by helping her build science projects. At Roosevelt High School, Jackson enrolled in accelerated programs in both math and science, having the intellectual and psychological skills needed to excel in college. After graduating as valedictorian of her class in 1964, she attended MIT. Jackson earned a bachelor's degree in 1968, writing her thesis on solid-state physics, the study of the properties of matter in the solid state, a subject then at the forefront of theoretical physics.

Earns Ph.D.

Although she was accepted at Brown, Harvard, and the University of Chicago, Jackson decided to stay at MIT for her doctoral work because she wanted to encourage more African American students to attend the institution. Her activism on campus increased the black enrollment there to nearly one hundred graduate students, many of whom have received their doctorates. For her Ph.D., which she completed in 1973, Jackson studied elementary particle theory under James Young, the first African American tenured full professor in the MIT physics department. Jackson's thesis, "The Study of a Multi-peripheral Model With Continued Cross-Channel Unitarity," was subsequently published in the *Annals of Physics* in 1975.

Studies subatomic particles

Jackson's area of interest in physics is the study of the subatomic particles found within atoms (the tiny units of which all matter is made). Subatomic particles, which are usually very unstable and short-lived, can be studied in several ways. One method is using a particle accelerator, a device in which nuclei are accelerated to high speeds and then collided with a target to separate them into subatomic particles. Another way is by detecting their movements though the use of certain kinds of nonconducting solids. When some solids are exposed to high-energy particles, the crystal lattice structure of its atoms is distorted. This phenomenon leaves marks or tracks that can be seen with an electron microscope. Photographs of the tracks are then enhanced, and by examining these photographs physicists like Jackson can make deductions about what kinds of particles have caused the marks.

Continues research

As a postdoctoral student of subatomic particles during the 1970s, Jackson studied and conducted research at a number of prestigious physics laboratories in both the United States and Europe. Her first position was as research associate at the Fermi National Accelerator Laboratory in Batavia, Illinois (known as Fermilab), where she studied hadrons (medium to large subatomic particles, baryons and mesons among them). In 1974 Jackson became visiting scientist at the accelerator lab at the European Center for Nuclear Research (CERN) in Switzerland. There she explored theories of strongly interacting elementary particles. In 1976 and 1977 she lectured in physics at the Stanford Linear Accelerator Center and became a visiting scientist at the Aspen Center for Physics.

Joins AT&T Bell Laboratories

Jackson joined the Theoretical Physics Research Department at AT&T Bell Laboratories in 1976. The research projects at this facility are designed to examine the properties of various materials in an effort to discover useful applications. Within two years Jackson had become part of the Scattering and Low Energy Physics Research Department, then in 1988 she moved to the Solid State and Quantum Physics Research Department. At Bell Labs Jackson explored theories of charged density waves and the reactions of neutrinos, one type of subatomic particle. On these and various other topics she has prepared or collaborated on over one hundred scientific articles.

Receives awards and honors

Jackson has received many scholarships, including the Martin Marietta Aircraft Company Scholarship and Fellowship, the Prince Hall Masons Scholarship, the National Science Foundation Traineeship, and a Ford Foundation Advanced Study Fellowship. She has been elected to the American Physical Society and selected a CIBA-GEIGY Exceptional Black Scientist. In 1985 Governor Thomas Kean appointed her to the New Jersey Commission on Science and Technology. Then in the early 1990s Governor James Florio awarded her the Thomas Alva Edison Science Award for her contributions to physics and for the promotion of science. Jackson is an active voice in numerous committees of the National Academy of Sciences, the American Association for the Advancement of Science, and the National Science Foundation, where her aim has been to promote women's roles in science.

Jackson is actively involved in university life at Rutgers University as well, where in addition to being professor of physics she is also on the board of trustees. She is a lifetime member of the MIT Board of Trustees and was formerly a trustee of Lincoln University. Jackson is also involved in civic organizations that promote community resources and developing enterprises. She is married and has one son.

Further Reading

American Men and Women of Science, 13th ed., Volume 3, Bowker, 1976.

Blacks in Science and Medicine, Hemisphere, 1990, p. 130.

Carwell, Hattie, *Blacks in Science: Astrophysicist to Zoologist,* Exposition Press, 1977, p. 60.

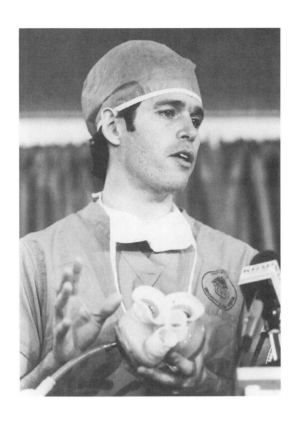

Robert K. Jarvik

Born May 11, 1946
Midland, Michigan

Surgeon and biomedical engineer Robert K. Jarvik invented the Jarvik-7 artificial heart.

Physician Robert K. Jarvik is designer and biomedical engineer of the first artificial heart permanently implanted in a human being. The device, named Jarvik-7, was implanted in Barney Clark on December 2, 1982, at the University of Utah Medical Center. Clark lived 112 days after the artificial heart was implanted. Jarvik has also performed research on other artificial organs and holds a number of patents on other medical devices.

Finds his direction

Robert Koffler Jarvik was born on May 11, 1946, in Midland, Michigan, the son of physician Norman Eugene Jarvik and Edythe Koffler Jarvik. He was raised in Stamford, Connecticut, where he was a tinkerer and inventor as a teenager. Jarvik watched his father performing surgery, and even before he graduated from high school he had invented an automatic surgical stapler. Used during surgery, the device would replace the process of manually sewing up living body tissue.

Jarvik entered Syracuse University in 1964 and took courses in mechanical drawing and architecture. However, his father's heart disease prompted him to change his course of study. Jarvik began premedical course work, graduating in 1968 with a bachelor's degree in zoology. His immediate plans were stalled when only average grades prevented him from acceptance into an American medical school. As an alternative he attended medical school at the University of Bologna in Italy. After two years he returned to the United States to pursue a degree in occupational biomechanics (the study of the mechanics of biological processes such as muscular activity) at New York University in New York City. He received a master's degree in 1971.

Embarks on career

Shortly after graduation Jarvik was hired as an assistant design engineer at the University of Utah, in Salt Lake City, by Willem Kolff, a leading expert in the development of artificial organs. Kolff had been working on inventing an artificial heart since the mid-1950s. He had recently been appointed head of a new division at the university, which became known as the Institute of Biomedical Engineering. Its primary project was to develop an artificial heart.

Jarvik's achievements in biomedical engineering are closely tied to his employment at the institute, as it was headed by a world expert on man-made organs who had been working on developing an artificial heart for more than fifteen years. Jarvik's inventive genius soon solved several problems associated with the devices. By the early 1980s he had developed an artificial heart that could be implanted in a human being. In 1976, while working at the institute, Jarvik received his medical degree from the University of Utah.

Problems of the heart

The artificial heart program at the Utah institute aimed to recreate the lower two chambers, or ventricles, of the heart,

Barney Clark was a sixty-one-year-old retired dentist suffering from cardiomyopathy (a degenerative disease of the heart muscle). Realizing he was terminally ill, he believed that having an artificial heart implanted in his body would give him hope and would also contribute to the progress of medical science. In a seven-and-a-half hour operation performed by surgeon William C. DeVries with assistance from Robert K. Jarvik, Clark's ventricles were replaced by the Jarvik-7, which was driven by an outside air-compressor connected to the artificial heart by tubes. The surgery received worldwide publicity. Shortly after the operation, Clark suffered from disabling brain seizures. He died less than four months later. The artificial heart itself (except for a malfunctioning valve, which was replaced) functioned throughout and was still pumping when Clark died of multiple organ failure.

which comprise the pumping portion of the organ. Creating the pump with a suitable power source was the major obstacle facing the project. The ideal solution was considered a single unit containing both the pump and the power source that would be completely encased in the recipient's body. Before Jarvik arrived Kolff had worked hard to create an electrical power source and, after failing at that, a nuclear one. When this strategy also failed, Kolff decided to concentrate on the pump and to rely on power from compressed air from a machine outside the body connected by tubes to the artificial heart. Scientifically, the decision was sound, as it divided a complex problem into two simpler parts. Practicaly, however, it meant that recipients of the artificial heart would be permanently attached by tubes to a machine.

Develops the Jarvik-7 artificial heart

When Jarvik arrived at the institute he immediately began working on the "Kwann-Gett heart," which was designed in 1971 by a member of Kolff's team, Clifford S. Kwann-Gett. This device used a rubber diaphragm as the pumping element that forced blood in and out of the artificial heart. The diaphragm represented an improvement in that it lowered the possibility of mechanical failure. However, it also caused blood to clot on its surface, which could result in death. Jarvik's improved version, called the "Jarvik-3," was shaped to better fit the anatomy of the experimental animals. In addition, the rubber of the diaphragm had been replaced by three highly flexible layers of a smooth polyurethane (a substance used for coating), called "biomer," which eliminated the clotting problem.

By the mid-1970s Jarvik was working on a version intended for the human body. The plastic and aluminum device would replace the lower pumping chambers, known as the ventricles, and would be attached to the two upper chambers of the heart, known as the atria, which receive blood from the veins. Such a device, called the "Jarvik-7," was implanted into Barney Clark on December 2, 1982.

Ventures into manufacturing artificial organs

In 1976 Jarvik became a vice-president of Symbion, Inc., originally known as Kolff Associates, an artificial organs research firm founded by Kolff. An aggressive officer of the company, Jarvik was appointed president in 1981. In search of venture capital (money to start a new business), Jarvik arranged a deal with an outside investment firm whereby Kolff was to be deliberately excluded from direct management of the company. The move became a source of friction between Kolff and Jarvik that was eventually resolved. Under Jarvik's direction, the company branched out to include development and manufacturing of other organs, including an artificial ear.

After Clark's surgery a number of other modified Jarvik hearts were implanted, but none of the recipients lived more than 620 days. The Jarvik-7 was also frequently and more successfully used as a temporary measure for patients awaiting a natural heart transplant. After Jarvik's own departure from the University of Utah and Symbion in 1987, the Jarvik-7 artificial heart did not fare well. Federal funding for the Jarvik project stopped in 1988, and artificial heart implantation was restricted to temporary implantation only. In 1990 the Food and Drug Administration (FDA) withdrew approval for the experimental use of the Jarvik-7, citing Symbion's poor quality control in the manufacturing process and inadequate service of equipment.

In 1987 Jarvik moved to New York City, where he became president of his own company, Jarvik Research, Inc. In the same year he married Marilyn vos Savant, a writer who is reported by the *Guinness Book of World Records* as having the highest IQ score in the world and whose well-known col-

Christiaan Barnard, South African Heart Surgeon

Robert K. Jarvik's experiments with artificial heart transplants followed Christiaan Barnard's (1922–) pioneering work in human heart transplantation. Barnard rose to international prominence when he performed the world's first human heart transplant at Groote Schuur Hospital in Cape Town, South Africa, on December 3, 1967. Fifty-five-year-old Louis Washkansky, recipient of the first transplanted heart—that of a young woman who became brain dead following an auto accident but whose heart was still beating—recovered well enough to sit up in bed and eat steak and eggs. But eighteen days after his surgery he died of double pneumonia. His immune system, suppressed by drugs and radiation so pneumonia would not attack his new heart, had been unable to fight the infection.

Barnard's heart transplant surgery opened a host of ethical questions, which were widely discussed in forums such as newspapers and magazines. The initial enthusiasm for heart transplant surgery faded quickly, not over ethical quandaries (confusion), but because heart recipients continued to succumb to infection. Amid criticism that he had rushed too hastily into a risky procedure, Barnard continued to perform and perfect the transplant procedure. As the operation became more routine, more patients survived longer. By 1983 sixty-three successful heart transplants had been done at Groote Schuur under Barnard's direction.

umn appears in *Parade* magazine. Jarvik had been previously married to journalist Elaine Levin, with whom he had two children, Tyler and Kate.

Jarvik has continued artificial heart research, concentrating on the Jarvik 2000. Based on principles quite different from the Jarvik-7, both the pump and its power source would be implanted entirely inside the heart. Jarvik has received numerous awards, including two citations of "Inventor of the Year" from Intellectual Property Owners in 1982 and from National Inventors Hall of Fame in 1983. Jarvik also holds honorary doctorates from Syracuse and Hahnemann Universities, presented in 1983 and 1985 respectively.

Further Reading

Altman, Lawrence K., "U.S. Halts the Use of Jarvik Heart," *New York Times,* January 12, 1990, p. A20.

Baumgold, Julie, "In the Kingdom of the Brain: How Love Changed the Smartest Couple in New York," *New York,* February 6, 1989, pp. 36–43.

Berger, Melvin, *The Artificial Heart,* F. Watts, 1987.

Current Biography Yearbook: 1984, H. W. Wilson, 1985, pp. 201–04.

Shaw, Margery W., *After Barney Clark: Reflections on the Utah Artificial Heart Program,* University of Texas Press, 1984.

Teague, Paul E., "Robert Jarvik: Courage to Test Medicine's Frontier," *Design News,* July 11, 1994.

Robert K. Jarvik

Steven Jobs

Born February 24, 1955

"My self-identity does not revolve around being a businessman, though I recognize that is what I do. I think of myself more as a person who builds neat things."

Steven Jobs is an American electronics engineer. He was the founder, along with Stephen Wozniak, of Apple Computer, Inc., perhaps the most innovative force behind the personal computer revolution of the 1980s. Unlike large, established computer companies, Apple aimed from the beginning to bring computers into every household. Its watchword was "user-friendly," and this user-oriented philosophy is generally cited as a key to its phenomenal early success. Only six years after Jobs and Wozniak created the prototype (test model) for the Apple I, their company appeared on the Fortune 500 list of top corporations. Jobs was the business force behind Apple Computer, while Wozniak provided the engineering intelligence. Jobs became a powerful presence at Apple during the late 1970s and early 1980s, heading the Macintosh division until his departure in 1985. Widely recognized for his contributions to the computer field, Jobs, along with Wozniak, was presented with a National Medal of Science in 1985.

Develops entrepreneurial skills

Born February 24, 1955, Jobs was raised by his adoptive parents, Paul Jobs, a machinist at Spectra-Physics, and Clara Jobs, in San Francisco, California. Jobs's early interest in machines was inspired by his father's work. As a child he was generally bored with school until he became excited by several positive experiences. Among them was a school field trip to a Hewlett-Packard plant in Palo Alto, where he had his first encounter with a desk-top computer. A short time later Jobs telephoned William Hewlett, the cofounder of Hewlett-Packard, to ask for help in constructing a school project. Hewlett agreed to provide Jobs the necessary parts; then he offered the high-school freshman a summer job.

That summer, in 1968, Jobs met Stephen Wozniak, a college drop-out and electronics wizard five years his senior, at Hewlett-Packard. Wozniak had graduated from the high school Jobs attended, and together they began developing and peddling several electronic devices. Some—including the "blue box," a device for making free long-distance phone calls—were illegal. Jobs also repaired and sold stereos during his high school years, further developing his entrepreneurial skills. Yet he was clearly not headed for a conventional marketing career.

Creates the Apple I computer with Wozniak

After graduating from Homestead High School in Los Altos and spending a year at Reed College in Portland, Oregon, Jobs went to India to live in a commune in the summer of 1974. During his stay he practiced meditation, studied eastern culture and religion, and even shaved his head. But by the fall he had become ill with dysentery (an intestinal disease) and was forced to return to the United States. After this experience with alternative lifestyles, Jobs became a consultant for the Atari video game company. He also attended weekly meetings of the Homebrew Computer Club, one of many computer user groups springing up in the San Francisco Bay area.

Wozniak, an original member of Homebrew, was working at Hewlett-Packard during the day and constructing a computer at night. Encouraged by Jobs, Wozniak devised a crude but relatively powerful circuit board (a sheet of insulating material that carries electrical circuit elements and terminals) with a $25 microprocessor and a few memory chips (small wafers of semiconductor material that store information for later retrieval). It was the original Apple I computer.

Develops Apple II

Jobs began the difficult process of marketing and publicizing the computer, using contacts from the Homebrew club to sell the product. After scraping together investment capital and moving their small operation into his father's garage, Jobs worked with Wozniak to develop a more powerful computer—the Apple II—that would have a keyboard and video display (terminal). As the Apple II gained attention, Jobs and Wozniak formed Apple Computer, Inc. Within a short time investors were providing financial backing, and experienced executives were joining the fledgling (new) company. Jobs created a sleek design for the Apple II using a plastic casing and introducing the Apple logo: the image of an apple with a missing bite. The bitten apple was a play on the word "byte," one of the central units of information in computer languages.

Apple II becomes industry standard

The Apple II was introduced in 1977 and, after further refinements, became the standard for personal computers. Several factors contributed to its success. The Apple allowed the addition of such items as a modem (a device that converts computer signals to a form that is compatible with the telephone) and a music synthesizer (a computerized electronic device that produces music). Also, models built after mid-1978 included a disk drive (a device for reading and writing on magnetic computer disks) developed and engineered by Wozniak. In 1979 computer engineers at the Massachusetts Institute of Technology (MIT) in Cambridge, Massachusetts, developed a spreadsheet program (a ledger layout for accounting purposes) that made Apple II attractive to businesses.

With the success of the Apple II, Jobs found himself as the majority shareholder in a multimillion-dollar company. When Apple became a publicly held corporation (a company that sells shares to the public) in 1980, Jobs's holdings were valued at $165 million. For the next two years Apple led the market in personal computers, and as the company grew it invited competition. International Business Machines (IBM) introduced its first personal computer in 1981, within two years capturing nearly one-third of the market. Apple introduced several models intended to compete with IBM, but the Apple II remained the company's best-selling computer throughout the early 1980s.

IMPACT

When the Apple II computer, introduced by Steven Jobs and Stephen Wozniak, hit the market in 1977, it had impressive first year sales of $2.7 million. In one of the most phenomenal cases of corporate growth in U.S. history, the company's sales grew to $200 million within three years. Jobs and Wozniak had introduced an entirely new product—the personal computer—thus bringing the computational speed of business systems into people's homes and beginning a new era in information processing.

Introduces "Lisa" and Macintosh

In 1979 Jobs launched a project designed to revolutionize the way people used computers. Called the "Lisa" (Local Integrated Software Architecture), it was the first computer model to use a mouse (a small, hand-operated device that controls movement of the cursor on the computer display screen). Priced at $10,000, however, the machine was too expensive for the home market. The mouse technology developed for the Lisa eventually led to the creation of the Macintosh computer division of Apple, which Jobs headed in the early 1980s.

The new Macintosh had a dramatic impact on the information-processing industry. Equipped with easy-to-use software (programs, procedures, and related instructions and information) and a point-and-click mouse, the computer simplified the operation of word processing, spreadsheets, and graphics for people who had little experience with computers. Other innovative features of the Macintosh were icons (graphic sym-

Seymour Cray, American Electronics Engineer

Seymour Cray (1925–), one of the founding fathers of the computer industry, paved the way for Steven Jobs and other computer technology innovators. Cray's work includes developing the semiconductor as a component to store and process information, and he designed the first computer employing a freon cooling system to prevent chips from overheating. Cray's most significant contribution, however, was what many consider the first supercomputer, the CDC 6600, which he built while working for Control Data Corporation. To such fields as engineering, meteorology, and eventually biology and medicine, the large and powerful supercomputer represented a technological revolution akin to replacing a wagon with a sports car.

In 1972 Cray founded Cray Research Corporation. His advances in computer technology enabled him to corner the market on the supercomputer industry for many years with the Cray-1 and Cray-2. The advent of parallel processing, however, allowed others in the industry to make inroads into the same market. Utilizing hundreds of mini-computers to work on individual aspects of a problem, parallel processing is a less expensive approach to solving huge mathematical problems. Although Cray for many years denounced parallel processing as impractical, he eventually accepted this approach and made plans with other companies to incorporate it into his computer research and business.

bols that indicate computer functions) and windows (areas on the computer screen that permit displays of different types of information). The Macintosh also provided a simple alternative to the complicated "C:\>" prompt (combination of symbols) used in IBM compatibles (computers not made by IBM that can run IBM software). Indeed, within a decade of its 1984 release, the operating system called "Windows" (see **Bill Gates** entry), which is capable of being run on IBM-compatible machines, borrowed many of the Macintosh features.

Leaves Apple to start NeXT

The success of Macintosh did little to calm a highly charged and uncertain atmosphere at Apple. The company was increasingly threatened by IBM competition, and Apple employees were angered that most of the company's efforts were being devoted to the Macintosh division. In 1985 Wozniak resigned, and Jobs was demoted by John Sculley, the former Pepsi-Cola Company president whom Jobs had brought in to run Apple in 1983. After some hesitation Jobs left Apple to begin NeXT Company, an operation that would focus on educational computing. Jobs's departure brought more trouble, however, when Apple filed a lawsuit that accused him of stealing the company's research and some of its key employees for his new endeavor.

After settling his problems with Apple out of court, Jobs turned to the task of developing the NeXT computer. In 1988 he introduced the NeXT at a gala event in San Francisco. Initial reactions were generally good: the computer, which was designed primarily for students and educators, was user friendly, with a fast processing speed, impressive graphics displays, and an excellent sound system. Other innovations included an optical disk drive (which uses a light-sensing device instead of floppy disks) and a special sound chip to provide the fidelity of a compact disc. The computer, even though it sold poorly, resulted in a 1989 Software Publishers Association Lifetime Achievement Award for Jobs.

In 1986, in the midst of his struggle at Apple, Jobs bought a tiny Richmond, California, computer company, Pixar Animation Studios, that would cause a sensation nine years later with its computer-generated blockbuster *Toy Story*. Many say the movie—the first ever entirely generated by computer—will change forever the way animated films are created and how they look. *Toy Story* has a three-dimensional appearance, not two-dimensional such as cartoons like *Aladdin.* Work is underway at Pixar on a second film, *Bugs,* to be released in the late 1990s.

In 1991 Jobs married Laurene Powell; the couple has three children. He continues to head NeXT, researching, developing, and marketing new computer technology. In 1993 he announced the development of NextStep for Intel Processors, a development platform designed to aid users in creating custom applications. Two years later he introduced NeXT's WebObjects, which allows for the rapid creation of interactive sites on the World Wide Web of the Internet computer network. Having started a revolution in information processing in America, Jobs remains one of the most important innovators in American technology today.

Further Reading

Butcher, Lee, *Accidental Millionaire: The Rise and Fall of Steve Jobs at Apple Computer,* Paragon House, 1988.

Fortune, September 18, 1995.

Greenberg, Keith Elliot, *Steven Jobs and Stephen Wozniak: Creating the Apple Computer,* Blackbirch Press, 1994.

Kaplan, David A., "High Tech in Toon Town," *Newsweek,* December 14, 1995, pp. 54–56.

Lasseter, John, and Steve Daly, *Toy Story: The Art and Making of the Animated Film,* Hyperion, 1995.

Rolling Stone, April 1996; June 16, 1994.

Rogers, Adam, "In Search of a Sequel," *Newsweek,* September 4, 1995, p. 52.

Stross, Randall E., *Steve Jobs and the Next Big Thing,* Atheneum, 1993.

Donald Johanson

Born June 23, 1943
Chicago, Illinois

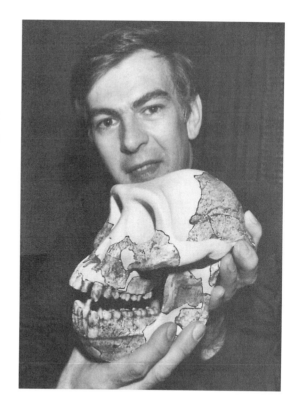

In 1974 anthropologist Donald Johanson found a partial, human-like skeleton in Ethiopia that proved to be more than three million years old. It was the fossilized remains of a young female, whom Johanson and his coworkers named Lucy. Johanson has since won wide agreement with his claim that Lucy and her kind were the ancestors of modern humans.

Anthropologist Donald Johanson discovered the oldest fossilized, human-like remains.

Befriends anthropologist

Donald Carl Johanson was born on June 23, 1943, in Chicago, Illinois, where his parents had emigrated from Sweden. His father died when he was two years old. Soon afterward Donald and his mother moved to Hartford, Connecticut, where she supported them by working as a cleaning woman. As Johanson grew up in Hartford, he found an older man, an anthropology teacher named Paul Leser, who took an interest in his upbringing. In Leser's apartment Johanson found shelves and shelves of books on anthropology (the science that onald Johanson believes that Lucy and her peers—*Australopithecus afarensis*—were the ancestors of two lines, later australopithecines and humans, that had split off from each other. The earliest australopithecines were almost twice as old as the counterparts of *Homo habilis,* about 3.5 to 4 million years. The australopithecines became extinct, while the human line evolved into *Homo habilis, Homo erectus,* and finally *Homo sapiens,* or modern man.

studies human beings, especially their origin, development, divisions, and customs). Many of the books were about fossils, the bones left behind by once-living things that have turned slowly into rock over hundreds of thousands of years. Some fossils are millions of years old, and have to be excavated with great care. When they are unearthed, they serve as "documents" that anthropologists and others can use to find out about creatures that lived long before our time.

For several decades anthropologists had been finding fossils of early hominids (human-like creatures) in Africa. Believing humans evolved from apes, scientists have focused their attention on that continent, which is the home of many species of apes, as the place where early humans first evolved. When Leser went off on trips to Africa, Johanson found his own curiosity and excitement stirred.

Decides on course of study

Johanson knew he wanted to be a scientist when he grew up, but Leser warned him against a career in anthropology, which does not offer high-paying jobs. So when he began college, at the University of Illinois, Johanson chose chemistry as his major. He quickly became bored by the subject, however, and recalled an article he had read about anthropology in high school. Written by famed anthropologist **Louis S. B. Leakey** (see entry), the article described Leakey's discovery in 1959 of a two-million-year-old hominid skull at Olduvai Gorge in Tanzania, Africa. Another skull of the same age was found in the same area in 1964, and Leakey's discovery pushed the date of humankind's suspected presence on Earth back at least one million years earlier than anyone had thought. Excited by Leakey's work, Johanson switched his major to anthropology. After finishing college, he began graduate work at the University of Chicago with Clark Howell, a leading American anthropologist.

Investigates humankind's early ancestors

Johanson's work as a graduate student was supposed to focus on chimpanzees and what can be learned from studying their teeth. Yet what he really wanted to look at were the skulls that had been found in Africa. He needed an excuse. The hominid skulls were still being studied, and Johanson told Howell that he might be able to put together a helpful catalog of them. Because hominid skulls, including teeth, are very similar to those of chimps, Howell gave Johanson permission. So in early 1970, a very excited Johanson left for a summer in Africa.

In Africa Johanson met **Mary Leakey,** Louis's wife, and their son **Richard Leakey** (see combined entry), who were both also leading anthropologists. In fact it was Mary who had actually found the famous hominid skull in 1959. Johanson spent some time helping at a dig that Howell was leading at Omo, Ethiopia. Here Johanson got used to camp life and learned anthropological methods as he watched the scientists handle the fossils that were found, including some very ancient skulls. Slowly he began to regard the finds as living, breathing beings who actually walked around, ate food, had children, and died on the African plains millions of years ago.

Goes to Afar Triangle

At the end of his second season of research Johanson met a young French geologist named Maurice Taieb, who was studying the geology of a region in Ethiopia called the Afar Triangle. As Taieb described his work, it dawned on Johanson that the area sounded like a perfect place to find very old fossils. Layers of rock as old as four million years had been pushed to the surface, where they were being worn away by Ethiopia's seasonal rains. Taieb said that fossil bones were simply lying there waiting to be found after heavy rains had washed the surrounding dirt away. It did not take Johanson

Raymond A. Dart, Australian Anatomist and Anthropologist

An early pioneer in the field of paleoanthropology, Raymond A. Dart (1893–1988) discovered the first fossils of *Australopithecus africanus,* or the "southern ape of Africa." In 1923 he was appointed chairman of the anatomy department of the School of Medicine at the University of Witwatersrand in Johannesburg, South Africa. Dart found the school in dire need of equipment, facilities, and a collection of bones with which to create a proper anatomy museum. To acquire the necessary bones, Dart encouraged his students to search for fossils during holidays. In the summer of 1924 a fossilized baboon skull was brought to Dart's attention. The fossil had been detected by a mining company employee on a sheet of limestone at Taungs (now Taung) in the Bechuanaland Protectorate, where other fossil baboon skulls had been discovered as early as 1920.

His interest piqued, Dart asked his colleague, geology professor R. B. Young, to look for similar specimens. By November 28, 1924, Dart had in his hands a fossil skull that would change the face of paleoanthropology. Young had sent back two crates full of bones, one of which held a face and skull and the internal cast of a cranium found by one of the quarry workers. After extensive examination over several months, Dart found that the face exhibited features of humanoid rather than anthropoid (apelike) characteristics. Dart believed he had found the "missing link" between ape and man and that his discovery might bear out the theory of English naturalist **Charles Darwin** (see entry) that man's origins were linked to Africa. He named the creature *Australopithecus africanus.*

Dart's views were immediately met with derision by the general public and adamant disagreement by many of his own colleagues. Some insisted that the skull belonged to a gorilla or a chimp. Many were appalled that the discovery was made in Africa, since Asia was seen as the cradle of humankind. Yet Dart did have his defenders, particularly Scottish anthropologist Robert Broom. Broom's discoveries of Taung-like fossils in Sterkfontein in 1936 and Kromdraii in 1938 would turn the tide of evidence in favor of Dart's South African ape-man.

long to decide that he was going to be the one to study the bones. He arranged to join Taieb the following spring, before the season's digging at Omo began.

Borrowing camping equipment and two battered Land Rovers (heavy-duty, Jeep-like vehicles), Johanson and Taieb headed into the rugged Afar region in early 1972. It was everything Johanson had hoped it would be. The bones he found seemed to be about two to three million years old. There were fossil bones of pigs, elephants, and even the nearly complete skeleton of an ancient monkey. Experts could tell how old the animal bones were by their shapes. Pigs, for example, had evolved by stages that were well known. A fossilized pig bone or tooth was like a yardstick for measuring the age of a hominid fossil found in the same layer of rock. If hominid fossils were found nearby, the bones of other animals would help date them. While it was unusual for a young student to go off on his own like this, Johanson was determined to lead a full-scale expedition into the Afar region. By fall 1973 Johanson had raised enough money to assemble a team and set up camp at Hadar, next to the Awash River in the Afar Triangle.

Gambles career leading first expedition

Johanson was staking his whole career on the expedition. He did not even have his graduate degree yet. If he failed to come through with a worthwhile find, he would gain a reputation for bad judgment, and finding money for future research would be next to impossible. Such were the worries he was pondering one day as he dug up what looked like a hippopotamus rib with his foot. Then he looked more closely. It was the upper end of a shinbone, and a few yards away he saw its mate, the lower end of a thighbone. From the size of the bones, he figured they belonged to a monkey. As he put them together to make a knee joint, he suddenly knew from the way they fit what he had discovered: the knee joint of a creature that had walked upright on two legs, unlike any ape or monkey. It was the knee joint of a hominid who had lived between three and four million years ago.

Finds Lucy

With this incredible find, Johanson was able to get enough money to continue at Hadar the following year, in the fall of

1974. Before much time had gone by, several hominid jaw-bones had been turned up. One day Johanson had gone out with an assistant, Tom Gray, to examine a nearby gully. Finding nothing and feeling frustrated, they were about to leave. Johanson, however, took one last look around and spotted a small piece of what looked like an arm bone, which was near a piece of skull and part of a thighbone. All appeared to belong to the same hominid. Three weeks later, when the whole area had been carefully excavated, the team had collected nearly half of a complete female skeleton, the first discovery of its kind. In addition to being more complete, this skeleton was also much older than any found previously. They named her Lucy, after the Beatles' song "Lucy in the Sky With Diamonds," which someone played over and over at the camp celebration.

Discovers "First Family"

Lucy made headlines and secured a place for Johanson at the very top of his field. He was offered a job at the Cleveland Museum of Natural History in Cleveland, Ohio. After completing his graduate degree, he began teaching. The following year, in 1975, the Hadar expedition found even more spectacular fossils—about 350 pieces of bone from at least thirteen individual hominids, which became known as "the First Family." In 1976 they discovered a number of primitive stone tools that were about 2.5 million years old. The tools had probably been fashioned by the hominids classified as *Homo habilis,* meaning "handy man," who belonged to one of the first classes of hominids and were the ancestor of modern man. Unfortunately, war in Ethiopia prevented the team from returning.

Classifies Australopithecus afarensis

After finding Lucy and the First Family, Johanson and his coworkers had to determine their identity. If Lucy were a previously unknown genus, or class, they also had to name her. It would take several years of careful measurement, thought, and, as it turned out, argument. They knew she was a hominid, because she clearly had walked upright. At first

Arthur Keith, Piltdown Hoaxer?

Scientists have often feuded and have been scandalized in their search to find the origins of the human species. One famous case of fraud might have directly involved prominent Scottish anatomist and physical anthropologist Arthur Keith (1866–1955). During the late nineteenth and early twentieth centuries many Europeans believed that humankind could have originated in Europe, and English paleontologists thought that evidence for the existence of prehistoric humans would be found in England. This belief appeared to be justified by the announcement in late 1912 of the discovery, made by amateur scientist Charles Dawson, of fragments of a prehistoric human skull at Piltdown, England. The skull comprised what was apparently a humanlike brain case and a simianlike (apelike) jaw. Although the discoverers conceded that the skull and jaw probably did not come from the same individual, they proposed that they came from two examples of the same species. They used fossils found nearby as evidence of the age of the fragments.

Keith had reservations about the Piltdown jaw, which at that time was lacking its canine teeth, which were crucial to the determination of the human nature of the jaw. The teeth were supposedly found, along with several other fragments, in 1913, the same year Keith was elected into the Royal Society. Basing his conclusions on plaster casts of the fragments, Keith determined that the teeth were apelike, not humanlike as he had expected. But Keith also argued that the large cranial capacity was similar to that of modern humans. (Keith believed brain size—not teeth shape or the ability to walk on two feet—was the essential mark of humans.) Ultimately, Keith dated the fragments to be a little more than 1.5 million years old and said the discovery was "of equal, if not of greater, importance than any other yet made." He never questioned the authenticity of the fragments, and his presence at the 1912 public unveiling, giving his stature in the scientific community, lent credence to the proceedings.

In the decades after the discovery, numerous scientists cast doubt on the authenticity of the Piltdown fragments, feeling that the apelike mandible could not have come from an individual with the configuration of the rest of the skull. It was not until 1953 that, by means of analysis of the fluorine content of the fragments, the Piltdown man was proven to be a forgery, the combination of a human skull and an orangutan jawbone. Speculation about the identity of the forger still exists, but some researchers say Keith himself conspired with Dawson to perpetrate the hoax in order to provide evidence for his own theories on the antiquity of humans. Ronald Millar, author of *The Piltdown Men,* suggested that Keith's prestige had protected him from suspicion in the case.

Johanson thought she was an early human. Soon after finding Lucy, however, he had begun working with a graduate student named Tim White, whose judgment he had come to value highly. White argued that Lucy was not a human at all. In the end White persuaded Johanson that he was right. In 1979 the two published a landmark paper that introduced Lucy as humanity's oldest ancestor: *Australopithecus afarensis,* the southern ape from Afar.

Contradicts Leakey find

Johanson's success at Hadar created a rift that scarred the world of anthropology. Before Lucy, anthropology had been dominated by the glamorous Leakey family. Louis and Mary Leakey had worked at Olduvai since the 1930s, making major breakthroughs in knowledge about human origins. Their brilliant son Richard had carried on the family's work, as well as its talent for publicity. Announcements by any member of the Leakey family always got headlines.

Louis and Mary Leakey had always insisted that humanity was very old, and that the australopithecines were not our ancestors at all, but our cousins. They believed that our real ancestors, creatures that were basically human, had lived just as early as the australopithecines. Their discovery of *H. habilis*—skeletal remains that could be recognized as human—supported this idea.

But Johanson's anthropological ability matched the Leakey's, as did his own knack for publicity. What caused the tension was that Johanson's findings went directly against that of the Leakey's. Johanson found that Lucy and the other earliest australopithecines were almost twice as old as *H. habilis,* about 3.5 to 4 million years, compared with 2 million years for the oldest *H. habilis* remains. This age difference in the finds has led most anthropologists to support Johanson's claim that *Australopithecus afarensis* was the ancestor—not just the cousin, as the Leakey's claimed—of *H. habilis* and later humans.

Founds Institute for Human Origins

Since 1981 Johanson has headed the Institute for Human Origins in Berkeley, California, which he founded to pursue his research. Johanson has also written several books and hosted a *Nova* television series titled "Ancestors: In Search of Human Origins." Johanson's first two marriages failed because of the time he had to put into his work, including long field trips. However, his third wife, Lenora, who is an award-winning documentary filmmaker, has interests that allow them to work together, for instance, on the *Nova* series. In 1992, after years of refusal, the government of Ethiopia that had come to power in the late 1970s allowed Johanson to return to dig at Hadar. Johanson made several important finds, including the nearly complete skull of a male *Australopithecus afarensis.*

Further Reading

Johanson, Donald, and Maitland Edey, *Lucy: The Beginnings of Humankind,* Simon & Schuster, 1981.

Johanson, Donald, and others, *Ancestors: In Search of Human Origins* (companion volume to *Nova* series), Villard, 1994.

Lewin, Roger, *Bones of Contention: Controversies in the Search for Human Origins,* Simon & Schuster, 1987.

McAuliffe, Sharon, "Lucy's Father," *Omni,* May 1994, p. 34.

James Prescott Joule

Born in 1818
Manchester, England
Died in 1889

English physicist James Prescott Joule made important contributions to the fields of heat energy, electricity, and thermodynamics.

James Prescott Joule was perhaps the greatest amateur scientist of all time. The proprietor of a successful brewery, he never held an academic post—in fact, he never completed an undergraduate degree. Joule made valuable contributions to the fields of heat energy, electricity, and thermodynamics (the branch of physics concerning the transformation of heat into energy). Having established the mechanical theory of heat, he was the first to recognize the relationship between heat energy and mechanical energy. Today he is recognized as an important contributor to the field of thermodynamics. The mechanical unit of work is named for him.

Began course of self-education

Joule was born in Manchester, England, in 1818. He was a sickly child who suffered from a chronic spinal injury. His father, a wealthy brewer, was eager to please his young son; he provided as many books as the child could read and eventually built a home laboratory for him. Joule was entirely self-educated; taking from his books only the information that interested him, he quickly gained a working knowledge of physics and chemistry. At the age of seventeen he briefly attended Manchester University but left shortly thereafter to pursue his own studies.

Formulates Joule's Law

During his early years Joule had developed a passion for measurement, and as he became an adult that passion turned to fanaticism. He reportedly spent most of his honeymoon comparing the temperature of water at the top of a nearby waterfall to its temperature at the bottom. The purpose of this experiment—the transformation of kinetic (motion) energy into heat energy—would not be fully appreciated for several years. Joule's scientific momentum was slowed in 1833 when his father's illness forced him to take greater control of the family brewery. Nevertheless, within seven years he made his first important scientific discovery.

It was well known at that time that a wire would heat up when an electrical current was passed through it. However, no scientist had determined the principles that governed this process. In 1840 Joule announced that the heat produced was proportional to the square of the current's intensity as multiplied by the circuit's resistance. This formula has come to be known as Joule's law.

Calculates mechanical equivalent of heat

Having become fascinated by heat, Joule set out to measure the heat produced by every process he could construct in the laboratory. Using paddles, he churned water and measured its temperature increase. He forced water through small holes and measured the heat caused by friction. In his most famous experiment he used a falling weight to drive a paddle that would stir water; by measuring the distance the weight dropped, Joule could calculate the precise amount of work that went into raising the temperature of water.

s the result of James Prescott Joule's discovery of the mechanical equivalent of heat, a researcher could calculate precisely the amount of work that was converted into heat. Joule had proven that the amount of potential energy always equaled the amount of kinetic energy. In previous experiments, a small amount of energy was lost during the experiment, probably to friction. Joule had thus found the principle of conservation of energy.

This experiment became the basis of Joule's calculation for the mechanical equivalent of heat. He determined that 41,800,000 ergs (from the Greek word *ergon,* for work) of work were required to increase the temperature of 1 gram of water by 1 degree Celsius (this amount of heat is called a calorie). Joule had made a landmark discovery, since no other scientist had achieved so accurate a measurement.

Supported by Thomson

Joule set out to publish his findings in 1847. Unfortunately, no science journal would accept his essay, principally because he was a brewer and a wealthy eccentric, not a scientist. He ultimately introduced his research at a small public lecture in Manchester, afterward begging a local paper to publish the text. Several months later Joule was allowed to speak before a crowd of doubtful academicians, all but one of whom took little or no interest. The only person who recognized the importance of Joule's work was a young scholar named **William Thomson** (see entry), who would go on to become the preeminent physicist Lord Kelvin. Although Thomson was only twenty-three, his opinion was held in high regard by his peers, so with his support Joule's research was quickly accepted.

Unit of work named for Joule

Joule was not the first to come up with a figure for the mechanical equivalent of heat, but his was considered the most precise. In his honor the principle unit of work—equal to 10,000,000 ergs—was named the joule. On the basis of Joule's findings, 4.18 joules is equal to 1 calorie.

The determination of the mechanical equivalent of heat was an important step in the eventual development of the con-

Hermann von Helmholtz, German Physiologist and Physicist

James Prescott Joule's theory that the amount of potential energy always equals the amount of kinetic energy was proven—and clarified—by Hermann von Helmholtz (1821–1894). One of few scientists to master two disciplines (medicine and physics), Helmholtz conducted breakthrough research on the nervous system as well as the functions of the eye and ear. In the field of physics he is recognized (along with two other scientists) as the author of the concept of conservation of energy. The concept of conservation of energy was introduced by Julius Mayer in 1842, but Helmholtz was unaware of Mayer's work.

Helmholtz based his theories of energy upon his previous experience with muscles. It can be observed that animal heat is generated by muscle action as well as chemical reaction within a working muscle. Helmholtz believed that this energy was derived from food and that food got its energy from the Sun. He therefore proposed that energy could not be created spontaneously, nor could it vanish—it was either used or released as heat. This explanation was much clearer and more detailed than the one offered by Mayer, and thus Helmholtz is often considered the true originator of the concept of conservation of energy.

cept of conservation of energy. For example, researchers could compare the amount of potential energy in a weight held aloft to the amount of kinetic energy generated as that weight falls to the ground. In previous experiments, a small amount of energy was lost during the experiment, probably to friction.

After the announcement of Joule's number, a researcher could calculate precisely the amount of work that was converted into heat, and it was realized that the amount of potential energy always equaled the amount of kinetic energy. However, final proof would be provided by the German physicist Hermann von Helmholtz (see box).

Discovers Joule-Thomson effect

Joule was at least partially responsible for two other important discoveries. Along with Thomson he showed that a gas, when allowed to expand, would drop in temperature, sometimes significantly. They conducted a number of experiments with low temperatures, succeeding in the liquefaction (reduction to a liquid state) of certain gases. Their discovery is known as the Joule-Thomson effect, which forms the basis of the modern science of cryogenics (study of low temperatures). Using techniques based upon Joule and Thomson's work, scientists can now liquefy hydrogen, helium, and other gases. In 1846 Joule also discovered that an iron bar, when magnetized, would change in length. He called this phenomenon magnetostriction, and it has since been used in connection with the formation of ultrasonic sound waves.

Receives recognition

Joule was elected to the prestigious British Royal Society in 1850 and received its highest honor, the Copley Medal, in 1866. He also served as president of the British Association for the Advancement of Science. He remained a brewer all his life, however, and when his business failed in 1878 he was given a pension by Queen Victoria. Joule died in 1889.

Further Reading

Cardwell, D. S., *James Joule: A Biography,* St. Martin's, 1989.

Percy L. Julian

Born April 11, 1899
Montgomery, Alabama
Died in 1975

P ercy L. Julian is best known for discovering how to synthesize (produce in the laboratory) physostigmine, a chemical
used to treat the eye disease glaucoma. He also developed
an economical method for producing sterols (or steroid alcohols, found in fatty tissues of plants and animals), making it
possible for many people with arthritis to afford cortisone to
relieve their pain. An African American who eventually grew
frustrated with the discrimination he faced in academia, Julian
turned to industry and worked at the Glidden Company in
Chicago, Illinois, before starting his own business.

American organic chemist Percy L. Julian discovered how to synthesize the chemical physostigmine, used in the treatment of glaucoma.

Achieves academic distinction

Percy Lavon Julian was born in Montgomery, Alabama,
on April 11, 1899, to James and Elizabeth Adams Julian. His
father was a railway clerk and his mother was a schoolteacher.
His paternal grandfather was a former slave who had two fingers cut off his right hand for learning to write. Julian was one

≋IMPACT≋

Percy L. Julian synthesized progesterone and testosterone, both of which are hormones essential to the body's endocrine system, which regulates body functions. His discoveries helped treat cancer and relieve problem pregnancies and menstrual disorders. He later developed a low-cost method of producing cortisone, which made treatment available to countless rheumatoid arthritis patients. The victim of racial discrimination throughout his academic career, Julian eventually found both respect and success in private industry, where after becoming the first African American to head a major industrial laboratory, he eventually established his own company. He was elected to the Inventors Hall of Fame in 1990.

of six children, all of whom earned university degrees. Julian attended public school until the eighth grade, but because there was only one public high school in Alabama that accepted African American students, he attended a private school called the State Normal School. He graduated at the top of his class in 1916 and was admitted to DePauw University in Greencastle, Indiana. Because his high school education had not been satisfactory, however, for two years Julian had to take remedial classes in addition to a regular course load. He lived in the attic of a fraternity house during this time and earned money by waiting on tables downstairs. He also played in a jazz band and tended furnaces. Despite his heavy workload, Julian graduated in 1920 with a degree in chemistry; he was class valedictorian and a member of Phi Beta Kappa, a scholastic honorary society.

Encounters racial discrimination

When Julian had decided to major in chemistry, his father had tried to persuade him to become a physician instead, feeling that Julian would not find many career opportunities in chemistry beyond teaching because of his ethnicity. His father's concerns proved well founded. Although Julian wanted to go to graduate school, the head of his department told him that an African American would not find work in the field. Julian was denied fellowships by the same people who had been his role models.

Julian taught chemistry at Fisk University in Nashville, Tennessee, for the next two years. In 1922 he received the Austin Fellowship in chemistry at Harvard University, which enabled him to earn his master's degree in chemistry by 1923. Despite his high grades, however, Harvard did not offer Julian a teaching assistantship because white students from the American South might object to having an African American teacher. Julian therefore took various research assistantships in order to continue to work toward his doctorate. He stayed at Harvard until 1926, studying biophysics and organic chemistry.

Studies in Vienna

From 1926 to 1927 Julian taught at West Virginia State College, then in 1928 he went to Howard University in Washington, D.C., as associate professor and head of the chemistry department. By this time Julian had begun to follow research that was being done at the University of Vienna by Ernst Spath, who had developed methods for synthesizing nicotine and ephedrine (a crystalline alkaloid extracted from the ephedra, a desert shrub). In 1929 Julian received a fellowship from the General Education Board and went to Vienna to study with Spath. While in Vienna he became interested in the soya bean, which was then being used in Germany to manufacture certain drugs, including physostigmine and sex hormones. In 1931 he received his Ph.D. from the University of Vienna. Upon returning to Howard, Julian resumed teaching and was promoted to full professor.

Synthesizes physostigmine

Working with two colleagues from Vienna who had come back to Howard with him, Julian began to investigate the structure and synthesis of physostigmine, a crystalline substance extracted from the Calabar bean. Physostigmine was used to treat glaucoma, an eye disease that eventually leads to blindness by slowly damaging the retina. In 1932, just as he and his colleagues had begun to see results, a disagreement with the Howard administration forced Julian to leave. A former professor arranged for Julian to return to DePauw as a research fellow and teacher of organic chemistry. At DePauw he was able to identify the chemicals that led to the formation of physostigmine. In 1934 Julian presented his findings to the American Chemical Society, challenging the work of Robert

Robinson, the head of the chemistry department at Oxford University. By early 1935 Julian had accomplished the first successful synthesis of physostigmine, thus proving his method and research to be valid.

Pioneers use of soya protein

Despite his achievements, Julian continued to face discrimination. He was denied two positions, one at DePauw and one at the University of Minnesota, on the basis of his race. Deciding to seek employment at an industrial laboratory, he accepted a position as director of research and chief chemist at the Glidden Company in Chicago. He became the first African American in United States history to direct a major industrial laboratory.

In 1936 a milk protein called casein was being used to coat paper. Because this process was expensive, Julian's first task at Glidden was to extract protein from the soya bean. Soya protein was cheaper but equally effective for use in textiles, paints, and paper coating. The results of his work proved profitable for Glidden, and in one year the company went from a deficit of $35,000 to a profit of $135,000. Julian's experiments with soya protein also yielded a new product, "Aero Foam," which was used to extinguish oil and gas fires.

Perfects hormone extraction process

One of Julian's most important achievements was the synthesis of sex hormones from sterols extracted from soya beans. Progesterone (a female sex hormone) was used to prevent miscarriages, while testosterone (a male sex hormone) was used to treat older men for diminishing sex drive. Both hormones were also important in the treatment of cancer. Traditionally, these hormones were made by using cholesterol from the brains and spinal cords of cattle. German scientists had developed a process to extract sterols from the soya bean and convert them into hormones, but it was slow and very expensive. From watching how plaster of Paris puffed up into a porous, foamy mass after the addition of quicklime, Julian

developed a method to convert the soya bean oil into a porous foam from which sterols could be easily extracted. He was able to synthesize progesterone and testosterone from the sterols, increasing the supply of these chemicals and reducing their cost.

Makes synthetic cortisone

Cortisone (a steroid secreted by the adrenal cortex) had recently been found to be effective in treating rheumatoid arthritis (a chronic disease causing painful swelling and deformity in the joints), but the method of production made it extremely expensive and unaffordable for most patients. For instance, the bile of 14,600 oxen was needed to produce enough cortisone to treat one patient for one year. Julian perfected an economical method for synthesizing cortexolone from soya beans. The difference between cortisone and cortexolone, which Julian called Substance S, was one oxygen atom. The process Julian devised to add this missing atom to cortexolone—and the resulting synthetic cortisone—was just as effective in the treatment of arthritis as the organic form.

Starts his own company

In 1954 Julian left Glidden to open his own plant and company, Julian Laboratories Inc. in Chicago, and the Laboratorios Julian de Mexico in Mexico City, Mexico. He had found that wild yams were more effective than soya beans in the production of Substance S. Within a few years Julian Laboratories had become a world leader in making drugs with wild yams. In 1961 Julian sold his Chicago plant to Smith, Kline & French. He stayed on as president until 1964, when he founded the Julian Research Institute and Julian Associates Inc. in Franklin Park, Illinois.

Elected to hall of fame

In 1947 Julian received the Spingarn Medal from the National Association for the Advancement of Colored People, and in 1949 he was presented the Distinguished Service Award from the Phi Beta Kappa Association for his work with Substance S and synthetic cortisone. In 1990 he was elected to the National Inventors Hall of Fame, along with agricultural chemist **George Washington Carver** (see entry). Julian and Carver were the first African Americans to be so honored since the institution was created in 1973. Julian married Anna Johnson, who held a Ph.D. in sociology, in 1935. They had a daughter and a son. Julian continued to investigate synthetic drugs and the chemistry of various substances until his death in 1975.

Further Reading

Cobb, W. Montague, "Percy Lavon Julian," *Journal of the National Medical Association,* March 1971.

Current Biography, H. W. Wilson, 1947.

Haber, Louis, *Black Pioneers of Science and Invention,* Harcourt, 1970.

Toppin, Edgar Allen, *A Biographical History of Blacks in America Since 1528,* McKay, 1971.

C. G. Jung

Born July 26, 1875
Kesswil, Thurgau, Switzerland
Died June 6, 1961
Kuessnacht, Switzerland

"My life is a story of the self-realization of the unconscious."

C. G. Jung was the best known and most influential member of the early psychoanalytic movement, which consisted of students and followers of the famous Austrian psychoanalyst **Sigmund Freud** (see entry). Psychoanalysis is the branch of psychology that focuses on the unconscious dimension of an individual's personality. Contributions made by Jung and his fellow pioneers in the exploration of human behavior and thought processes revolutionized the age-old quest for emotional well-being and inner peace.

Drawn to the field of psychiatry

Carl Gustav Jung (surname pronounced yung) was born on July 26, 1875, to Paul Jung and Emilie Preiswerk Jung. His formative years were tainted by his mother's ongoing struggle against various physical ailments and emotional disorders. Her illnesses also had an impact on Jung's father, a scholar turned Evangelical minister whose increasing sorrow, bitterness, and despair led him to a profound religious crisis. As a young man Jung found himself pondering questions of faith. His lifelong communion with nature, heightened by his reflections on his dreams and fantasies, helped him to develop a concept of God that was quite different from his father's dark, traditional Christian teachings.

Jung began his studies at the University of Basel in Switzerland intent on pursuing a career in medicine. But his fascination with mental and spiritual matters remained undeniable. He even conducted a two-year study of a young girl who practiced spiritualism (a belief that spirits of the dead communicate with the living). Then, while reading a textbook by German neurologist Richard Krafft-Ebing, Jung became completely convinced of his calling to the field of psychiatry. "It had become clear to me in a flash of illumination that for me [this was] the only possible goal," he stated, as quoted in the introduction to *The Portable Jung.*

Originates theory of psychological complexes

After completing his medical studies in 1900, Jung joined the staff of the Burghoelzli Hospital in Zurich, Switzerland, where he worked with patients suffering from schizophrenia (a mental disorder characterized by personality disintegration). In 1903 he married Emma Rauschenbach, a psychoanalyst; they eventually had five children: Agathe, Gret, Franz, Marianne, and Helene. Around this time Jung began to study the existence of thoughts, feelings, memories, and perceptions organized around a central theme, which he called psychological complexes. This entire direction of research was prompted by his experience with word association, a technique whereby words presented to a patient spark other word responses that reflect related thoughts or associations in the patient's mind. The responses, in turn, give clues to the patient's psychological state. Jung's work in this area increased the reliability of word association tests in treating patients.

Uses Freud's concepts

Jung sent a copy of his word association studies to Freud and in 1904 began integrating aspects of Freud's psychoanalytical technique into his own method of treating patients. Psychoanalysis hinges on "free association," a sort of "talking cure," that allows patients to express their feelings, needs, and desires to the doctor, who uses the conversation to arrive at a diagnosis of psychological problems. Freud invited Jung to Vienna, Austria, in 1906. This marked the beginning of a professional relationship that lasted for several years. In fact, during the course of their association Freud formed a special bond with Jung and favored him over his other followers in the psychoanalytic movement. Clearly the elder physician saw in his young protégé a worthy and capable successor.

In spite of Freud's support, however, Jung sensed important differences in their beliefs. For instance, Freud wanted Jung to accept Freudian sexual theory (that all human behavior is based on sexual impulses) as a stand against "occultism." But Jung was interested in exploring the influences of philosophy, religion, and the fledgling science of parapsychology (the study of supernatural psychological events) on the human mind. These, however, were the very forces that Freud felt had no bearing on psychiatric study.

Formulates dream theory

One area of agreement between Freud and Jung was the importance of the interpretation of dreams, a field for which Jung became famous. One of his best-known theories centers on the concept of symbols. While observing his patients Jung noticed that symbols occurring in their dreams sometimes caused highly emotional reactions. He determined that the symbols had no real meaning for the patient; he was unable to determine any significance of the symbols through word association. Finally he came to realize that many of the same symbols seem to reappear throughout history in religion, the arts, folktales, and other forms of human expression.

Jung came to view the source of these constantly recurring symbols as the "collective unconscious," a cross-generational pool of inherited psychological associations that originated with the beginning of the human race. According to Jung, every human has access to the collective unconscious; common experiences, therefore, form universal images and mental connections in all people. Jung distinguished the collective unconscious as being different from the "personal unconscious," which he felt was a storehouse of associations unique to each individual.

Formulates theory of individuation

The unification of the various aspects of the human mind —our dark side, our feminine nature, our masculine nature— serves as the core of Jung's psychiatric theories. According to Jung, people crave psychic wholeness and seek to join all parts of their personalities by integrating elements of the personal unconscious with the collective unconscious. He called the method of achieving this unity the process of "individuation" (becoming a whole, distinct individual)—a process that relies heavily on the identification of symbols and the interpretation of dreams.

Within the psychological community it became apparent that Jung's theories of the unconscious and individuation could be applied to other areas of human experience outside the realm of psychology. Indeed, his approach went beyond the scope of Freud's theory, which was concerned primarily with treating neurosis (an emotional or mental disorder that affects only part of the personality). Jung's ideas could be applied to psychotics (people with severe emotional or mental disorders that cause a loss of contact with reality), the mentally disturbed, and even "normal" individuals in all aspects of their lives.

Clarissa Pinkola Estés, Jungian Psychoanalyst

C. G. Jung's theories have attracted many followers since his death in 1961. Among them is Clarissa Pinkola Estés (1943–), a Jungian psychoanalyst who served as the executive director of the C. G. Jung Center for Education and Research in the United States. She is also a *cantadora* (a keeper of old stories) in the Hispanic tradition, and a poet. In 1992 she published her masterwork, *Women Who Run With the Wolves: Myths and Stories of the Wild Woman Archetype,* in which she explores the nature of the psyche through psychoanalytic commentary and the use of her own literary stories and fairy tales from Magyar, Mexicano, European, Asian and Greek traditions. In *Women Who Run* Estés shows how the "wild woman archetype"—portraying the female as instinctual, playful, devoted to family and community, and possessing great endurance and strength—is damaged by a stifling culture that does not value feminine characteristics. She also demonstrates how women can find inner power of self-determination that will lead to strength and freedom. Her other published works include *The Gift of Story* and *The Faithful Gardener* and an extensive series of audio works.

Breaks from Freud

In formulating his concepts Jung relied on observations of his patients as well as an intensive analysis of his own experience. His self-analysis, in fact, is said to have brought him to the edge of insanity. This flurry of professional activity and personal crisis coincided with the collapse of his relationship with Freud. By 1913, when Jung published his book *The Psychology of the Unconscious,* the former comrades had reached a permanent break. Freud openly criticized the importance Jung gave to symbols, and he felt personally betrayed because Jung had departed from Freudian theory. Jung was left bewildered by Freud's failure to support the work that seemed to be a logical result of their mutual efforts.

Classifies personality types

The clash with Freud was deeply painful for Jung. Some researchers claim that the entire psychoanalytic community ended up turning on him. Attempting to understand the reasons for such an intense reaction, Jung devised a method of classifying personality types. He described these classifications in his 1921 book *Psychological Types,* identifying two basic categories—introverts and extroverts—to explain a person's orientation toward the world. An introvert is inner-directed, whereas an extrovert is outer-directed. He further identified four modes of psychological functioning: thinking, feeling, sensation, and intuition. Jung applied these theories to his own experience with Freud, labeling Freud an extrovert and himself an introvert. He thus explained their rift as being the conflict of different personality types.

Continues work

Jung emerged from his battle against the psychoanalytical establishment with a renewed commitment to his own theories. Calling his approach analytical psychology, he continued treating patients and expanded his study to such diverse subjects as alchemy (a medieval chemical science of transformation), Zen Buddhism (a branch of Buddhism that stresses meditation), folktales, extrasensory perception (ESP), astrology, and the occult. However, the psychiatric community ignored Jung's contributions to the understanding of the human mind. Freud's followers regarded him as a traitor and others dismissed him as being overly mystical, saying his work placed too much emphasis on religion and was too populated by demons, fairy tales, and mythical figures.

Considers his work complete

After his break with Freud, Jung developed his own following. During the last decades of his life, beginning in 1933, scholars throughout the world met each year at Lake Magiore, Switzerland, for the Eranos Lectures. They read and discussed papers on Jungian thought, and Jung himself presented some of his most important theories. He treated patients while working on his last major writings, *Aion,* and a thirty-year study of alchemy titled *Mysterium Coniunctionis.* After completing these books Jung reportedly said, "My psychology was at last given its place in reality and established upon its historical foundations. Thus my task was finished, my work done, and now it can stand." Jung died on June 6, 1961, in Kuessnacht, Switzerland.

Further Reading

Campbell, Joseph, ed., *The Portable Jung,* Viking, 1971.

Gallo, Ernest, "Synchronicity and the Archetypes," *Skeptical Inquirer,* Summer 1994.

Goode, Erica E., "The Man Behind the Mythology," *U.S. News & World Report,* December 7, 1992.

Goode, Erica E., "Spiritual Questing," *U.S. News & World Report,* September 20, 1993.

Goode, Stephen, "Freud Is Losing Out to the Jung-at-Heart," *Insight on the News,* September 20, 1993.

Heller, Scott, "Flare-Up Over Jung," *Chronicle of Higher Education,* June 15, 1995.

Jung, C. G., *Memories, Dream, Reflections,* Vintage Books, 1961.

Kerr, John, *A Most Dangerous Method: The Study of Jung, Freud, and Sabina Spielrein,* Random House, 1993.

Pederson, Loren E., *Dark Hearts: The Unconscious Forces That Shape Men's Lives,* Shambhala Publications, 1990.

Sheperd, Linda Jean, *Lifting the Veil: The Feminine Face of Science,* Shambhala Publications, 1993.

Stevens, Anthony, *On Jung,* Routledge, 1990.

Ernest Everett Just

Born August 14, 1883
Charleston, South Carolina
Died October 27, 1941
Washington, D.C.

Zoologist Ernest Everett Just performed groundbreaking work on the embryology of marine invertebrates, or the early life stages of water animals without spines. He conducted research on fertilization, as well as the development of unfertilized eggs in a process known as parthenogenesis. His most important achievement was the discovery of the role protoplasm plays in the development of a cell. An African American, Just conducted his research despite widespread discrimination. He spent most of his career at Howard University when that institution was still little more than a college, with few graduate students and fewer facilities. In addition to his international reputation as a zoologist, Just was a dedicated teacher whose scientific successes inspired many younger men and women.

"I have a feeling that anything in the way of sacrifice is worthwhile; somebody appreciates my striving and learning."

Achieves academic distinction

Just was born on August 14, 1883, in Charleston, South Carolina, to Charles and Mary Just. His father was a dock builder who died when Just was still a young boy, and his mother was a schoolteacher who supervised his education. After his mother sent him to the Colored Normal, Industrial, Agricultural, and Mechanical College in South Carolina, she enrolled him at a northern preparatory school called Kimball Union Academy, in Meriden, New Hampshire. Just was an excellent student, completing the four-year course in three years while serving as editor of the school newspaper and president of the debating society.

After graduation Just entered Dartmouth College, which was only a few miles away from Kimball. At Dartmouth he found himself the only black in a freshman class of 288 students. Although he performed exceptionally well in Greek during his first year, he decided to major in biology. By the time he graduated with a bachelor's degree in 1907, he had taken all the courses the college offered in biology. He had even supplied studies and drawings of frog embryo formation for a zoology textbook being written by the head of the biology department, William Patten. In recognition of his superior performance as an undergraduate, Just was elected to Phi Beta Kappa, a scholastic honorary society. Receiving special honors in zoology and history, he was also the only student in his class to graduate *magna cum laude* (with high honors). Just then joined the faculty at Howard University in Washington, D.C., first as a teacher in the English department and then as professor of zoology and physiology (the study of the functions of living things) in the medical school.

Studies at Woods Hole

Although Just was teaching at a university, he lacked a higher degree. He therefore began graduate training in 1909 at the Marine Biological Laboratory (MBL) at the Woods Hole Oceanographic Institute at Woods Hole, Massachusetts. This world-famous research institution gives scientists an opportunity to pursue their investigations during the summer without the interruptions of teaching or other duties. Since Just carried a heavy teaching load at Howard, he conducted most of his research at Wood's Hole for the next twenty years. He was often called upon for advice by other scientific investigators in the study of marine (water) organisms.

In 1911 Just became a research assistant to the director of the MBL, Frank Rattray Lillie (see box), who was also head of the zoology department at the University of Chicago. Their research focused on the fertilization process, or the union of a male egg and a female egg to initiate a new individual, in the sandworm *Nereis*. In 1912 Just published his first paper, a description of the results of research on the fertilized egg of the *Nereis*. His study showed that when the egg cell undergoes its first division, the polar bodies (the cells that separate from the female egg that contain a nucleus but very little cytoplasm) control development of the embryo, together with the point of entrance of the spermatozoan (the male germ cell).

Wins first Spingarn Medal

In 1915 the National Association for the Advancement of Colored People presented Just with the first Spingarn Medal, an award the organization had created to honor men and women of African descent. The recognition encouraged his efforts to pursue research despite the obstacles presented by an effectively segregated society. At the time of the award, Just had not yet earned his doctorate. Lillie had arranged for him to enter the doctoral program at the University of Chicago, but his teaching duties delayed completion of his dissertation and the awarding of his Ph.D. until 1916.

Contributes to understanding of parthenogenesis

The study of parthenogenesis (reproduction without fertilization) had been pioneered by German-born American physiologist Jacques Loeb, who discovered that sea urchin eggs and frog eggs could be induced to develop without being fertilized by sperm. Development could begin after the eggs were pricked with a needle or subjected to certain kinds of salt-water solutions. Just conducted numerous experiments on invertebrate (animals without a backbone) eggs, subjecting them to outside influences, such as various concentrations of seawater and butyric acid (a fatty acid). On the basis of the results of his experiments, Just came to question aspects of Loeb's procedures, as well as his theory of parthenogenesis in general.

As Just returned to Woods Hole year after year, he became an established member of the Corporation of the Marine Biological Laboratory. He also served as an associate editor of the laboratory publication, *Biological Bulletin*. In addition, he became associate editor of the *Journal of Morphology, Physiological Zoology*, and the German journal *Protoplasma*. In recognition of his professional achievements, he was elected to such scientific organizations as the American Society of Naturalists, the American Ecological Society, the American Association for the Advancement of Science, and the American Society of Zoologists. In 1920 the philanthropist Julius Rosenwald supported Just's research work with an individual financial grant that was to continue for a number of years. In 1928 Rosenwald gave an overall grant of $80,000 to Howard University. This expanded Just's work in the zoology department, allowing him to travel to European centers of research.

Publishes important work on cell biology

In 1939 Just published *The Biology of the Cell Surface,* which was the result of research he had conducted at Woods Hole in the 1920s and in Europe during the 1930s. Prior to his research on cell biology, scientists had believed that all the activities of the cell were controlled by the nucleus, which houses the cell's chromosomes and genes. Just established the important role played by the living substance that lies outside the nucleus in a cell, known as the protoplasm. He also emphasized the importance of the ectoplasm, the more rigid outer layer of the protoplasm.

Frank Rattray Lillie, Canadian-born American Biologist

Ernest Everett Just was a marine biology research assistant to Frank Rattray Lillie (1870–1947), one of the founders of the Woods Hole Oceanographic Institute at Woods Hole, Massachusetts. Perhaps most famous for his work on sex hormones, Lillie was also lauded for his research in morphology, the study of plant and animal structures. While teaching at various universities and researching at Woods Hole, Lillie developed his theories about the physiology (physical and chemical reactions) of fertilization and early development of invertebrate eggs. In 1914 he turned his microscope on mammals. Lillie's research, which developed from analyzing twin calf fetuses, introduced biologists to the nature, origin, and action of sex hormones. It also led to Lillie's study of the freemartin, a sterile female calf twinborn with a male. With F. C. Koch at the University of Chicago, Lillie isolated the first known androgens, or male sex hormones. That finding, in turn, led to a greater understanding of the role sex hormones play in animal behavior.

Drawing on two decades of observing the activity of the ectoplasm in the egg cells of marine animals undergoing fertilization, Just was able to demonstrate the important influence the ectoplasm exerts even before the nucleus of the sperm fuses with the nucleus of the egg. Just concluded that the combined influence of the ectoplasm and the nucleus on the protoplasm contributes to the actions of the genes in determining heredity. He further claimed that the factors influencing heredity are already present in the protoplasm and are then extracted from it by the genes.

Seeks "exile" in Europe

Although Just was frequently consulted on the selection of members of the National Academy of Sciences, he himself was never elected to the society. During his career he became increasingly bitter about racial discrimination in the United States. The fellowships and research grants he won never lasted long enough to give him a sense of security, and despite his success in the laboratory he was never granted an appointment at a major research institution. In 1929 Just traveled to Europe for an extended stay, and he frequented the continent often for the rest of his life. First invited to study at the Kaiser Wilhelm Institute for Biology in Berlin, Just also studied at the Sorbonne in Paris and the Stazione Zoologica in Naples. He died in the United States from cancer on October 27, 1941, at the age of fifty-eight. He was survived by his wife, Ethel Highwarden Just, and three children.

Further Reading

Cobb, W. Montague, "Ernest Everett Just, 1883–1941," *Journal of the National Medical Association,* Volume 49, 1957.

Haber, Louis, *Black Pioneers of Science and Invention,* Harcourt, 1970.

Manning, Kenneth R., *Black Apollo of Science: The Life of Ernest Everett Just,* Oxford University Press, 1983.

Louis Keith

Born April 24, 1935
Chicago, Illinois

The motivation that inspires physician Louis Keith, one of America's leading experts on twins, is a very personal one —he is an identical twin himself. He and his twin brother, Donald, founded the Center for the Study of Multiple Birth in 1977. Based in Chicago, Illinois, the nonprofit organization was the first major multi-birth research facility in the United States. The Center has become a national clearinghouse for information about twins, triplets, and other multiple births (multiples). Its purpose is to stimulate and support medical and social research on multiples, make information available about multiples, and publish books on twins. The center receives as many as one hundred inquiries a week, ranging from questions from families coping with the demands of raising two or more babies at once to interview requests from reporters. The center is affiliated with Northwestern University Medical School, where Keith is a professor of obstetrics (the branch of medicine dealing with birth) and gynecology (the branch of medicine dealing with the female reproductive

"There are many things the general population learns from twin studies. One of the most important is the difference between nature and nurture."

IMPACT

Louis Keith and his twin brother, Donald, founded the Chicago-based Center for the Study of Multiple Birth in 1977. The first major multi-birth research facility in the United States, the center has a goal of stimulating and supporting medical and social research on multiples. Twins—particularly identical twins—are useful in examining the effects of heredity versus the environment on medical and behavioral development. Scientists reason that because identical twins share the same genes, differences between them must be due to environmental factors.

system). He serves as president of the center, and his brother is the executive director.

Becomes a doctor

The only children of Russian immigrants, Louis Gerald Keith and Donald Keith were born in Chicago on April 24, 1935. As children they received quite a bit of attention due to their status as twins. Yet their parents encouraged them to develop their own personalities. At age twelve Louis decided he would be a physician. Five years later, he and his brother went their separate ways. Louis entered the University of Illinois, where he earned a bachelor of science degree, and Donald joined the army.

After graduating from the Chicago Medical School (now University of Health Sciences—Chicago Medical School) in 1960, Keith completed an internship and residency at Cook County Hospital in Chicago. Then he joined the U.S. Public Health Service, and he was stationed in Puerto Rico. After being certified by the American Board of Obstetrics and Gynecology in 1967, he returned to Chicago and served on the faculty of the Chicago Medical School. In addition he was attending physician at Cook County and Mt. Sinai Hospitals in Chicago. In 1975 he became professor of obstetrics and gynecology at Northwestern University Medical School and an attending physician at the Prentice Women's Hospital and Maternity Center in Chicago. He is now obstetrician in chief of the Chemical Dependency Clinic at the hospital.

Studies twins

Keith undertook his first project involving twins in 1969. After the twin brother of a colleague died of lymphoma, the colleague asked Keith what was known about cancer in twins.

He reviewed the literature, then reported his findings to the First International Symposium on Twin Studies. His interest in twin research grew, culminating in 1977, when his brother convinced him to begin the Center for the Study of Multiple Birth.

Keith and his fellow physicians at Prentice Women's Hospital have published several major studies on the demographics (population statistics) and results of multiple births at the hospital. These reports have informed the medical community about the dangers of multiple pregnancy and childbirth to both the infant and the mother. For example, the researchers have discovered that, more often than single-birth infants, twins begin their lives in double jeopardy. The risk of losing the baby in twin gestation is at least three times greater than in a single birth, and the mortality rate for twins is about five times greater than single children in the first five years of life. Keith has also found that the second-born twin has a greater chance of dying in infancy. A woman who is pregnant with multiples is medically considered a high risk. Complications such as hemorrhaging (severe bleeding) or high blood pressure are an ever-present danger, necessitating the care of physicians with expertise in handling high-risk births.

Reports on multiple-birth risks

Many twin pregnancies are not detected until late in the pregnancy or at the time of the birth. According to a report from the Center for the Study of Multiple Birth, most twin pregnancies were not discovered until the seventh, eighth, or even ninth month. In nearly 24 percent of the cases, the presence of multiples was not found until labor had begun. In the United States, 50 percent of multiple pregnancies are not discovered until about two weeks before delivery, Keith said. Ultrasound (a procedure that uses sound waves to create a picture of internal organs) can detect twins early in pregnancy, but it is not used routinely in many areas of the country.

Another factor in the high mortality rate of twins is the fact that multiple pregnancies are more likely to result in pre-

Wilhelm Weinberg, German Geneticist

Wilhelm Weinberg (1862–1937) was an early pioneer in research on multiple births. An obstetrician in private practice at the beginning of the twentieth century, Weinberg was the first to apply to observable human characteristics the laws of heredity formulated by **Gregor Mendel** (see entry). Weinberg collected data on multiple births, genetic diseases, and mortality, using these statistics to derive generalized mathematical laws and statistical relationships. The most notable was the Hardy-Weinberg law, which has become one of the fundamental laws of genetics and is now widely used to predict gene frequency within a population.

In 1901 Weinberg developed the "difference method," a mathematical rule geneticists use to determine the proportion of identical versus fraternal twin births within a population. He did not invent the difference method and he acknowledged that it had been used previously, but he was the first to apply the method without unnecessary alteration of data. Weinberg also discovered a number of differences between fraternal and identical twins, and he concluded that women could inherit a tendency to bear fraternal twins but not identical twins.

mature birth, before the thirty-seventh week of a forty-week pregnancy. About 50 percent of the three thousand twins born yearly arrive prematurely and have a low chance of survival. More than 75 percent of triplets are born prematurely. Researchers do not know what causes the high incidence of pre-term labor in multiple pregnancies, but the weight of the two babies and the increased stress both to the mother and the babies appear to play a role. If detected early, pre-term labor can be stopped by bed rest or medication in some cases. The survival of premature twins often depends on where the babies are born, Keith said. Major medical centers with specialists in high-risk pregnancy and experience in caring for premature babies have better success than smaller community hospitals.

One in fifty persons is a twin

More than 30,000 sets of twins are born annually in the United States. Throughout the world, there are an estimated

100,000,000 twins. About 1 in 90 births results in twins; 1 in 50 persons is a twin. Triplets occur in 1 in 8,000 births, quadruplets in one in 730,000, and quintuplets in 1 in 60,000,000. Identical twins, also called monozygotic, result when one fertilized egg splits within days of conception, forming two embryos. Identical twins share the same genes and, except in extremely rare instances, are the same sex. About one-third of twin pairs are identical. Fraternal, or dizygotic, twins result when two eggs are released and fertilized by different sperm. This type of twinning can result in same sex or different sex children whose genes are no more alike than any other siblings.

The occurrence of identical twins appears to be an accident of nature, and the rate is the same throughout the world, about 4 in 1,000 births. However, the rate of fraternal twinning increases with the age of the mother, the number of pregnancies, and the use of fertility drugs. Fraternal twining appears to run in families and is higher in blacks than whites. People from Asian countries have the lowest incidence of twins.

Other twin studies reinforce Keith's findings

Scientists theorize that identical twins reared apart have more similarities than those brought up in one family where families tend to encourage their children to develop their own identities. Director of the Minnesota Center for Twin and Adoption Research at the University of Minnesota Thomas Bouchard and his colleagues conducted week-long medical and psychological tests on 350 pairs of twins and 44 pairs of identical twins reared apart (adopted as infants by different families). The group reported in 1987 that personality is based more on heredity than had been previously assumed. Genetic factors appear to play a role in such personality traits as social potency, alienation, well-being, and harm avoidance. Expressive behaviors, such as style of walking, standing, and gesturing, also appear to be influenced by heredity.

The Louisville Twin Study, organized in 1957 at the University of Louisville School of Medicine, focuses on the environmental and genetic components of child development.

Jim Lewis and Jim Springer, Identical Twins

The Minnesota Center for Twin and Adoption Research at the University of Minnesota has conducted extensive tests on some 350 pairs of twins and 44 pairs of identical twins reared apart (adopted as infants by different families). Some of the twin pairs in the project who were reared apart show eerie similarities. Take the case of Jim Lewis and Jim Springer. These identical twins were adopted as infants by different families in Ohio and grew up forty miles apart. Once reunited in 1979, they learned that each had married and divorced a woman named Linda and then married a woman named Betty. Each had an adopted brother named Larry. Lewis had named his first son James Allan, Springer named his first son James Allan. Each had a dog named Toy. Each vacationed at the same beach in St. Petersburg, Florida, drove the same model blue Chevrolet, chain-smoked the same brand of cigarettes, and had similar headache patterns.

Louisville researchers have looked into language and reading ability, blood typing, color blindness, and ways of detecting accident-prone children. The International Twin Study, founded in 1981 at the University of Southern California in Los Angeles, uses twin pairs to study environmental causes of cancer, multiple sclerosis, diabetes, and other chronic diseases.

Acknowledges personal interest

Keith's personal experience has increased his understanding of parents with twins. "Parents of twins assume new responsibility, that of having to raise their children as individuals without destroying the natural bond of twinship," he wrote in the forward to *Having Twins* by Elizabeth Noble. "It is said that the bond between twins is closer than the bond between mother and child." And Keith told an interviewer that his personal involvement makes his work even more worthwhile: "Had it not been for my being a twin, I would not have devoted a major portion of my academic intellectual life to the study of twins. It was the fact that I was an identical twin that has made [it] all so personal and all so meaningful." As research on twins yields new information, Keith continues to make it known to the general public. The Center for the Study of Multiple Births offers support to families coping with raising more than one child at the same time.

Continues studies

Throughout his academic career Keith has published scientific articles on a wide range of topics in obstetrics and gynecology, including breast disease, pelvic inflammatory disease, fertility, sterilization, and sexually transmitted disease. Since 1980 his major research interest, along with multiple birth, has been the effects of cocaine use during pregnancy. In 1994 he coauthored a book on premature birth, and in 1996 he wrote, with his brother Donald and others, *Multiple Pregnancy: Epidemiology, Gestation and Prenatal Outcome.* Keith is a member of numerous professional organizations, including the International College of Surgeons, the International Council of Sex Education and Parenthood, and the American Association of Medical Writers. He is a founding member of the International Society of Twin Studies.

Further Reading

Castile, Kay, *Twins: Nature's Amazing Mystery,* Atheneum, 1982.

Noble, Elizabeth, *Having Twins,* Houghton, 1980.

Theroux, Rosemary, and Josephine Tingley, *The Care of Twin Children: A Common-Sense Guide for Parents,* Center for the Study of Multiple Birth, 1978.

Twins Magazine, July-August 1984; January-February 1985; September-October 1987.

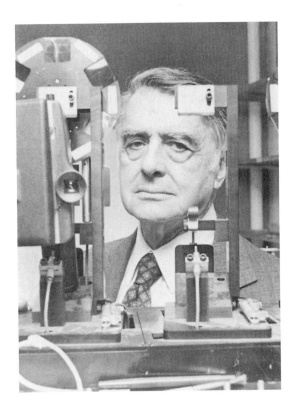

Edwin H. Land

Born May 7, 1909
Bridgeport, Connecticut
Died March 1, 1991

Edwin H. Land invented the Polaroid camera and developed many uses for polarized glass.

American inventor Edwin H. Land was the driving force behind the Polaroid Corporation's engineering and marketing successes. He founded the company to manufacture his inventions, such as polarized windows and sunglasses, and he also produced revolutionary optics for the military during World War II. It was his development of the instant camera, however, that made his company famous and allowed him to dominate the instant-photography market with cameras that first produced pictures in sepia tones, then black and white, and finally in color. Routinely discarding conventional wisdom, Land believed that market research was not necessary; he claimed that any invention would sell if people believed it was something they could not live without.

Becomes interested in polarized light

An only child, Edwin Land was born to Martha F. and Harry Land on May 7, 1909, in Bridgeport, Connecticut. The family was prosperous and Land had a comfortable upbringing. In his youth he dreamed of being an inventor and idolized **Michael Faraday, Thomas Alva Edison,** and **Alexander Graham Bell** (see entries). Land was very interested in polarized light, or light filtered in a way to prevent its glare, from an early age. He entered Harvard University in Cambridge, Massachusetts, at age seventeen in 1926. While walking along Broadway in New York City that same year, he was overwhelmed by the glare from headlights and store signs that shone in his eyes. Land perceived safety hazards in all that glare, and he determined that polarized lights could reduce it. He left Harvard at the end of the school year to pursue this idea and did not return for three years.

Land stayed in New York and worked on his idea. He studied at the New York Public Library and even found a laboratory at Columbia University where a window was always left unlocked. He would climb in at night and conduct various experiments. During this period Land met Helen Maislen, a graduate of Smith College who began assisting him in his research. They were married in 1929, and Land returned to Harvard that same year. This time the university provided him with a laboratory to conduct his research.

Develops commercial method to polarize light

It had been known since the eighteenth century that certain kinds of crystals (clear colorless glasses of superior quality) could affect the direction of light waves. In his effort to develop a method for polarizing light, Land was searching for a crystal that could not only reduce glare but was stable and economical enough to be produced commercially. He conceived the idea of two plates that would absorb the light waves that were not wanted and transmit those that were. He then succeeded in aligning millions of microscopic iodine crystals in one direction, thus creating the first polarizer. Land presented a paper on his discovery at a physics colloquium (meeting) at Harvard in February 1932. In June he left the university, one semester short of a degree, and never returned.

Invents "Polaroid"

With a Harvard graduate student named George Wheelwright, who had been one of his teachers, Land formed Land-Wheelwright Laboratories, Inc., in June 1932. The two men worked on developing methods of manufacturing polarized sheets made of crystals trapped in nitrocellulose (any of several nitric-acid esters of cellulose used for making explosives, plastics, and varnishes). On November 30, 1934, the camera company Eastman Kodak gave Land-Wheelwright an order for $10,000 worth of polarizing filters. The company wanted a polarizer laminated between two sheets of optical glass, but neither Land nor Wheelwright had any idea how to manufacture such an item. Nonetheless, they accepted the order—a decision typical of the way Land would work in the future. Their persistence paid off, and Land-Wheelwright Laboratories invented what they called "Polaroid," with which they fulfilled their contract with Eastman Kodak.

Land had a flair for the dramatic that he put to good use in marketing his inventions. For example, when he was trying to sell his polarizers as sunglasses, he rented a room at a hotel and invited executives from the American Optical Company to meet him there. The late afternoon sun produced a glare on the windowsill; Land put a fishbowl on the sill and the glare rendered the goldfish inside it invisible. When the executives arrived Land handed them each a sheet of polarizer, and they were able to see the fish instantly. Land told them that from now on their sunglasses should be made with polarized glass, and the company bought the idea.

Starts the Polaroid Corporation

Land gave his first press conference on polarization on January 30, 1936, at the Waldorf Astoria Hotel in New York. He repeated it for the National Academy of Sciences and the New York Museum of Science soon afterward. On August 10, 1937, a group of investors, impressed with Land-Wheelwright's accomplishments, invested $375,000 to fund the Polaroid Corporation. Furthermore, they gave Land controlling interest in the company. With the money Land purchased competing patents on polarization.

Land decided that the 1939 New York World's Fair would be an excellent place to demonstrate to automakers and the American public the virtues of polarized headlights. The Chrysler Corporation rented space to Polaroid in one of its booths, and Land played a three-dimensional movie he had invented that graphically illustrated the improvements of polarized headlights. The twelve-minute film was well received by the public; 150,000 people saw it during the first two months, but Detroit automakers never bought Land's system. Polaroid nevertheless enjoyed success with Polaroid Day Glasses and the dual polarized windows they installed on Union Pacific's Copper King rail cars. By January 1940 the company had about 240 employees, and it moved its headquarters from Boston to nearby Cambridge.

IMPACT

In addition to inventing successful consumer items, Edwin H. Land manufactured many products for science and the military. In 1948 he developed a new optical system for the Sloan-Kettering Cancer Institute that enabled scientists to observe living human cells in their natural color. In 1953 he invented a microscope that used light invisible to the human eye for illumination. Both of these inventions were a great aid in cancer research. He also headed the 1954 U-2 rocket bomb project that utilized several Polaroid developments, and he provided the U.S. Army and Navy with various types of goggles and gunsights made of polarized glass.

Invents instant photography

By 1943 Land had a three-year-old daughter named Jennifer. While they were vacationing in Santa Fe, New Mexico, just before Christmas, she asked him why they could not see the pictures they had taken during the day. Land pondered the question and came up with a solution. On February 21, 1947, Land demonstrated his instant camera at the winter meeting of the Optical Society of America. Although the images were in sepia (a brownish color), public reaction was so enthusiastic that Polaroid came under much pressure to manufacture the camera quickly. The camera also had another revolutionary feature: it linked aperture size and shutter speed, which eliminated much of the guesswork in using the camera. (The aperture is the lens opening, which lets in light; the shutter controls how much light is let in.)

In 1952 Polaroid introduced true black-and-white film for the instant camera. But unlike the sepia prints, which held their images well, the black-and-white prints faded over time. Land pressed his company to find a solution, which they found in only four weeks. Yet he was not happy with it, since it required swabbing the photo after pulling it from the camera; Land wanted his instant camera to require only one step. In addition, research had continued simultaneously to develop an instant camera that produced color photos. Land even had his own private laboratory where he did much work on the project.

Finally, in April 1972, Land was able to reveal to the public a long-time dream brought to reality: the SX-70 instant color camera. The introduction of color had meant overcoming a host of technological obstacles. His achievement was recognized with the October 27, 1972, cover of *Life* magazine, which showed Land taking pictures of children from behind his SX-70.

Receives honors and awards

Land was awarded the Hood Medal from the Royal Photographic Society in London in 1935. Five years later he was named one of America's Modern Pioneers by the National Association of Manufacturers. In 1963 Land received the Presidential Medal of Freedom, awarded by Lyndon Johnson. President Johnson also presented the National Medal of Science to Land in 1967. Land, who received 533 patents during his lifetime, was inducted into the Inventor's Hall of Fame by the American patent office in 1977.

During the 1960s Land started an inner city program for disadvantaged blacks youths as well as the Rowland Foundation. He later founded the Rowland Institute for Science. His financial gifts to various institutions, such as the Massachusetts Institute of Technology (MIT) and Harvard University, were always anonymous. He was a visiting professor at MIT, a member of Harvard visiting committees for astronomy, chemistry, and physics, and a fellow at the MIT School for Advanced Study. Land received honorary doctorates from such notable institutions as Yale, Tufts, Columbia, Loyola, and Washington Universities. From 1951 to 1953 he served as president of the American Academy of Arts and Sciences. Land retired in 1982 and died on March 1, 1991.

Further Reading

Berg, Howard C., "Edwin H. Land," *Physics Today,* April 1992, p. 106.

Olshaker, Mark, *The Instant Image,* Stein & Day, 1978.

Pace, Eric, "Edwin H. Land, Dies at 81; Invented Polaroid Camera," *New York Times,* March 2, 1991.

Wensberg, Peter C., *Land's Polaroid,* Houghton, 1987.

Jaron Lanier

Born in 1961
New Mexico

Jaron Lanier will go down in history as the man who coined the phrase "virtual reality." Beginning in the mid-1980s the software designer and inventor almost singlehandedly brought high-tech thinking within the reach of the ordinary citizen. Revered by enthusiasts of the technical age, Lanier has left an indelible mark on the field of computer science.

Shows talent for both math and music

A self-taught computer genius who might be considered eccentric, Jaron Lanier grew up in an environmentally friendly geodesic dome home (see **R. Buckminster Fuller** entry) in New Mexico, where he pursued his two main interests: mathematics and music. As the son of a science writer father and a concert pianist mother—she died when he was nine—Lanier was exposed to both the arts and sciences from a very early age. He once said that he was always "consumed by math's beauty," but at the same time he studied several musical

Computer Simulation: Fly a Plane, Design a Kitchen

Computer simulation began nearly fifty years before Jaron Lanier created virtual reality. In the 1930s Edwin A. Link designed the famous Link trainer, a flight simulator that taught people how to fly airplanes. More complex flight simulators began making use of computer graphics in 1968, when David Evans and Ivan Sutherland designed a program for ARPA, the Advanced Research Projects Agency. Sutherland went on to start his own company at Lincoln Laboratory, where he founded the field of interactive computer graphics. Another pioneer in computer simulation is Myron Krueger, who created programs such as CRITTER, a virtual reality cartoon featuring a four-legged yellow creature that interacts with the user.

The tremendous practical potential of computer simulation is just beginning to unfold. Matsushita Corporation of Japan is using virtual reality to help customers shop for custom-built kitchens. The customers can "tour" three-dimensional images of their proposed kitchens, using headsets and gloves, suggesting changes before actual installation takes place. Architects and aerospace engineers will be using more simulations in their work as well. Boeing has already developed a new airliner designed and engineered entirely by computer. Researchers in drug companies are generating models of molecules to tailor specific drugs for specific medical conditions. Computer simulation may even become the newest form of entertainment. VPL Research, Lanier's old company, has formed a joint venture with MCA, Inc. to build a series of test theaters using virtual reality on a large scale.

instruments. Although he later dropped out of high school, Lanier was allowed to attend college courses at the age of fourteen. According to an article in *Business Week* magazine, "By the age most kids enter college, he had already progressed to graduate level courses."

Founds his own company

Drawn to computer science, Lanier moved to California in 1980 and took a job designing video games. He soon earned a reputation for high-quality work. As a programmer in demand, he eventually acquired the money he needed to form his own company, VPL Research Inc., in 1984. At that time nnovative software designer Jaron Lanier pioneered the concept of virtual reality, a computer-simulated environment that mirrors the external world. His invention has practical uses in the medical, aerospace, automotive, and construction fields, and it has also opened new doors in the burgeoning computer game arena.

the technologies involved in virtual reality (an artificial computer-created environment that seeks to mimic reality), also known as VR, were already in place and in use. However, the software was expensive and limited to just a few applications, such as flight simulators. Seeing the possibilities for making the technology available to the average computer user, Lanier developed virtual reality software for relatively inexpensive systems. He designed computers, gloves, and goggles that commercial users could adapt to their own software applications.

To experience Lanier's virtual reality world, the user would simply strap on the special goggles containing tiny liquid crystal screens, and the headset would project a computer-generated landscape onto the lenses. Since the image projection program is sensitive to the user's movements, it alters the perspective of the viewed scene as the user's head moves, producing stunningly realistic images. Lanier also created the DataGlove, which has optical fibers and sensors that can measure the position and movement of the fingers. The glove allows the wearer to move or grab things in the artificial world presented on the headset. A simplified version of the glove, known as the PowerGlove, is sold by Mattel for use with the popular Nintendo video games.

Brings virtual reality to the world

Lanier's notion of virtual reality for the masses was accepted quickly. By the 1990s any ordinary person could strap on a special helmet, don a power glove, and travel through space and time under the influence of computer-generated environments. "You might be in a Moorish temple," Lanier explained in an interview, "or a heart that's pumping. You might be watching a representation of hydrogen bonds

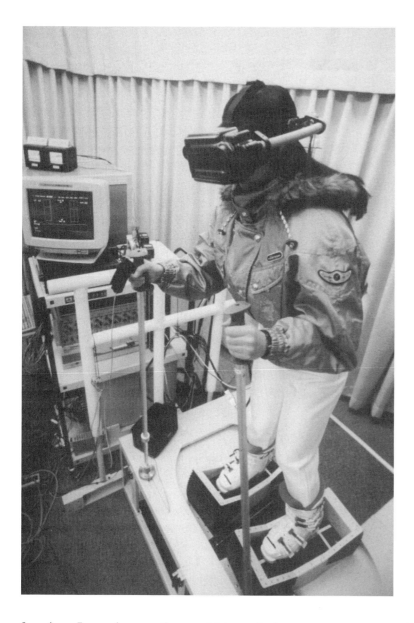

forming. In each case the world is entirely computer generated. Now, imagine that you had the power to change the
world quickly—without limitations. If you suddenly wanted to
make the planet three times larger, put a crystal cave in the
middle with a giant goat bladder pulsing inside of that and tiny
cities populating the goat bladder's surface ... you could build
that world instead of talking about it!"

Jaron Lanier

ELIZA: Computer as Psychiatrist

A predecessor to virtual reality was the "talking" computer, which was used in the field of psychology. A man named Joseph Weizenbaum began a friendship with psychiatrist Kenneth Colby that resulted in a revolutionary leap in psychoanalysis. Colby, who had become disenchanted with traditional one-to-one counseling, believed that computers could offer a way of gaining new insights into neurotic behavior and perhaps aid in the development of new therapeutic methods. Several question-answer machines had already been developed, but Weizenbaum decided to create a new one. The result was ELIZA (named after the character in the musical *My Fair Lady,* a rags to riches tale about a woman who learns to speak properly). The program was designed to simulate the conversation between patient and psychoanalyst, with the machine playing the role of the doctor. The psychoanalytic program was such a success that many people began telling their problems to computers. The key to ELIZA was its natural responses. When puzzled by a statement, it would say, "I see," or "That's very interesting," much as humans do in similar situations.

Becomes a celebrity

As brilliant as Lanier is within the realm of high-tech computers, he was unfamiliar with the business world. In 1992 he lost his control of VPL Research Inc. to the French technology giant Thomson-CSF, which had loaned him money to start the company. Thomson seized all VPL patents and intellectual property (plans and designs), leaving Lanier with nothing. Lanier responded by forming a new company, Domain Simulations. He now serves as the chief technical officer in a working studio filled with both computer equipment and musical instruments. Lanier's interest in music has enhanced his image. Whenever he is recognized—and Lanier is not easy to forget because of his large frame and distinctive blond dreadlocks—he is treated much like a rock star. He is especially popular in Europe, where the use of virtual reality is widespread. His fans even sell Jaron Lanier psychedelic posters, and in Japan he was actually mobbed while walking down the street.

Sees bright future for virtual reality

Lanier is somewhat surprised by his cult status and the enthusiasm his invention has generated, for virtual reality has not yet met his original expectations. Nevertheless he predicts the technology will eventually fulfill its potential by creating an environment that can be perceived as actually being "real" by the computer user. Lanier told a *Time* magazine interviewer, "The internal experience of reality is much more a product of your central nervous system than of the actual external world. That's why virtual reality works. Provide enough visual clues [on the screen], and million of years of evolution will kick into gear."

Further Reading

Elmer-DeWitt, Philip, "(Mis)adventures in Cyberspace," *Time,* September 3, 1990.

Hamilton, Joan O., "Trials of a Cyber-Celebrity," *Business Week,* February 22, 1993.

"Jaron Lanier Is Virtually Sure," *New Yorker,* December 27, 1993.

Lanier, Jaron, "Music From Inside Virtual Reality: The Sound of One Hand," *Whole Earth Review,* Summer 1993.

Lanier, Jaron, "Unmuzzling the Internet: How to Avoid the Censors, and Make a Statement, Too," *New York Times,* January 2, 1996.

Levy, Steven, "Brave New World," *Rolling Stone,* June 14, 1990.

Maglitta, Joseph E., "One on One With Jaron Lanier," *Computerworld,* June 20, 1994.

Stewart, Doug, "Jaron Lanier," *Omni,* January 1991.

Antoine Lavoisier

Born in 1743
Paris, France
Died May 8, 1794
Paris, France

Antoine Lavoisier universalized the language and method of identification used in chemistry.

Prior to the late eighteenth century and the influence of Antoine Lavoisier, scientific experiments were generally conducted haphazardly and results were often invalid. Lavoisier, a French chemist and physicist, established the practice of accurate measurement that underlies all valid quantitative experiments. He also developed the first rational system for naming chemical compounds—a system that is still used today. A brilliant scientist with wide-ranging interests, Lavoisier is known as the father of modern chemistry.

Chooses to study science

Antoine-Laurent Lavoisier grew up in Paris, France, the product of a sophisticated urban culture and a well-to-do bourgeois (middle-class) lifestyle. His father was an influential attorney who followed the family tradition of practicing law. Lavoisier's mother adored her first-born, and after her untimely death Lavoisier received equally doting care from his young aunt. He received an excellent education at an exclusive school, where he proved to be a brilliant student.

Although Lavoisier earned his law degree, he never became intrigued by the profession. Instead, he studied with some of France's most distinguished scientists in the fields of astronomy, mathematics, botany, geology, and chemistry. By the time he began his scientific career, he had gained entrance into the leading intellectual circles of the day and had been exposed to a great variety of scientific pursuits.

The breadth of Lavoisier's curiosity is reflected in his earliest research. Before he turned twenty-five, he had collaborated in producing a geological atlas of France, explored the possibility of using street lights in large French towns, and discovered the composition of the mineral gypsum (plaster of Paris). Lavoisier's experiments with gypsum illustrate one of his strengths as a chemist—accurate measurement. By carefully measuring the amount of water given off when gypsum was heated, Lavoisier showed that the mineral is composed partly of water. Although a few scientists had earlier paid careful attention to measurement, it was Lavoisier who convinced the majority of chemists that accurate measurements are essential to experimental success and scientific progress. Lavoisier was elected to France's Academy of Sciences in 1768.

As a member of the scientific academy, Lavoisier served on many boards and committees that were appointed by the government to improve public welfare. He set up a model farm where new scientific methods could be applied to agriculture. He helped standardize the national system of weights and measures, which laid the foundation for today's metric system. He even investigated prison reform.

In 1771 Lavoisier married Marie Paulze, who was barely fourteen years old and not only beautiful but also intelligent. She soon began to collaborate with her husband in his scientific work, translating English works into French for him, and illustrating his works. Although Lavoisier was fairly wealthy, scientists earned little money in those days, and he was forced to invest his funds in a profit-making venture in order to support his research. Unfortunately, he chose to invest in a private agency, of which Marie's father was an executive, that collected taxes for the government. French peasants viciously hated tax collectors, who were notorious for extorting extra profits. Although the money Lavoisier made allowed him to continue with his scientific research, the affiliation would later play a role in his death.

Discovers content of diamonds

In 1768 Lavoisier had dispelled the ancient notion that earth could be created from water. People thought this was possible because a solid sediment appears when water is heated for several days. Lavoisier conducted a long, tedious experiment to disprove this idea. By carefully weighing the glass container and the water it held before and after his test, he proved that the sediment was made up of material that had been eaten away from the container during heating.

During the early 1770s Lavoisier began heating substances in air to see whether they would burn. Using two large magnifying lenses, he placed a diamond in a ray of sunshine that was filtered through the lenses. The diamond slowly disappeared and carbon dioxide gas (containing one part carbon and two parts oxygen) accumulated. This test proved that diamonds are made of carbon, or at least contain carbon. Lavoisier also showed that diamonds would not burn without air. Intrigued by the process of combustion (a rapid chemical process requiring oxygen that produces heat and light), Lavoisier went on to burn other substances such as phosphorus and sulfur. Again, by carefully measuring the materials and containers, he showed that these elements gain weight when they are heated in air.

Challenges accepted theories

According to the accepted theory of the day, phlogiston (a substance believed to allow a material to burn) was released during combustion. But Lavoisier realized that instead of losing phlogiston, the materials were combining with a portion of the air, which increased their weight. Around the same time, English clergyman and chemist **Joseph Priestley** (see entry) had isolated a gas that greatly promoted combustion. He called it dephlogisticated air because it absorbed phlogiston so readily. Lavoisier realized this gas was precisely the same as the part of the air which reacts with substances during combustion.

After repeating and expanding Priestley's experiments, Lavoisier announced his new theory. Stating that phlogiston is required if an object is to burn, he renamed Priestley's gas "oxygen" and argued that air also contains a second gas, which does not support combustion. Although Lavoisier called the gas "azote," it was soon given the modern name of nitrogen. Lavoisier's discovery additionally implied that the total weight of the substances taking part in a chemical reaction remains the same before and after the reaction. Today we call this fundamental concept the law of conservation of mass. A popular version states that matter can be neither created nor destroyed.

Builds renowned laboratory

In 1775 Lavoisier was put in charge of the government's gunpowder-manufacturing operation. He and his wife moved to the arsenal, where they lived for many years. Using his investment earnings, Lavoisier set up a magnificent private laboratory—the best in Europe at that time. One of his most valuable pieces of equipment was a chemical balance that could weigh objects with great precision. Leading scientists from France met regularly at Lavoisier's laboratory, and world-renowned figures such as American statesmen and amateur scientists Thomas Jefferson and Benjamin Franklin also visited.

As an offshoot of his studies of combustion, Lavoisier began to explore the process of respiration (supplying oxygen to cells and relieving them of carbon dioxide). Working with French physicist Pierre Laplace, Lavoisier measured the heat given off when guinea pigs and sparrows digest food. These experiments, reported in 1789, showed that animals' energy and warmth depends on oxygen intake. Lavoisier and Laplace also demonstrated that nitrogen plays no part in respiration; it is only the oxygen in the air that is needed to support animal life.

Introduces chemical classification system

As his reputation grew, Lavoisier was recruited to pursue more research avenues. Louis-Bernard Guyton de Morveau, a colleague who was trying to write a history of chemistry, turned to Lavoisier for help. Lavoisier soon pinpointed the biggest problem—language. For centuries alchemists (scientists who tried to change base metals into gold) had deliberately tried to keep their discoveries secret from common people, so they gave new substances absurd names, such as butter of arsenic or sugar of lead, that were meaningless to the uninitiated. In collaboration with other chemists, including Claude Berthollot, Lavoisier developed a new, logical system for naming chemical substances in 1787. They decided that a chemical name should indicate the elements that make up the compound; for example, hydrogen sulfide contains hydrogen and sulfur. This revolutionary system, which is still used today, provided an understandable and rational method of compound identification.

Publishes works

In 1789, just two years after introducing the chemical classification system, Lavoisier published the first truly modern chemical textbook, *Elementary Treatise on Chemistry*. In the book he not only stated the law of conservation of mass, but also revived the definition of an element, which had been suggested earlier by English physicist and chemist Robert Boyle (see box). Lavoisier also listed all substances thought to

Robert Boyle, English Physicist and Chemist

The ancient Greeks proposed that all things were made of only four elements—air, earth, fire, and water—which could be changed, or transmuted, into other substances. Later, people believed that only three substances existed in nature: salt, sulfur, and mercury. English physicist and chemist Robert Boyle (1627–1691) was the first to set science on the right track by asserting the true nature of elements and compounds. In 1661 he published his most famous work, *The Sceptical Chymist*, which revolutionized scientific thought and formed the basis of modern chemistry. In this work, Boyle defined an element as the simplest form of matter, one that cannot be broken down into any simpler form or changed into a different substance. According to Boyle, none of the substances the ancients believed were elements were true elements.

Boyle argued that elements could be identified only by scientific experimentation. He also pointed out that a compound will usually have chemical properties that are very different from parent elements. Boyle's concept of an element rose from his experiments with gases. Antoine Lavoisier revived Boyle's definition of an element a century later and lent it credence in his *Elementary Treatise on Chemistry*.

be elements at that time, emphasizing that the list probably contained some compounds that could be decomposed only with advanced scientific techniques. Overall, the list was remarkably accurate.

Anxious to prove himself, Lavoisier often discredited the contributions of other chemists to his work. For example, even though Lavoisier deserves full credit for figuring out the combustion process, he neglected to mention the information he got from Priestley. Similarly, he repeated research done by English physicist and chemist Henry Cavendish, who discovered inflammable air and burned it to produce water. When Lavoisier named this gas "hydrogen," he failed to point out that Cavendish had performed the original experiments. Possibly these omissions were not intentional; Lavoisier simply wanted, very badly, to discover an element himself—a goal he would never accomplish.

Executed by revolutionaries

With the outbreak of the French Revolution in 1789, in which the French peasants rose up against the aristocracy, Lavoisier's position as an administrator in the government's tax collection agency automatically made him a target of hatred. After being barred from his laboratory, he fled his home but was caught and arrested a few months later. When he protested that he was a scientist, not a tax man, he was told the Republic did not need scientists. Lavoisier was charged with ridiculous crimes. Testifying against him was an old enemy, Jean-Paul Marat, whom Lavoisier had prevented, with good reason, from joining the Academy of Sciences. Eager for revenge, Marat accused Lavoisier of diluting commercial tobacco and cutting off the Paris air supply by building a defensive wall around the city. On May 8, 1794, Lavoisier was sentenced to death and executed on the guillotine.

Further Reading

Donovan, Arthur, *Antoine Lavoisier: Science, Administration, and Revolution,* Cambridge University Press, 1996.

Gould, Stephen Jay, "The Passion of Antoine Lavoisier," *Natural History,* June 1989, p. 16.

Grey, Vivian, *The Chemist Who Lost His Head: The Story of Antoine-Laurent Lavoisier,* Coward, McCann, Geogheghan, 1982.

Guerlac, H., *Lavoisier—The Crucial Year: The Background and Origin of His First Experiments on Combustion in 1772,* Gordon & Breach, 1990.

McKie, Douglas, *Antoine Lavoisier,* Da Capo Press, 1990.

Louis S. B. Leakey

Born August 7, 1903
Kabete, Kenya
Died October 1, 1972
London, England

Mary Leakey

Born February 6, 1913
London, England

Richard Leakey

Born December 19, 1944
Nairobi, Kenya

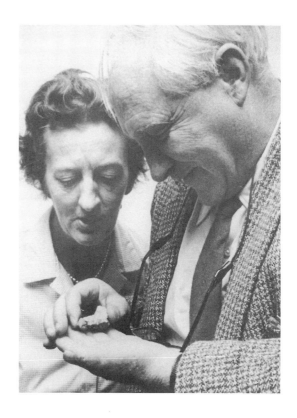

Mary and Louis Leakey

Anthropology is the science of the way humans have lived and developed over the ages. In the field of paleoanthropology, the branch of anthropology that deals with the study of fossil man, there is no name better known to experts and the general public alike than Leakey. Louis and Mary Leakey completed important early excavations—or archeological "digs," in which they unearthed and studied ancient material remains of past civilizations—at the Olduvai Gorge in the eastern African country of Tanzania. In the 1970s their middle son, Richard, made equally significant discoveries at Lake Turkana (also known as Lake Rudolf) along the border between Kenya and Ethiopia. The work of this pioneering family of scientists has expanded knowledge of the stages of human evolution and the conditions under which they occurred. As a result of the Leakeys' dedication and perseverance over more than sixty years, the story of the pre-history of human beings has revealed itself to be far more ancient and complex than ever before imagined.

"There have been thousands of living organisms, of which a very high percentage has become extinct. There is nothing, at the moment, to suggest that [humans] are not part of the same pattern."

—Richard Leakey

The Leakey family is in a great part responsible for the increased anthropology activity during the late twentieth century. As a result of Louis and Mary Leakey's work, research emphasis shifted from Asia to Africa, and experts came to accept that humanity's evolutionary descent took much longer than anyone had ever dreamed. Even though their *Zinjanthropus* find in 1959 led Louis to draw some conclusions that were later proven incorrect, the discovery is still considered the event that launched the modern scientific study of man. And Richard's work at Turkana provided the first solid evidence to support his and his father's contention that evolution did not progress in a linear, or neatly sequential, way. Instead they showed it was an overlapping process during which several types of humans and near-humans lived side by side. For these reasons, the Leakey name has become virtually synonymous with the search and discovery of the fossilized remains of the earliest human ancestors.

Louis Leakey uncovers the origins of man

Louis Seymour Bazett Leakey was the oldest of four children born to Anglican Church missionaries Harry and Mary Bazett Leakey on August 7, 1903, in the village of Kabete, outside of Nairobi, Kenya. He spent his entire childhood and adolescence among members of the Kikuyu people and absorbed their traditions and language to the point that the tribal chief once described him as "the black man with a white face." His early interest in bird-watching gave way to a fascination with archaeology after he came across some stone arrowheads and tools during one of his explorations in the wild.

Leakey later pursued his formal education in archaeology and anthropology at Cambridge University in England. When he was twenty-one he accompanied a British Museum archeological expedition to Tanganyika (now Tanzania). From that moment on, he was convinced that there was much more to be uncovered in east Africa about the origins of humans. His professors tried to discourage him; at that time Asia, not Africa, was widely accepted as the birthplace of the human race. But throughout the late 1920s and early 1930s Leakey alternated work on his doctorate at Cambridge with additional field research in east Africa, primarily Kenya.

In 1929 Leakey accidentally stumbled across a 200,000-year-old hand ax that convinced him he was indeed on the right track. A 1931 expedition led him to the remote Olduvai Gorge, an 800-foot-deep, 20-mile-long dry canyon that slices through what was once a shallow lake in northern Tanzania. On Leakey's first day there, he uncovered some prehistoric stone tools and a few fossilized human remains. It was merely a hint of what he might encounter with more serious study. Thus Olduvai Gorge, which would turn out to be one of the richest troves of fossilized human and animal bones in the world, became the center of Leakey's existence for virtually the rest of his life.

Mary Leakey begins archaeological career

During one of his stays in England in 1933, Leakey met a young archeologist and illustrator named Mary Douglas Nicol. Born in London, England, on February 6, 1913, she was the only child of Cecilia Marion Frere Nicol and Edward Nicol, an artist. Her father's profession kept him on the road a great deal, and as a result Mary had a rather unconventional childhood. For example, she did not attend a regular school until she was a teenager. Her father taught her to read, and he also instilled in her a love of ancient relics and monuments. On several occasions while the family was living in southwestern France, she was able to visit various prehistoric caves and excavation sites and view magnificent cave paintings. She even received permission from French archaeologists to sort through objects they had unearthed. It was all Mary needed to persuade her to pursue an archeological career.

The collaboration begins

From 1930 until 1934, Mary Leakey served as an assistant to archaeologist Dorothy Liddell at a major Neolithic (late Stone Age) site in southern Britain. She typically spent summers in the field and winters attending lectures in geology and archaeology at the University of London and the London Museum. Having inherited a considerable amount of artistic talent from her father, she also began to do some drawings of the stone tools uncovered at the excavation. When the drawings appeared in several scientific publications, they caught the eye of another archeologist, Gertrude Caton-Thompson, who asked the budding artist to illustrate a book she was writing on Egyptian stone tools. Caton-Thompson subsequently

Louis and Mary Leakey dig for fossils at the Olduvai Gorge in July 1961.

introduced Mary Nicol to Louis Leakey, who also asked for her help with some illustrations for his 1934 book *Adam's Ancestors*. Despite a ten-year age difference (as well as the fact that Louis was already married and the father of two children), they soon became constant companions. They made their first journey together to Olduvai in April 1935, and in December 1936, after Louis obtained a divorce from his first wife, they married and left again for Africa.

The Leakeys conducted excavations at various east African sites until World War II erupted in 1939; Louis Leakey then suspended his fieldwork to serve with the British military intelligence in Nairobi. Mary continued the excavations on her own throughout the war years. During this time she gave birth to their sons Jonathan and Richard, and to a daughter, Deborah, who died in infancy. (A third son, Philip, was born in

1949.) Mary uncovered thousands of stone tools from various periods, including some that were the oldest known at the time. She also found samples of Iron Age (beginning sometime before 1000 B.C.) pottery and the bones of numerous, unusual extinct animals, but she unearthed no human remains.

Make revolutionary find

After the war Louis Leakey was named full-time director of the Coryndon Museum in Nairobi, leaving him with only a few weeks each year to devote to excavating Olduvai. Funds were a problem, too, since research grants for such work were scarce. Then, in 1948, while digging at a site on the island of Rusing in Lake Victoria, Mary discovered a fossilized skull and other bones that turned out to be those of an apelike creature about twenty-five to forty million years old. Called *Proconsul africanus,* it had humanlike jaws and teeth and walked on its hind legs. The first significant find to suggest that humans may have originated in east Africa, this discovery focused world attention on the Leakeys and encouraged them to begin digging in earnest at Olduvai around 1952.

Seven years later, on July 17, 1959, a day when a feverish Louis was resting in his tent, Mary spotted some fossilized molars protruding from a small slope. Days of painstaking excavation with dental picks and brushes followed, uncovering a complete, humanlike skull some 1.75 million years old—nearly twice as old as scientists had estimated the human species' age to be. Because Louis initially believed the remains to be a distinct, new form of hominid (upright walking human ancestors), he gave it the name *Zinjanthropus,* or "East Africa man." He also proclaimed that he and his wife had found the long-sought missing link between the more apelike *Australopithecus* (discovered some years before in South Africa) and modern human beings. This was later shown to be incorrect—*Zinjanthropus* is now regarded as another form of *Australopithecus* and has been renamed accordingly. Because of its age, however, the *Zinjanthropus* remains a revolutionary find.

Another revolutionary find

The publicity resulting from the *Zinjanthropus* discovery brought the Leakeys worldwide acclaim as well as much-needed funding from the National Geographic Society, which allowed them to live and work at Olduvai on a year-round basis. In 1960 and 1962 they unearthed fossil fragments, a skull, and some tools of a new species they named *Homo habilis,* or "handy man," in recognition of the fact that he made tools. More humanlike than *Zinjanthropus* but of roughly the same age, *Homo habilis* was at that time considered the earliest known ancestor of the genus (or biological classification) *Homo. Homo* includes the later *Homo erectus* and modern *Homo sapiens,* our own species. Also in 1962, at an excavation site forty miles east of Lake Victoria, Louis discovered a fourteen-million-year-old fragment of jaw and teeth belonging to an apelike creature similar to Mary's *Proconsul* find. He called it *Kenyapithecus* (also known as *Ramapithecus*).

By the mid-1960s the Leakeys felt they had assembled enough evidence to prove that early humans had existed in Africa at least two million years ago—and perhaps as many as fourteen million years ago. Louis Leakey created a controversy in the archeological world by stating that, contrary to the scientific opinion of the day, different strains of *Homo sapiens* and near-human species had existed side by side in the same time frame. Throughout the remainder of the 1960s, Leakey spent more and more of his time away from Olduvai on lecture tours, driving himself at such a furious pace that it affected his health. He also began making some unproven claims that Mary, who was always the more conservative scientist of the pair, found difficult to support. And he was growing estranged from his middle son, Richard, the only child who showed any interest in carrying on the family's research. No longer physically able to work in the field after surgery for an arthritic hip in 1968, Louis remained active on the lecture circuit. While in London for a speaking engagement on 1972, he suffered a fatal heart attack.

Richard Leakey, in November 1972, displays fragments of a Homo habilis *skull he unearthed east of Lake Turkana.*

Richard Leakey joins in the field

While Mary carried on the research at Olduvai, Richard Erskine Frere Leakey was starting to generate some headlines of his own. Born in Nairobi on December 19, 1944, he had since infancy accompanied his parents on various excavations. As a youngster he was able to identify fossils and rattle off appropriate anthropological jargon at will. While the subject fascinated Richard, he had no interest in trying to make a name for himself in the same field as his strong-willed father. Nor did he have any desire to go to college and study something else. So he dropped out of high school and found work as a safari guide. (He already had years of experience escorting scientific visitors around Olduvai.)

Within just a few years Richard was making an excellent living but was thoroughly bored with the work. After quitting the safari business around 1963, he started doing some excavation in northeastern Tanzania and unearthed the lower jaw of an *Australopithecus*. Realizing that if he truly wanted to pursue anthropology he needed to broaden his background, Richard went to London to complete two years of high school in seven months. He then passed his university entrance exams but ran out of money before he could start classes. So he returned to Kenya and concentrated on gaining his education in the field.

Carrying on the family tradition

In 1967 Richard joined an expedition his father had organized in southern Ethiopia, not far from the border of Kenya. While piloting his plane around the area, he spotted a desolate stretch of land along the shores of Lake Turkana that he thought looked like a promising place for some research. Accompanying his father to a business meeting with the National Geographic Society in 1968, the brash twenty-three-year-old asked for funds so he could investigate the site. The committee agreed, and before the end of the year Richard was established at Turkana in a camp named Koobi Fora, which has turned out to be what one newspaper reporter called "an anthropological mother lode" even richer than Olduvai.

Almost immediately the young and ambitious Leakey found a wealth of fossil evidence suggesting life had thrived in the Turkana area at least four million years ago. At first he and his team uncovered only animal bones, but then they located *Australopithecus* jaw fragments and a skull. Finally they found some crude tools about 2.6 million years old that had not been made by the vegetarian *Australopithecus* but by a more humanlike hunting hominid alive in the same area at the same time. In 1971 Richard discovered the remains of *Homo habilis,* which supported the theory that this humanlike creature existed alongside the apelike *Australopithecus.* More proof of the theory surfaced the next year with the discovery of a *Homo habilis* skull called "1470" (after its registration number). It was eventually determined to be 1.9 million years old. Richard's find was the oldest *Homo habilis* specimen at that time, making it a revolutionary discovery that rivaled his mother's *Zinjanthropus* in importance. Based on what he had uncovered at Turkana, Richard concluded that at least three kinds of early humanlike species coexisted in east Africa approximately two to three million years ago: *Homo habilis* and two varieties of *Australopithecus.*

Richard Leakey receives recognition

Richard Leakey's discoveries brought him instant acclaim, moving him to the forefront of experts researching the origins of man. His success led to resentment on the part of academically trained anthropologists, who looked on him as an untrained upstart. Richard's fame also strained relations with his father, who had dominated African anthropology for so many years. Their feud ended just a few days before Louis Leakey's death in 1972, after he paid a visit to Turkana and expressed genuine excitement and pride at Richard's 1470 find and predicted even greater achievements for him in the future.

Since his big discovery, Richard Leakey has uncovered more evidence at Turkana that several varieties of early humans coexisted there. In 1975, for example, in a layer of deposits that had already given up some *Australopithecus* remains, he found a *Homo erectus* skull approximately 1.5 million years old. Richard's hope is that anthropologists will one day be able to demonstrate a common origin for humans and thus put superficial differences between people, such as skin color, into proper perspective.

Mary Leakey continues her work

Throughout the 1970s and into the early 1980s, Mary Leakey continued her work at Olduvai and gradually emerged from behind the shadow of her flamboyant husband to become an effective and popular speaker and a fund-raiser in her own right. She also made another exciting and significant discovery in 1978 when she came upon a beautifully preserved stretch of hominid footprints—apparently of two adults and a child—at Laetoli on the Serengeti Plain in Tanzania, about thirty miles south of Olduvai. Nearby excavations at the same level as the footprints unearthed human fossils dating back some 3.5 million years and similar to the well-known "Lucy" skeleton (properly known as *Australopithecus afarensis*). Also about 3.5 million years old, Lucy was discovered in Ethiopia in 1974 by **Donald Johanson** (see entry). Anthropologists are still arguing over whether the bones at each site represent one or two species.

Richard Leakey heads wildlife agency

In 1982 Mary Leakey lost the vision in one of her eyes, prompting her to cut back on research in the field. She eventually turned over the Olduvai Gorge camp to the Tanzanian Department of Antiquities and moved to Nairobi, where she still resided in the mid-1990s. Richard, meanwhile, gave over much of the research at Turkana to his wife, Maeve Epps, and focused his efforts on another Leakey tradition: conservation work. Not long after his twenty-year tenure as director of the National Museums of Kenya ended in 1989, the lifelong environmental activist was named head of the Kenya Department of Wildlife Services. He cracked down on corruption in the agency that allowed poaching to flourish, taking the first major step toward preserving the endangered elephant population. He also sought to revitalize the country's wildlife parks and do a better job of attracting and spending tourist dollars.

Leakeys divided by political conflict

In 1994 Richard lost both of his legs in an airplane crash and now walks on artificial limbs. This was not his first brush

with death. During the late 1970s he was dying from kidney disease, and his life was saved only when his brother Philip (who had not spoken to Richard for nearly ten years) gave him a kidney. Richard's tenure as director of the Kenya Department of Wildlife Services ended with his resignation in 1994, after five years of conflict with the Kenyan government (which he accused of being corrupt). He and his wife continue to live with their daughter, Louise, in their desert camp in northern Kenya. Richard Leakey has since become involved in a democratic movement, the newly formed Safina party—Safina is the Swahili term for Noah's Ark—placing himself in yet another dangerous situation in a highly volatile political climate.

As an environmentalist Richard Leakey has made political enemies among both black and white members of the ruling party led by Kenyan president Daniel Arap Moi. While Richard's campaign for democratic reforms is widely supported by black Kenyans (many hope he will be the first white president of Kenya), his movements are closely monitored by

Richard Leakey and his partner, Kamoya Kimeu, turn up facial bones of a fossil Homo erectus *on the western shore of Lake Turkana in October 1985.*

L. S. B., M., and R. Leakey

government security forces. In fact, the government has tapped the telephones of the entire Leaky family, including Mary, Jonathan, and Philip. Richard's activities have once again put him at odds with Philip, who was the first white member of the Kenyan parliament and who is one of Richard's most vocal opponents.

The search continues

Anthropologists continue to search for the true origins of man, if indeed the origins can ever be identified with certainty. In January 1991, for example, scientists working in Ethiopia reported finding an older version of a "Lucy" who walked upright, dating back four million years. Thus, known human origins were pushed back at least another 500,000 years. In February 1992 another group of scientists succeeded in dating a *Homo habilis* skull fragment originally discovered in 1965 in Kenya. Only recently subjected to modern dating techniques, it proved to be 2.4 million years old. The fragment is therefore half a million years older than 1470, the skull Richard Leakey found in Turkana, which was the previous record-holder for *Homo habilis*. And in March 1992 theories about east Africa being the center of evolution were turned upside down when anthropologists announced the unearthing of a thirteen-million-year-old jawbone belonging to an apelike creature in Namibia in southern Africa. This astonishing and unprecedented find suggests evolution in apes and humans actually has occurred over a much broader geographic area than previously believed.

Further Reading

"Can He Save the Elephants?" *New York Times Magazine,* January 7, 1990.

Detroit News, February 20, 1992; March 12, 1992.

Grand Rapids Press, January 11, 1991; February 20, 1992.

"An Interview with Kenya's Zookeeper," *Audubon,* September 1990.

Leakey, Louis, *By the Evidence: Memoirs, 1932–1951,* Harcourt, 1974.

Leakey, Louis, *White African: An Early Autobiography,* originally published in 1937, reprinted, Ballantine Books, 1973.

Leakey, Mary, *Disclosing the Past,* Doubleday, 1984.

Leakey, Richard, *One Life: An Autobiography,* Salem House, 1984.

Morell, Virginia, *Ancestral Passions: The Leakey Family and the Quest for Humankind's Beginnings,* Simon & Schuster, 1995.

"The Most Dangerous Game," *New York Times Magazine,* January 7, 1996.

Konrad Lorenz

Born November 7, 1903
Vienna, Austria
Died February 27, 1989
Altenburg, Austria

"The truth about nature is always far more beautiful even than what our great poets sing of it, and they are the only true magicians that exist."

The discoveries of Austrian zoologist and ethologist Konrad Lorenz advanced the field of ethology, or the scientific and objective study of animal behavior under natural conditions. He developed such concepts as imprinting and the innate releasing mechanism, and he studied the fixed-action pattern of animals. He published several important books, some of which sparked controversy at the time of their release. Nonetheless, in 1973 Lorenz and two other ethologists accepted the Nobel Prize for physiology or medicine for their research in animal behavior.

Inspired by Darwin

Konrad Lorenz was born on November 7, 1903, in Vienna, Austria, the younger of two sons of Adolf Lorenz and Emma Lecher. Lorenz received his education in Vienna at a private elementary school and at the Schottengymnasium, one of the city's best secondary schools. His love of animals began outside of school, primarily at the family's summer home in Altenburg, Austria. Lorenz's parents indulged his interests, allowing him to have many pets as a youth. He became more interested in science at the age of ten, when he read about evolutionary theory, which was formulated by **Charles Darwin** (see entry). Darwin's theory states that in the struggle for survival, successive generations of a species pass on to their offspring the characteristics that enable the species to survive. Darwin named this process natural selection.

Begins studying animals

Although Lorenz wanted to study animals, his father insisted he study medicine. In 1922 Lorenz began premedical training at Columbia University in New York City, but he soon returned to Austria to continue the program at the University of Vienna. Despite his medical studies, Lorenz found time for animal studies. He kept a detailed diary of the activities of his pet bird Jock, a jackdaw (a black and gray bird related to but smaller than the common crow). In 1927 his career as an animal behaviorist was launched when an ornithological (dealing with the study of birds) journal printed his jackdaw diary. The following year he received a medical degree from the University of Vienna, where he then became an assistant to a professor at the anatomical institute. In 1933 he earned a Ph.D. in zoology at the University of Vienna.

Develops concept of imprinting

Lorenz developed his best-known theories, and advanced the field of ethology, early in his career, from 1935 to 1938. He spent what he called his "goose summers" at the Altenburg home, concentrating on the behavior of greylag geese and confirming many hypotheses he had formed while observing his pet birds. While working with the geese, Lorenz developed the concept of imprinting. Imprinting occurs in many species, most noticeably in geese and ducks. Within a short, genetically set time frame an animal will accept a foster mother in the place of its biological mother, even if that foster mother is a different species.

Konrad Lorenz played a leading role in developing the field of ethology and helped raise the stature of observation to a recognized and respected scientific method. Inspired by the theories of English naturalist Charles Darwin, Lorenz believed that the innate animal behavior pattern, like physical characteristics, had evolved through natural selection. He drew criticism when he suggested what some scientists felt were improper comparisons between human and animal behavior, such as fighting. Nonetheless, his studies—particularly of greylag geese—led to important discoveries in animal behavior.

Lorenz raised goslings that, when removed from their parents, bonded instead with Lorenz. They accepted him and attached themselves to him as they normally would to their mother. Lorenz was often photographed in Altenburg walking down a path or rowing across the water with a string of goslings following, single file, behind him. He similarly found that mallard ducks would imprint on him, but only when he quacked and presented a shortened version of himself by squatting.

Develops concept of the innate releasing mechanism

Lorenz and Nikolaas Tinbergen (see box), future Nobel Prize cowinner, developed the concept of the innate releasing mechanism. Lorenz found that animals have instinctive behavior patterns, or fixed-action patterns, that remain dormant until a specific event triggers the animals to exhibit this behavior for the first time. (The fixed-action pattern is a specific, ordered series of behaviors, such as the fighting and surrender postures used by many animals.) He emphasized that fixed-action patterns are not learned but are genetically programmed. The stimulus is called the releaser, and the nervous system structure that responds to the stimulus and prompts the instinctive behavior is the innate releasing mechanism.

Lorenz later devised a hydraulic (water-operated) model to explain an animal's motivation to perform fixed-action patterns. With the model he showed that energy for a specific action builds up in the animal either until a stimulus occurs or until there is so much energy that the animal displays the fixed-action pattern spontaneously. Lorenz first witnessed the spontaneous performance of a fixed-action pattern when he was a boy. He watched his pet starling suddenly fly off its

Nikolaas Tinbergen, Dutch-born English Zoologist and Ethologist

Zoologist, animal psychologist, and ethology pioneer Nikolaas Tinbergen (1907–1988) is best known for his studies of stimulus-response processes in wasps, fishes, and gulls. He shared the 1973 Nobel Prize in physiology or medicine with Konrad Lorenz and **Karl von Frisch** (see entry). During the 1930s Tinbergen and Lorenz began conducting research on the fixed-action pattern, a repeated, distinct set of movements or behaviors triggered by something in the animal's environment. In some species of gulls, for instance, hungry chicks will peck at a decoy with a red spot on its bill, a characteristic of the species. Tinbergen also showed that in some animals learned behavior is critical for survival. The oystercatcher, for instance, has to learn which objects to peck at for food by watching its mother.

Tinbergen and Lorenz demonstrated that animal behavior can be the result of contradictory impulses as well, and that a conflict between drives may produce a reaction strangely unsuited to the stimuli. For example, an animal defending its territory against a formidable attacker, caught between the impulse to fight or flee, may begin grooming or eating. Tinbergen made many nature films during his lifetime and wrote several children's books, including *Kleew* and *The Tale of John Sickle*.

perch to the ceiling of the room, snap at the air in the same way it would snap at an insect, then return to the perch to beat the "insect," and finally swallow it.

While continuing his research, Lorenz accepted an appointment in 1937 as lecturer in comparative anatomy and animal psychology at the University of Vienna. In 1940 he became professor of psychology at the University of Königsberg in Germany, but a year later he volunteered to serve in the German army. In 1944 Lorenz was captured by the Russians and sent to a prison camp. After his release in 1948 he returned briefly to the University of Vienna. Then the Max Planck Society for the Advancement of Science awarded him a small stipend that enabled him to resume his studies at Altenburg.

Establishes the Institute for Behavioral Physiology

In 1955 Lorenz, along with ethologist Gustav Kramer and physiologist Erich von Holst, established the Institute for Behavioral Physiology in Seewiesen, Bavaria, near Munich. During the ensuing years at Seewiesen, Lorenz drew criticism for the comparisons he drew between human and animal behavior, which many scientists felt were improper. He also continued his work on instinct, giving support to ethologists who believed that the innate animal behavior pattern, like physical characteristics, had evolved through natural selection. Lorenz's theory caused a stir among many animal psychologists who contended that all behavior is learned. Following the deaths of codirectors Holst and Kramer, Lorenz became the sole director of the Seewiesen institute in 1961.

Publishes books and receives criticism

Throughout his career, Lorenz published several books about his theories on the evolution of animals. *King Solomon's Ring* (1952) provided an account of animal behavior in easily understood terminology. In his book *On Aggression* (1966) Lorenz drew comparisons between the survival instincts of animals and man. *The Year of the Greylag Goose* is an account of the period from 1935 to 1938 when Lorenz spent his "goose summers" developing the concept of imprinting. Finally, in *The Foundations of Ethology* (1982), Lorenz recalled the period of around 1928 when he received his medical degree from the University of Vienna and began studying phylogenetic (evolutionary) comparison.

Despite the importance of Lorenz's work, much of it was considered controversial, and he endured considerable criticism. For instance, some scientists felt his paper titled "Disorders Caused by the Domestication of Species-Specific Behavior" contained strong pro-Nazi overtones, even though Lorenz repeatedly condemned Nazi ideology. (The Nazis were an extremist political party that came to power in Germany under Adolf Hitler in 1933. Espousing racist doctrines, they claimed the superiority of the "Aryan," or Germanic, race over all others, particularly the Jewish and black peoples, who belonged to races they considered inferior.) Furthermore, critics said *On Aggression* encourages the acceptance of violence in human behavior. In the book Lorenz draws comparisons between the fighting instinct of animals and man. He writes that this instinct aids the survival of both the individual and the species, in the latter case by giving the stronger males the better mating opportunities and territories. Lorenz says only humans purposefully kill each other—a fact he attributes to the development of artificial weapons that have out-paced the human evolution of killing inhibitions.

Wins Nobel Prize

In 1973 Lorenz, Tinbergen, and ethologist **Karl von Frisch** (see entry), who studied bee communication, jointly accepted the Nobel Prize for their behavioral research. In the same year Lorenz retired from the Seewiesen institute. He then returned to Altenburg, where he continued writing and directed the department of animal sociology at the Austrian Academy of Science. In addition, the Max Planck Society set up a research station for him at his home in Altenburg.

In 1927, the same year his career-launching diary was published, Lorenz married childhood friend Margarethe "Gretl" Gebhardt, a gynecologist. They had two daughters, Agnes and Dagmar, and a son, Thomas. Lorenz died on February 27, 1989, in Altenburg.

Further Reading

Evans, Richard I., *Konrad Lorenz: The Man and His Ideas,* Harcourt, 1975.

Lorenz, Konrad, *King Solomon's Ring,* New American Library, 1952.

Lorenz, Konrad, *On Aggression,* translated by Marjorie Kerr Wilson, Harcourt, 1966.

Lorenz, Konrad, *The Year of the Greylag Goose,* translated by Robert Martin, Harcourt, 1978.

Nisbett, Alec, *Konrad Lorenz,* Harcourt, 1976.

Time, March 13, 1989, p. B6.

Washington Post, March 1, 1989.

Wasson, Tyler, ed., *Nobel Prize Winners,* H. W. Wilson, 1987, pp. 645–47.

James E. Lovelock

Born July 26, 1919
Letchworth, Hertfordshire, England

Although climatologist and inventor James E. Lovelock has patented sixty inventions, including the diathermy machine and the electron capture detector, he is best known as the proponent of the Gaia hypothesis. According to this hypothesis, Earth functions as a "superorganism" that regulates itself for the survival of life. Lovelock's work has led to increased scientific inquiry and popular interest in the environment.

Influenced by father

James E. Lovelock was born on July 26, 1919, to Thomas A. Lovelock and Nellie A. E. (March) Lovelock in the English village of Letchworth, Hertfordshire, where he spent his early life roaming the country fields and rolling hills. Crediting his father with his interest in nature, Lovelock has described how his father would take him on long walks and point out various birds, insects, and plants.

After graduating in 1938 from the Strand School in London, Lovelock enrolled at the University at Birkbeck College, also in London, where he took a series of evening courses. After several years of night school, Lovelock became a full-time student at the University of Manchester; he majored in chemistry, earning a B.S. degree in 1941. The following year he married Helen M. Hyslop. The advent of World War II interrupted his studies, and it was not until 1949 that he obtained a Ph.D. in medicine from the University of London. Lovelock also holds a Ph.D. in biophysics from the university, which he earned in 1959.

Invents diathermy machine

During World War II Lovelock was hired as a staff scientist with the National Institute for Medical Research (NIMR) in London. He remained there for the next two decades, becoming involved in a large number of projects. Many of the NIMR projects were hindered by a wide variety of technical problems, problems that led Lovelock to invent a number of devices. When he began investigating the effects of thawing and freezing on living tissue, he discovered that there was no machine that could effectively generate heat in living cells. He consequently invented such a device, called a diathermy machine.

Since then Lovelock has patented some sixty inventions, including a gauge for scuba divers to monitor blood pressure and other precision instruments. In 1957 he invented the electron capture detector, a device about the size of a pack of cigarettes designed to measure the level of chemical contamination in the environment. Marine biologist **Rachel Carson** (see entry) used it to measure the level of pesticides in the environment and based her 1962 book, *Silent Spring,* on the results. Lovelock himself used the instrument to prove the presence of chlorofluorocarbons (CFCs) in the atmosphere. His findings were a key factor in developing an understanding of global warming and the depletion of the ozone layer, the portion of the atmosphere that protects Earth from the Sun's harmful ultraviolet rays.

James E. Lovelock

James E. Lovelock is best known for putting forth the Gaia hypothesis, a highly controversial theory that suggests that organisms and ecosystems on Earth cause substantial changes to occur in the environment in a manner that maintains the living conditions of the planet. Despite some criticism leveled against it, the Gaia hypothesis is a useful concept because it emphasizes the diverse connections of ecosystems and the consequences of human activities that result in environmental and ecological changes. And as humans become a dominant force that causes large, often degradative changes to Earth's environments and ecosystems, unchecked changes brought by humans can disrupt Earth's delicate ecological balance.

Develops Gaia hypothesis

In 1961 Lovelock was hired by the U.S. National Aeronautics and Space Administration (NASA) to work with a group that was designing instruments and experiments to determine if life exists beyond Earth. Lovelock left England and moved to Houston, Texas, with his family. During his job with NASA Lovelock developed his Gaia hypothesis. In 1965 he and colleague Dian Hitchcock were at the Jet Propulsion Laboratory discussing the comparative atmospheres of Mars, Venus, and Earth. They noted that the atmospheres of Mars and Venus are close to equilibrium, whereas Earth's atmosphere is in a state of disequilibrium (imbalance), even though it remains able to sustain life over long periods of time. Lovelock hypothesized that life on Earth not only created the atmosphere but also regulated it to keep it hospitable. In other words, Lovelock suggested that Earth is like an organism with mechanisms that help to maintain its own environments so organisms can flourish. An English neighbor, author William Golding, suggested that he name his concept after the Greek goddess of the Earth, Gaia.

Receives criticism

Lovelock first published his hypothesis in a brief paper that appeared in a 1968 publication of the American Astronautical Society, but there was little reaction. The following year, however, he read another paper on his theory before a meeting on the origins of life in Princeton, New Jersey. This time the reaction was strongly negative; only University of Massachusetts biologist Lynn Margulis, who had edited the paper, and Swedish chemist Lars Gunnar Sillen lent their support to this hypothesis.

The Gaia concept was initially formulated by Scottish geologist James Hutton (1726–1797), who referred to Earth as a "superorganism." Viewing Earth's systems as affecting and being affected by a single organism, Hutton asserted that physiology would be the proper science to study the co-dependence of the planet's systems. He became known as the father of geology after he published his *Theory of the Earth,* which identified volcanism (the activity of volcanoes) as the primary force shaping Earth.

In 1979 Lovelock responded to criticism from his scientific colleagues by publishing a more expanded version of his theory, *Gaia: A New Look at Life on Earth.* Although he has won many converts to Gaia, including a number of environmentalists who fear that man has done and is continuing to do irreparable damage to Earth, the theory remains extremely controversial in scientific circles. Scientists believe that by claiming that Earth regulates itself to make the environment more hospitable to life, Lovelock is running counter to the laws of natural selection, which state that only individuals or groups that are best adjusted to their environment survive. Lovelock himself is aware that his theory might have shortcomings, but he continues to defend its importance.

Returns to England

After two years of working with NASA, Lovelock returned to England with his family. He now lives in the small English community of St. Giles on the Heath, and works in his own laboratory. Income from his many inventions allows him to avoid the bustle of big cities and large research facilities. His wife Helen died in 1989, and in 1991 he married the former Sandra J. Orchard. He is a fellow of the Royal Society, a Commander of the British Empire, and an Associate of the Royal Institute of Chemistry. From 1986 to 1990 he served as president of the Marine Biological Association.

Further Reading

Beardsley, Tim, "Gaia: The Smile Remains, But the Lady Vanishes," *Scientific American,* December 1989, pp. 35–36.

"Gaia: The Veiled Goddess," *Economist,* December 22, 1990, pp. 101–07.

Lovelock, James E., *The Ages of Gaia,* Norton, 1988.

Lovelock, James E., *Gaia: A New Look at Life on Earth,* Oxford University Press, 1979.

Lovelock, James E., *Healing Gaia,* Crown Publications, 1991.

Wiley, John P., Jr., "The Gaia Hypothesis—That Life Creates the Conditions It Needs Has Its Day in Court; The Jury Is Out," *Smithsonian,* May 1988, pp. 30–34.

Theodore Maiman

Born July 11, 1927
Los Angeles, California

Since the late 1950s one of the most contested issues in the scientific community has been about whom to credit for the light amplifier, popularly known as the laser. Designs for the laser were submitted by several prominent physicists, and many others contributed to the pool of knowledge from which those designs emerged. Theodore Maiman is credited with developing the first working model of the laser in 1960, although the American physicist Gordon Gould (see box) is now acknowledged as the true inventor of the laser. In 1961 Maiman founded Korad Corporation to further develop his invention, the ruby laser. Capable of producing an intense, monochromatic beam of visible light that can be directed with great precision, Maiman's lasers have demonstrated their usefulness in a variety of fields, from business to medicine.

American physicist Theodore Maiman constructed the first laser in the United States.

Inherits interest in electronics

Theodore Harold Maiman was born in Los Angeles, California, on July 11, 1927. His father was an electrical engineer

Theodore Maiman is credited with developing the first working model of the laser. The device is now used in a wide variety of fields, including the semiconductor industry, telecommunications, retailing, printing, the military, and medicine. Lasers are instrumental in producing computer components and circuit boards, long-distance telephone networks, bar code scanners, desktop printers, typesetting machines, and medical diagnostic tests and therapeutic treatments.

whose experiments yielded inventions such as a vibrating power supply for automobiles. Having inherited an interest in electronics from his father, Maiman earned money for his college education by repairing electrical appliances and radios. He entered the University of Colorado in 1945 and received a bachelor of science degree in engineering physics in 1949. He then transferred to Stanford University in Stanford, California, where he earned a master of science degree in 1951 and a doctorate in physics four years later. His doctoral advisor at Stanford was Willis E. Lamb, who won the Nobel Prize for physics in 1955.

Works on maser

After graduating from Stanford Maiman took a job at Hughes Research Laboratories, a division of Hughes Aircraft Company. While working at Hughes he became interested in the development of a coherent (controlled), high-density, monochromatic (consisting of one color or hue) light source. In the course of his research Maiman encountered experiments on the maser done in the United States by physicist Charles H. Townes and in the Soviet Union by physicists Nikolai Basov and Aleksandr Prokhorov. In 1953 Townes had invented a device for generating coherent, monochromatic beams of microwaves (radiation of very short wavelengths), a device that became known as the maser (Microwave Amplification by Stimulated Emission of Radiation). He and his colleague A. L. Schawlow suggested the possibility of making a similar device that would generate beams of visible light rather than microwaves. Maiman turned his attention to developing this concept at Hughes.

Experiments with rubies

Townes and Schawlow had originally considered using an alkali (soluble salt) vapor to generate the monochromatic

Charles H. Townes, American Physicist

Charles H. Townes (1915–) is generally considered the American inventor of the maser (an acronym for Microwave Amplification by Stimulated Emission of Radiation), an honor he shares with two Russian scientists, Aleksandr Prokhorov and Nikolai Basov. The microwave theories he introduced and pursued throughout the 1960s paved the way for such advances as the modern laser. After Townes joined the physics faculty at Columbia University in 1948, he began conducting research on microwave spectroscopy (the study of the basic structure of matter). He discovered that an oscillator was needed that would produce radiation of very short wavelengths (microwaves), but he knew existing technology could not produce such a device. (An oscillator is a device that can produce an alternating current, or an electric current that reverses its direction at regularly recurring intervals.) In 1951, while sitting on a park bench in Washington, D.C., it struck Townes that an extremely small oscillator might be made if he concentrated not on electrical circuits but on molecules. Frantically writing on the back of an envelope, he calculated that it would be possible to produce microwaves if ammonia molecules were "excited" by pumping energy into them. The molecules would then be stimulated to emit energy in a controlled (coherent) pattern. By 1953 Townes and his associate Schawlow had produced a working ammonia maser. One of its first uses was in a highly accurate timepiece called the "atomic clock."

Gordon Gould, American Physicist

Although Theodore Maiman has been credited with making the first working model of the laser in 1960, Gordon Gould (1920–) is now acknowledged as the true inventor of the device. Gould began working on laser theory several years before Maiman did his work. While Gould was studying for a doctorate at Columbia University in 1957, the idea for the laser came to him in a "flash of insight." Many scientists had been struggling to develop a laser since American physicist Charles H. Townes (see box) had invented the maser, but Gould's model was the first to put together all the available pieces. He had his design notes notarized, and in those notes he coined the term "light amplification by the stimulated emission of radiation" (laser). However, because of a mix-up at the patent office, Gould was led to believe that one had to exhibit a working model of a device to be awarded a patent. Thus, while he was in the laboratory building his machine, Townes and A. L. Schawlow quickly patented remarkably similar design notes. Gould spent the majority of twenty years fighting to get the patent back. Finally, in 1970, the U.S. Patent Office gave Gould the patent for his initial laser design.

light source. Maiman decided to take a different approach and use a solid instead of a gas, as proposed by physicists Nicolas Bloembergen, Saturo Sugano, Yukito Tanabe, and I. Wieder. For his experiments he chose a ruby-based device. Other scientists had used rubies (minerals composed of corundum and chromium) with mixed results. One of the most serious problems appeared to be that the amount of amplification obtained with the ruby was insufficient to produce the desired beam.

Designs the laser

Maiman continued to work with rubies, eventually making an important discovery: earlier calculations about the expected amplification required for beam generation had been incorrect. Using this new information, Maiman constructed his own ruby-based device, which consisted of a ruby rod with a silver coating on both ends. He fed an intense beam of light from a xenon lamp (xenon is a heavy, mainly inert gaseous element) into the rod. The rod then emitted a coherent, monochromatic beam of light. A successful modification of the maser process to generate light, Maiman's device was named the laser (Light Amplification by Stimulated Emission of Radiation).

Light produced by Maiman's first laser consisted of a very narrow beam of electromagnetic radiation with a wavelength of precisely 6943 angstroms. (An angstrom is a unit of length equal to one ten-billionth of a meter.) The beam had the ability to travel great distances without dispersing, thus making it ideal, for example, for measuring the distance from Earth to the Moon. Because the energy of the beam was so highly concentrated, it produced very high temperatures at the point where it came into contact with a material. The laser became useful in welding and cutting and in surgical procedures.

Continues laser research

Laser research and development have continued to be the focus of Maiman's professional interests. After Korad Corporation was acquired by Union Carbide in 1968, Maiman established Maiman Associates to specialize in optical and laser problems. Four years later he cofounded another company, Laser Video, for development of large-screen, laser-driven color video display systems. In 1976 Maiman became vice president for advanced technology at TRW Electronics. He has been honored for his work with a variety of awards, including the Ballantine Medal from the Franklin Institute, the Wolf Prize in Physics from the Wolf Foundation in Israel, and the Japan Prize. He has also been a member of numerous professional organizations, including the National Academy of Engineering and the Optical Society of America.

Further Reading

McGraw-Hill Modern Scientists and Engineers, Volume 2, McGraw-Hill, 1980, pp. 271–72.

Swinbanks, David, "International Winners of Japan's Version of Nobel Prize," *Nature,* February 26, 1987, p. 749.

"Wolf Prizes in Physics for Hahn, Hirsch, and Maiman," *Physics Today,* April 1984, pp. 93–94.

Guglielmo Marconi

Born April 25, 1874
Bologna, Italy
Died July 20, 1937
Italy

Italian physicist and engineer Guglielmo Marconi was responsible for the first transatlantic transmission of radio waves in 1901. A brilliant businessman, he realized his dream of linking the globe in a network of radio waves in 1927 when Earth was completely encircled with a short-wave radio network. He shared the 1909 Nobel Prize in physics with Carl Ferdinand Braun (see box) for their advancement of radio technology.

Italian physicist and engineer Guglielmo Marconi made possible the first transatlantic radio transmission.

Becomes interested in radio waves

Guglielmo Marconi was born on April 25, 1874, in Bologna, Italy. His father, Giuseppe Marconi, was a successful landowner who split his time between Bologna and his estate, the Villa Grifone, located in the town of Pontecchio. His mother, Annie (Jameson) Marconi, was an Irishwoman who had come to Italy to study opera. Life was very strict in the family household, where Marconi was educated in his early years. In 1886, at age twelve, he went to the Istituto Cavallero in Florence. The following year he enrolled in the Technical Institute in Leghorn.

In 1894 Marconi became acquainted with the work of the German physicist Heinrich Hertz (see box). He was so fascinated with Hertz's investigations of radio waves that he began auditing the courses of physicist and professor Augusto Righi, the expert on radio waves at the University of Bologna. Marconi never received any academic degrees in physics.

Accomplishes the first successful radio transmission

At Villa Grifone, in 1895, Marconi built his first crude transmitter and receiver. The transmitter consisted of Hertz's oscillator, in which an electrical circuit generated radio waves as a spark jumped back and forth across a gap between two metal balls. In order to work up the voltage to power such a spark, Marconi used induction coils—two sets of wires wrapped around a soft iron core—to increase the current from a low-voltage battery. In the receiver Marconi used a coherer—a glass tube full of metal filings connected to a battery—to pick up the radio signals. Then he introduced improvements of his own, such as insulated wire antennas and grounding (anchoring) of both the transmitter and the receiver. In the fall of 1895 Marconi succeeded in sending radio signals across his father's estate, a distance of about a mile.

Forms wireless telegraph company

Marconi's father, who until that point had been skeptical of the practicality of his son's experiments, realized that Marconi's discoveries should be publicized. After the Italian Minister of Post and Telegraph showed no interest in the invention, Marconi went to England in 1896. That same year, after a successful radio transmission on Salisbury Plain across

a distance of nine miles, Marconi gained fame as well as an offer to buy the rights to his system. On July 2, 1897, Patent Number 12,039 was granted for Marconi's invention of the "wireless," as radio was called then. Instead of selling his rights, however, he formed the Wireless Telegraph and Signal Company, which was renamed Marconi's Wireless Telegraph Company in 1900.

Guglielmo Marconi at age twenty-two, in 1896, seated before his first wireless receiver.

Convinces Lord Kelvin

In recognition of Marconi's achievement the English government invited him to become an English citizen so he could evade three years of required service in the Italian military. A lifelong Italian patriot, Marconi declined. Instead, through the support of Italy's ambassador in England, he

Heinrich Hertz, German Physicist

German physicist Heinrich Hertz (1857–1894) was best known for his work with electromagnetism (developed by a current of electricity) and electromagnetic radiation (a series of energy waves). In 1883, while working at the University of Kiel in Germany, Hertz became interested in the electromagnetic equations established by English physicist **James Clerk Maxwell** (see entry) when the Berlin Academy of Science had established a prize for work on a specific problem. In order to solve it, Hertz had to delve into the matter of oscillating (moving back and forth) electric currents, which Maxwell had studied in the 1860s and 1870s. Hertz bent a copper wire into a loop, leaving a small gap between the two ends. He then connected the loop to a circuit, discharged an induction coil (a wire wrapped around a soft iron core) into it, and was rewarded with a spark jumping the gap. Attaching spheres to the ends of the gap, he passed an electric current backward and forward, causing each sphere alternately to become charged. When the charge reached a specific level, the spark jumped.

Realizing that Maxwell had predicted that electromagnetic radiation with an extremely long wavelength should be emitted by such an oscillating charge, Hertz wondered if these invisible waves were being generated by his spark. To see if this were so, Hertz devised a simple test. He reasoned that in the same way an oscillating current in his loop created radiation, the radiation produced might set up an oscillating current in another loop. He bent another wire to serve as a "detector." Hertz was able not only to detect the radiation, but to determine the shape and intensity of the invisible waves by moving the receiving loop around the room. He found the wavelength of the "Hertzian waves" was 2.2 feet (66 centimeters), one million times greater than the wavelength for visible light.

Thus Hertz had detected a new type of radiation—the radio wave—and had shown that it behaved in accordance with Maxwell's theory. Hertz's discovery paved the way for the age of radio, television, and satellite communication. Within forty years Guglielmo Marconi and Russian physicists Alexandr Popov (1859–1906) and **Vladimir Zworykin** (see entry) had learned how to carry Morse code, sound, and even moving pictures on radio waves. The term "hertz," designating one single vibration or cycle per second, is named in Hertz's honor.

became a cadet in training in the Italian navy with the understanding that he could pursue his work without interruption. Returning to Italy, Marconi performed a ship-to-shore demonstration of his system for the Italian navy at Spezia, where he reached a limit of twelve miles for good reception. In 1898 he returned to England for another demonstration, increasing the range to eighteen miles. English physicist and mathematician **William Thomson, Lord Kelvin** (see entry), who had earlier disparaged radio communication, made the first paid wireless transmission in 1899 and thereafter became an ally.

Also in 1899, at the request of Britain's Queen Victoria, Marconi set up a system so that the royal family could receive news of the Kingstown regatta (boat race) in Ireland. This feat brought Marconi enormous publicity. Permanent radio stations were beginning to be put into place in England and France. In March 1899, with the cooperation of the respective governments, radio communications began between Chelmsford in England and Wimereux in France, a new record of eighty-five miles.

Transmits across the Atlantic

Unlike many scientists of his day, Marconi believed that radio waves would follow Earth's curve rather than shoot straight into space. He decided to prove his point by transmitting across the Atlantic Ocean. With the company he had created to finance him, he began to build stations at Poldhu, in Cornwall, England, and at Cape Cod, Massachusetts. Unfortunately, before Marconi was ready to test his theory, the antennas at both sites were destroyed in storms. Poldhu's antenna was soon repaired, but Marconi, impatient to get on with his tests, improvised an antenna in St. John's, Newfoundland, Canada, by lofting a kite four hundred feet into the air with a wire attached to it. The first signal coming out of Poldhu, the Morse code (a code used for transmitting messages by audible or visual signals) for the letter *s,* was heard in St. John's on December 12, 1901, at a distance this time of eighteen hundred miles. Marconi had proved to his own satisfaction that the curve of Earth was no obstacle.

Proves his invention

The Anglo-American Telegraph Company brought a suit against Marconi for trespassing on a monopoly it had been granted in Newfoundland. But if the business community were convinced of Marconi's success, the scientific community was not. Many scientists believed that the transatlantic transmission had been a hoax, or perhaps a fluke. No one knew then, as scientists later determined, that the type of radio waves Marconi generated are reflected by certain layers in Earth's atmosphere and thus can travel great distances despite the curve of Earth. Skepticism faded when in February 1902 Marconi, on the boat *Philadelphia* in front of technically reliable witnesses, received clear signals from Poldhu at 1550 miles and intermittent signals at 2100 miles. The Canadian government decided that Marconi could be licensed to operate in Newfoundland under the condition that he could charge no more than ten cents a word, a rate far lower than the cable companies charged.

Monopoly begins to slip

In 1902, when he was not yet thirty years old, Marconi had reached the pinnacle of his career. His company was operating on two continents. The transmission across the Atlantic had won him the awe and admiration of his fellow scientists. He had overcome the limitations of the coherer in his receiver by designing and patenting a superior radio wave detector that operated with magnets and wires. When Marconi returned to Italy in 1902, the Italian navy offered him a ship, the *Carlo Alberto,* as his first floating laboratory. Although he successfully transmitted messages between U.S. President Theodore Roosevelt and King Edward VII of England on January 19, 1903, Marconi was having a hard time convincing anyone that transatlantic communication could become more reliable and profitable. The Marconi company began making money that year, but not much. Furthermore, Germany was unhappy with the English domination of radio technology and began looking for ways to bypass the Marconi patents. The Marconi company's monopoly on radio broadcasting was beginning to slip.

Carl Ferdinand Braun, German Physicist

Theoretical physicist Carl Ferdinand Braun (1850–1918) performed research into the behavior of electricity that led him to produce several notable inventions. The most important was his modification of the cathode-ray tube (a form of vacuum tube) to create the oscilloscope, a device that displays a fluctuating electrical quantity. With improvements, it is still used in electronics today. Braun's research into the conductivity (the ability of a substance to conduct or transmit an electrical current) of minerals helped others to create electronic components made out of crystals, which initiated the development of solid-state (as opposed to electron tube) circuitry. After he became interested in radio waves, he redesigned the radio-transmitting system invented by Guglielmo Marconi, greatly increasing its range beyond the original twelve-mile limit. For this work Braun shared with Marconi the 1909 Nobel Prize in physics. Braun's interest in radio also resulted in unidirectional broadcasting antennas and the use of radio waves as beacons for boats at sea.

Receives Nobel Prize

In 1909 Marconi received the Nobel Prize in physics. He was puzzled, as were many others, as to why he was sharing his award for radio with Carl Ferdinand Braun, despite the fact that Braun's modifications on Marconi's designs had increased radio's range fivefold. Indeed, something very close to Braun's improvements had allowed Marconi to transmit across the Atlantic. In spite of the awkward circumstances, the two men became friends.

With the onset of World War I, Marconi became a technical consultant to the Italian military, which was badly in need of modernization. He was also attached to the Italian War Mission to the United States. During his service in Italy, a new benchmark for radio range was reached in 1918 when England made its first transmission to Australia. In 1919 the king of Italy sent Marconi as a delegate to the Peace Conference in Paris. He signed the treaties with Austria and Bulgaria for the Italian government. After the war Marconi bought a yacht he christened the *Elettra,* which became his laboratory and home.

Establishes worldwide short-wave radio network

In 1923 Marconi's experiments with short-wave radio began to pay off. He had been plagued by the greatly reduced performance of long-wave radio during daylight but did not understand the reasons for it—physics had not advanced to that stage. Yet in October of that year he found that waves thirty meters long—a tiny fraction of his original waves' length—could be transmitted across vast distances without interference from the Sun's radiation. In 1924 the Marconi company contracted with the British government to supply short-wave radio relay stations throughout the empire. By 1927 the world was completely encircled with a short-wave radio network.

In 1928 the Marconi company merged with the telegraph companies, making Marconi a wealthy man. In 1932 he proved that microwaves (waves less than one centimeter in length) could be received well beyond the horizon-line limit that the theory of the day mandated. It was not until after the technological advances produced by World War II that this discovery received commercial application. In 1934 he demonstrated a radio beacon, a primitive form of radar, with which he piloted the *Elettra* blind into a difficult harbor.

Meets Edison

Musically gifted, involved in Italian and international politics, and always featured on the society pages of the newspapers, Marconi was anything but one-sided. He managed not only to invent long-wave and short-wave radio transmission but also to run a company. With his business skill, scientific creativity, technical know-how, and determination, Marconi resembled another famous scientist-engineer, America's **Thomas Alva Edison** (see entry). Edison, in fact, greatly admired Marconi for his successful transatlantic radio transmission. In 1903 the two inventors met at Edison's home in Orange, New Jersey.

Despite Marconi's success, the last ten years of his life were difficult. After the annulment of his first marriage, he married Cristina Bezzi-Scali, a daughter of the Italian nobility, in 1927. They had a daughter, Elettra. By then Marconi had received the hereditary title of *Marchese* or Marquis from the Italian king. Unfortunately, his health was declining and he had become estranged from his ex-wife and the children from his first marriage. Furthermore, Marconi's involvement in politics became controversial. After Italy invaded Abyssinia in 1935 his public embrace of Italian dictator Benito Mussolini alienated much of the European and American public. On July 20, 1937, Marconi died after suffering from a heart condition.

Further Reading

Heathcote, Niels H. de V., *Nobel Prize Winners in Physics, 1901–1950,* Schuman, 1953, pp. 70–81.

Marconi, Degna, *My Father, Marconi,* McGraw, 1962.

Fitch, Richard D., "Inventors and Inventions," *Radio-Electronics,* March 1987, p. 86.

Reese, K. M., "Marconi's Floating Lab Being Recreated in Italy," *Chemical and Engineering News,* December 5, 1988, p. 78.

Schueler, Donald G., "Inventor Marconi: Brilliant, Dapper, Tough to Live With," *Smithsonian,* March 1982, p. 126.

James Clerk Maxwell

Born November 13, 1831
Edinburgh, Scotland
Died November 5, 1879
Cambridge, England

James Clerk Maxwell was the greatest physicist and theorist of the nineteenth century.

James Clerk Maxwell is considered to be the greatest theoretical physicist of the nineteenth century. He discovered that light consists of electromagnetic waves, proved the nature of Saturn's rings, set forth the principles of color vision, and established the kinetic theory of gases, which explains that heat results from the motion of molecules.

Shows early scientific genius

Born on November 13, 1831, in Edinburgh, Scotland, Maxwell was the only son of a well-to-do family. He showed a brilliance for mathematics at an early age and, at fourteen, had a paper on geometry read at the University of Edinburgh. Unfortunately, this accomplishment set him apart from his peers, who nicknamed him "Daffy." Maxwell did not let their taunting bother him, however. Two years later, in 1847, he was attending lectures at the university, and in 1850 he entered Cambridge University, where he excelled in his studies.

616

After six years in England, Maxwell returned to Scotland and was appointed professor at Aberdeen University at age twenty-five. He had already begun making valuable contributions to science at the age of eighteen when, in 1849, he resurrected a theory of English physician and physicist Thomas Young regarding color vision. Young believed the eye had three types of receptors that were sensitive to three primary colors of light. Maxwell showed how any color of the rainbow could be created by adding or subtracting the three primary colors of light: red, green, and blue. In 1861 he used his knowledge to make the first color photograph.

Discovers nature of Saturn's rings

Maxwell's first major contribution to astronomy related to the nature of the rings of Saturn. To the seventeenth-century Dutch astronomer and physicist Christian Huygens, who discovered them, the rings looked like a flat disc encircling the planet, yet that theory was not widely accepted and controversy regarding their composition had lasted well over a century. In 1857 Maxwell suggested the rings were neither solid nor liquid. If either were the case, they would break up due to mechanical forces. However, he added, if they were composed of tiny particles, as the Italian-born French astronomer Gian Dominico Cassini had guessed 150 years earlier, they would be stable.

In 1860 Maxwell consequently turned his attention to the tiny particles that compose gases on Earth. That gases were composed of molecules in constant motion was not in question, but how the molecules moved was a topic of conjecture. Using his mathematical background, Maxwell concluded that the molecules in a given gas do not all travel at the same speed. By applying statistical concepts to show the speeds of the molecules were random and were related to probability theory (the statistical chance that an event will occur), he became the father of statistical mechanics. Maxwell's kinetic theory of gases showed that the motion of molecules was responsible for the production of heat; when the average velocity (speed) of the molecules increased, so did the temperature of the gas. This finding dispelled the notion that heat was a kind of fluid.

With considerable reluctance Maxwell agreed to be appointed professor of experimental physics at Cambridge in 1871, for he lacked sound teaching skills. Nevertheless he went on to establish the Cavendish Laboratory, named for the English scientist Henry Cavendish. The Cavendish Laboratory would produce revolutionary studies of radioactivity (the spontaneous release of energetic particles by the disintegration of atomic nuclei).

Makes greatest contribution

Between 1864 and 1873 Maxwell made his greatest contribution to science by devising equations that unified electrical and magnetic phenomena. In the mid-1850s he had published a paper titled "On Faraday's Lines of Force," discussing some of the experiments of English physicist **Michael Faraday** (see entry). Faraday had sprinkled iron filings on a paper that he then held over a magnet. The filings consequently arranged themselves along what he called "lines of force." With the magnetic field now "visible," scientists began to wonder if space itself was filled with interacting fields of various types. Later Faraday discovered that an electric current flowing in a wire caused "lines of force" to expand outward, inducing an electric flow in a crossed wire. Obviously there was some kind of connection between electricity and magnetism; it just needed to be defined. Using a few simple equations, Maxwell proved that magnetism and electricity were distinctly related. His theory linking the two forces became known as the electromagnetic theory.

Maxwell also discovered that the oscillation (fluctuation) of an electric current would produce a magnetic field that expanded outward at a constant speed. By applying the ratio of the units of magnetic phenomena to the units of electrical phenomena it was possible to calculate the speed of expansion. The calculation came out to around 186,300 miles (300,000 kilometers) per second, nearly the speed of light. Unwilling to believe this result was just coincidental, Maxwell theorized that light itself was a form of electromagnetic radiation that traveled in waves. Since electric charges could be made to oscillate at many velocities (speeds), there should be a corresponding number of electromagnetic radiations. Therefore, visible light would be just a small part of the electromagnetic spectrum.

Improves existing theories

The existence of wavelengths of light beyond what was visible to the human eye was already known. In 1800 **William Herschel** (see entry) had discovered infrared (IR) wavelengths (those situated outside the visible spectrum at the red end). Ultraviolet (UV) wavelengths (situated beyond the visible spectrum at the violet end) had been discovered by the German physicist Johann Ritter. Irish mathematician and physicist George Gabriel Stokes had shown that UV light behaved just like visible light, and Macedonio Melloni had made the same discovery about IR light. What made Maxwell's theory remarkable was the prediction of electromagnetic radiation, of which no one had even dreamed—wavelengths below infrared (where radar and radio waves are found) and above ultraviolet (the location of X rays and gamma rays). Interestingly, the German physicist Heinrich Hertz, who discovered radio waves in the 1880s, thereby confirming Maxwell's theory, had become interested in electromagnetism because of Maxwell's original equations.

Some of his theories disproved

As brilliant as he was, Maxwell was not always correct. The laws of electrolysis (production of a chemical change by

IMPACT

James Clerk Maxwell secured his place in science as the father of electromagnetism when, from 1864 to 1873, he conducted experiments and devised equations that proved that magnetism and electricity were distinctly linked. From his calculations he also came to the theory that light itself was a form of electromagnetic radiation that traveled in waves, and that visible light was just a small part of the electromagnetic spectrum. Perhaps the greatest confirmation of Maxwell's equations came about following the work of German-born American physicist **Albert Einstein** (see entry). Einstein managed to overturn nearly all of the principles of classical physics, yet Maxwell's equations remained unchanged.

Edward Morley and Albert Michelson

In 1887 American chemist and physicist Edward Morley (1838–1923) and German-born American physicist Albert Michelson (1852–1931) disproved James Clerk Maxwell's theory of ether. As a professor at Case Western Reserve University in Cleveland, Ohio, Morley developed an obsession for precision and accuracy in measurements. He equipped his laboratory with the most sophisticated measuring devices of the time. Morley's collection, along with his natural passion for accurate measurement, attracted Case School of Applied Science professor Albert Michelson. Michelson had begun attempting to prove the existence of ether. Along with many other prominent scientists, he believed that light was an undulating wave, and that ether was the medium through which it traveled. Michelson had invented a device called the interferometer that would be able to detect the ether-wind as it affected the velocities of two beams of light.

Edward Morley

Michelson recruited Morley to help him conduct his groundbreaking research. The now legendary Michelson-Morley experiment of 1887 took five days to complete, and the results were undeniable: after nearly fifty hours of research and observation, absolutely no evidence could be found to support the ether-drift theory. Disgusted with this outcome, the two scientists pronounced the experiment a failure. The scientific community, however, saw their findings as proof that ether did not exist, and the tide of theory and research began to turn toward new hypotheses, eventually culminating in the special theory of relativity formulated by Albert Einstein.

Albert Michelson

passing an electric current through a charged liquid) that had been established by Faraday indicated that electricity had a particulate (relating to minute, separate particles) nature. Maxwell did not agree. Had he lived a little longer he would have seen the confirmation of Faraday's laws. It was proven that electricity did consist of particles, but that had no bearing on Maxwell's equations. In addition, Maxwell accepted the concept that an invisible "ether" existed everywhere, and he believed that magnetic lines of force were due to disturbances in the ether. Later experimentation by German-born American physicists Albert Michelson and Edward Morley (see box) disproved the concept of ether, but Maxwell's equations remained valid regardless of whether the ether existed.

Toward the end of his life Maxwell was responsible for the publishing of the electrical experiments of Henry Cavendish, showing that Cavendish had been at least fifty years ahead of his time. Maxwell also became an early, ardent supporter of American theoretical physicist and chemist Josiah Willard Gibbs, who was one of the founders of statistical mechanics. Maxwell died of cancer in Cambridge on November 5, 1879, just eight days before his forty-eighth birthday.

Further Reading

MacDonald, David Keith Chambers, *Faraday, Maxwell, and Kelvin,* Anchor Books, 1964.

Barbara McClintock

Born June 16, 1902
Hartford, Connecticut

Died September 2, 1992
Cold Spring Harbor, New York

"It never occurred to me that there was going to be any stumbling block. Not that I had the answer, but [I had] the joy of going at it."

Barbara McClintock was a pioneering American geneticist whose revolutionary discovery of mobile or "jumping" genes in the 1940s went against established theories of genetics. An independent person, McClintock spent nearly fifty years working apart from the mainstream of the scientific community. Yet her colleagues had such a high regard for her as an adherent to rigid scientific principles that they accepted her discovery of transposable genes decades before others could confirm her observations. McClintock was awarded the Nobel Prize in medicine or physiology in 1983 for her ground-breaking discovery.

Grows up solitary and independent

Barbara McClintock was born in Hartford, Connecticut, on June 16, 1902. She was the third of four children of Thomas Henry McClintock and Sara Handy. Because of family difficulties early in her life, McClintock became a solitary and independent person. Her father graduated with a medical degree from Boston University, but it took him several years to establish a solid and profitable practice. Furthermore, while McClintock was still very young, her mother began to have emotional problems. As a result, McClintock was required to live with an aunt and uncle in the country for long periods. There she spent her time roaming the outdoors, where she developed a love of nature that would last a lifetime.

In 1908 McClintock moved with her family to Brooklyn, New York, where she attended Erasmus High School. Thomas McClintock would not allow any of his children's teachers to give them homework because he felt six hours a day in school was enough time to study. As a result, McClintock had time to pursue other interests, such as playing the piano and ice skating. And when she wanted to wear boy's clothes as a child, her parents had no objection.

After graduating from Erasmus, McClintock enrolled at Cornell University in New York City in 1919. She had an active college social life, even playing tenor banjo in a jazz band. Having decided to remain an independent, single woman devoted to her work, she had little desire to marry or start a family.

Studies cytology

While she was at Cornell, McClintock became interested in cytology (the study of cells). She exhibited a keen intellect as an undergraduate and was invited to take graduate-level genetics courses while still in her junior year. She received her undergraduate degree in 1923, then entered graduate school at Cornell, where she majored in cytology with a minor in genetics and zoology. At that time geneticists favored studies of the fruit fly *Drosophila,* which produces new offspring every ten days. This rapid production of successive generations offered them the opportunity to see quickly the results of genetic traits passed on through crossbreeding.

It was studies of *Drosophila* that produced much of the early evidence of the relationship between genes and chromosomes (the strands of biological material seen at the time of cell division). Studies confirmed that chromosomes carry the genes that pass hereditary traits from one generation to the next. At Cornell the main focus of genetic research was maize, or corn, whose varicolored kernels, relatively long life spans, and larger chromosomes (which could be viewed more easily under a microscope) offered geneticists the opportunity to identify specific genetic processes.

Continues studying genetics

While still in graduate school McClintock refined and simplified a technique originally developed by John Belling to prepare slides for the study of chromosome structures under a microscope. McClintock made modifications to this technique that enabled her to apply it to detailed chromosomal studies of corn. After obtaining an M.A. degree in 1925 and a Ph.D. two years later, she was appointed an instructor in the Cornell botany department. Her research at that time focused on linkage groups (the inherited sets or groups of genes that appear on a chromosome). Geneticists had already discovered these linkage groups in *Drosophila,* and McClintock set out to relate specific groups to specific chromosomes in corn.

Publishes landmark study

In 1931 McClintock and fellow geneticist Harriet Creighton published a landmark study on a theory that geneticists had previously believed without proof: that a correlation existed between genetic and chromosomal crossover. Their study revealed that genetic information was transferred during the early stages of meiosis (pronounced mie-OE-sus; the process of cell division), when parts of homologous chromosomes (chromosomes on which particular genes are identically located) were exchanged in the same division that produced sex cells. Their groundbreaking work was later recognized as the cornerstone of modern genetic research.

Studies genetic transposition

During the 1940s McClintock was invited to work at the Cold Spring Harbor Laboratory in New York, where she would spend the rest of her career. By the summer of 1944 she had initiated the studies that would lead to her discovery of genetic transposition (the process whereby a gene can be released from one position on the chromosome and "jump" to a new position). McClintock had noticed different-colored spots that did not belong on the green or yellow leaves of a particular plant. She surmised that the larger the discoloration patch, the earlier the mutation had occurred, concluding that many large patches on a plant's leaves meant the mutation had occurred early in the plant's development.

From this observation McClintock determined that mutations occurred at a constant rate that did not change within a plant's life cycle. This led her to the concept of regulation and control in the passing on of genetic information. In her investigation of how this passage of genetic information could be regulated, McClintock next noticed that exceptions occurred in addition to these regular mutations, producing different types of mutations not normally associated with the plant. Convinced that something must take place at the early stages of meiosis to cause these irregular mutations, McClintock again worked with corn to identify the process.

When McClintock discovered kernels on a self-pollinated ear of corn that had distinctive pigmentation but should have been clear, she suspected a loss of some genetic information that normally would have been passed on to inhibit color. Finally, after two years, she found what she called a controlled breakage in the chromosome. In 1948 she coined the term "transposition" to describe how an element is released from its original position on the chromosome and inserted into a new position. As a result of this "jumping" gene, plant offspring could have an unexpected pattern of heredity due to a specific genetic code that other offspring did not have. In fact, two transposable genes were involved in the process: one, which she called a "dissociator" gene, allowed the release of the "activator" gene, which could then be transposed to a different site.

Thomas Hunt Morgan, American Geneticist

Barbara McClintock was encouraged to publish the results of her corn research by Thomas Hunt Morgan (1866–1945), a prominent pioneer in the field of genetics. Morgan believed that heredity was in some way central to understanding all biological phenomena, especially development and evolution. His persistence in trying to prove and develop heredity theories led to his winning the Nobel Prize for physiology or medicine in 1933. He was skeptical of the chromosome theories formulated by **Gregor Mendel** (see entry) in the mid-nineteenth century, however, because the conclusions were speculative, based on nothing more than observation, inference, and analogy.

Morgan's strong belief in experimental analysis attracted him to the mutation theory of Dutch botanist and geneticist Hugo de Vries (1848–1935). De Vries had physical evidence that large-scale variation in one generation could produce offspring that were of a different species than their parent plants. Testing de Vries's theory, Morgan conducted experiments using the fruit fly *Drosophila melanogaster.* In 1910 he noticed a natural mutation in one of the male fruit flies—it had white eyes instead of red. He began breeding the white-eyed male to its red-eyed sister and found that all of the offspring had red eyes. When Morgan bred those offspring, he found that they produced a second generation of both red-and-white-eyed fruit flies. Morgan was fascinated to find that all of the white-eyed flies were male. He traced this unusual finding to a difference between male and female chromosomes. The white-eye gene of the fruit fly was located on the male sex-chromosome.

By studying future generations of fruit flies, Morgan found that genes were linearly arranged on the chromosomes. His work with the fruit fly strongly backed Mendel's gene concept and, moreover, established that chromosomes definitely carried genetic traits. For the first time, the association of one or more hereditary characteristics with specific chromosomes was clear, thereby unifying Mendelian "trait" theory and chromosome theory.

Morgan went on to prove that traits found on the same chromosome were not always inherited together. This genetic "mistake" was called "crossing over" because one chromosome actually exchanged material with (or crossed over to) another chromosome. This process was an important source of genetic diversity. In 1915 Morgan, along with his students, published the culmination of his work, *The Mechanism of Mendelian Heredity.* The book provided the key to further work in the area of genetics and laid the groundwork for genetically based research.

Anticipates later discoveries

When McClintock published her research on transposition in 1950, it was not well received; her discovery contradicted the then-current theory that genes were stable components of chromosomes. In addition, few of her contemporaries could actually understand her work. It was not until the 1970s—when technology had been developed that enabled geneticists to study genes on the molecular, rather than cellular, level—that McClintock's ideas were truly comprehended by the scientific community. Her discovery anticipated many later discoveries, such as genetic imprinting, or the "presetting" of genetic activity. Her work was also used to explain inheritance patterns that seemed to lie outside the strict law originated by **Gregor Mendel** (see entry), which is based on simple ratios of dominant and recessive genes.

Receives Nobel Prize

For her studies of genetic transposition, McClintock was appointed to the National Academy of Sciences in 1944 and elected president of the Genetics Society of America the following year. In 1983 she was awarded the Nobel Prize for physiology or medicine for her discovery of mobile genetic systems. McClintock died on September 2, 1992, shortly after celebrating her ninetieth birthday.

Further Reading

Dash, Joan, *The Triumph of Discovery: Women Who Won the Nobel Prize,* Julian Messner, 1990.

Fink, Gerald R., "Barbara McClintock (1902–1992)," *Nature,* September 24, 1992, p. 272.

Keller, Evelyn Fox, *A Feeling for the Organism: The Life and Work of Barbara McClintock,* W. H. Freeman, 1983.

Kitredge, Mary, *Barbara McClintock,* Chelsea House, 1991.

Nature, August 20, 1992, pp. 631–32; September 24, 1992, p. 272.

Elijah McCoy

Born May 2, 1844
Colchester, Ontario, Canada
Died October 10, 1929
Eloise, Michigan

American engineer and inventor Elijah McCoy is best known for inventions that helped lubricate engines without having to shut them down.

The man whose invention is behind the phrase "the real McCoy," American engineer and inventor Elijah McCoy patented more than fifty devices during his career, most relating to the lubrication of locomotives. Although McCoy's design of a superior "lubricating cup" that would oil machinery automatically rather than manually was highly successful, McCoy, an African American, never received the recognition he deserved during his lifetime.

Studies to become a mechanical engineer

Elijah McCoy was born in Colchester, Ontario, Canada, on May 2, 1844. He was the son of George and Mildred Goins McCoy, fugitive slaves who escaped bondage on a Kentucky plantation via the Underground Railroad. McCoy and his eleven brothers and sisters were raised on a farm near Colchester and attended grammar school for black children. From an early age, McCoy had a fascination with mechanical devices and spent much of his free time tinkering with machines. More often than not, he succeeded in repairing broken ones.

McCoy was only sixteen when, with the moral and financial support of his parents, he traveled to Edinburgh, Scotland, to begin an apprenticeship in mechanical engineering. At that time, quality training was not available to blacks in either the United States or Canada. While he was away, the Civil War broke out and American slaves were freed. McCoy's family returned to the United States and settled near Ypsilanti, Michigan. Upon completing his studies in Scotland, McCoy joined them there. He spent many long and frustrating months searching for work in engineering before finally resigning himself to the menial job of a railroad fireman.

Invents the lubricating cup

As a fireman McCoy's primary responsibilities were to keep the firebox filled with coal and to oil the moving parts of the engine as well as the axles, wheels, and bearings of each car whenever the train was stopped. All heavy machinery must be lubricated periodically; without lubrication, the moving parts come into contact with each other, resulting in engine burnout. Covering the parts with a thin film of oil or grease greatly reduces the friction. At that time, the only way to oil or lubricate machinery was to shut it down. Every so often, trains would be stopped or factory machines turned off so that the oilman could do his job.

Recognizing the extraordinary inefficiency of this method of lubrication—both time and money were lost whenever trains and factory machinery were stopped—McCoy quickly went to work on an alternative. His original invention, which he described as a "lubricating cup," consisted of an oil cup built into a steam cylinder, with a hollow stem running from the bottom of the cup into the cylinder. Inside the stem was a rod with a valve at the upper end and a piston at the bottom. Steam entering the cylinder put pressure on the piston, causing the valve to rise and allowing the oil in the cup to drip out and lubricate the cylinder. In 1872 McCoy was issued a patent for his invention. Within a short time his automatic lubricator—dubbed "the real McCoy" to distinguish it from the horde of less effective imitations that soon flooded the market—had been installed on locomotives around the United States.

Modifies the lubricating cup

Soon McCoy began to work on an improved version of his steam engine lubricator. His second steam cylinder lubricator, patented in May 1873, was similar to the original but featured additional devices designed to oil the engine parts just at the point when the steam was exhausted from the cylinders. This was the most crucial time for lubrication. Despite initial skepticism from company owners, McCoy's lubricating cups were quickly adopted in factories around the country and gained wide acceptance among railroads and shipping lines on the Great Lakes and in the West. They were later used on transatlantic liners.

Continues inventing

In 1882 McCoy left his job with the Michigan Central Railroad to devote all of his time and energy to his inventions. He and his wife settled in an integrated neighborhood in Detroit, and he accepted a job as a mechanical consultant for the Detroit Lubricating Company. There he continued to wrestle with the problem that had originally captivated his attention —that of providing continuous and effective lubrication for railroad locomotives.

In early locomotives, the inability to equalize steam pressure within the engine made it impossible to provide proper lubrication to the cylinders while the locomotive was in operation. McCoy's solution was to equalize the steam pressure going into and out of the engine by attaching an overflow pipe that was independent from the steam supply pipe. This system made it possible for oil to flow freely into the cylinders, resulting in thorough lubrication of the engine. Along with his original lubricating cup, it was one of McCoy's most important and widely used inventions.

Patents more inventions

Other patented McCoy inventions include an independent lubrication system for a two-piston cylinder and a special method of protecting engine valves from dust and dirt, which helped to prevent accidents caused by displacement of parts. The inventor also patented a special attachment designed to ensure regular delivery of lubricant to the moving parts of cylinders in varying amounts according to the speed of the engine; an oil cup with a support and sight-feed arm; a special technique that made it possible to clean both the sight-feed glass and oil nozzle without removing them or the oil that controlled the valve; and a method of improving engine lubrication in cold weather.

After 1910 McCoy concentrated his efforts on designing lubrication systems for air brakes used in locomotives and other vehicles. Among his most successful inventions was a device that delivered two different lubricants to crucial areas within the brake system: a mixture of oil and graphite (a form of carbon) to the pistons in the steam cylinders. This invention resulted in a dramatic improvement in the safety and effectiveness of air brakes. By 1920 McCoy had established his own business, the Elijah McCoy Manufacturing Company, to manufacture and sell a number of his devices, including a popular graphite lubricator designed to oil a new locomotive, known as the "superheater."

Achieves recognition

By 1928 McCoy's health began to fail. After having used up his small savings in an ongoing effort to perfect his inventions, he entered an infirmary in Eloise, Michigan, for poor, elderly people. He died there on October 10, 1929, alone and

IMPACT

Throughout his life, Elijah McCoy worked on the problem of continuous lubrication in industrial and locomotive machinery. But he also turned his inventive genius to household matters. He invented the world's first folding ironing table and the lawn sprinkler. Other domestic inventions included a buggy top support and a tread for tires.

largely forgotten. Because he had sold most of his patents for a fraction of their worth, he was never able to capitalize on his own inventions. The devices he had labored over made others millionaires. However, his name lives on and his inventions are still used. In 1975, forty-six years after his death, the city of Detroit honored his life and work by placing a historic marker at the site of his home and by naming a nearby street Elijah McCoy Drive. Furthermore, versions of his original lubricating cup are still used in factories, mining machinery, construction equipment, naval boats, and even space exploration vehicles.

Further Reading

Haber, Louis, *Black Pioneers of Science and Invention,* Harcourt Brace Jovanovich, 1970, pp. 51–59.

Klein, Aaron E., *The Hidden Contributors: Black Scientists and Inventors in America,* Doubleday, 1971, pp. 58–63.

Towle, Wendy, *The Real McCoy: The Life of an African-American Inventor,* Scholastic, 1993.

Margaret Mead

Born December 18, 1901
Philadelphia, Pennsylvania
Died November 15, 1978
New York, New York

In 1928 the publication of Margaret Mead's *Coming of Age in Samoa* revolutionized anthropology, the scientific study of human beings. The result of her early fieldwork on the Polynesian island of Samoa, the book became a bestseller as its American readers wanted to learn about adolescent behavior and sexual patterns in an exotic society. With *Coming of Age* Mead moved to the forefront of American anthropology and American society, and she remained there for more than half a century by publishing penetrating, insightful works and speaking out on a variety of issues important to the American people.

"Life in the twentieth century is like a parachute jump—you have to get it right the first time."

Influenced by "advanced" upbringing

Margaret Mead was born the oldest of four children on December 18, 1901, in Philadelphia, Pennsylvania. Her parents were educators, and the family moved frequently during her youth. Experiencing somewhat advanced ideas for the time, Mead learned that women could have their own profes-

633

Margaret Mead pioneered research methods that helped turn social anthropology into a major science and made anthropology relevant to public policy. She specialized in the study of gender role-conditioning, cross-cultural communication, cooperation and competition among various cultures, and in comparative child psychology. Mead became a leading authority on American culture, whose frequent commentaries on the family, sex, the generation gap, and moral issues changed the opinions —and lives—of millions of people.

sion from her grandmother and her mother, who was a suffragette (a woman who advocated the right of women to vote). Her parents encouraged her to play with children of all racial and economic backgrounds, and she was taught early to closely observe others. She also learned to paint and dance. Mead recalls that she "took pride in being unlike other children and in living in a household that was in itself unique."

Becomes anthropologist

While attending Barnard College in New York City, Mead developed an interest in anthropology, a new science at the time and one based on statistical analysis. In a class with the famous anthropologist Franz Boas she realized the importance of studying cultures that were rapidly disappearing around the world. "That settled it for me. Anthropology had to be done now. Other things could wait," she said later. After graduating in 1923 Mead married Luther Cressman and entered Columbia University graduate school in New York City.

Two years later Mead left for a nine-month stay in Samoa, an island in the southwest central Pacific Ocean, to study adolescence and biological and cultural influences on behavior. She introduced a number of new observation techniques—including those used in disciplines such as psychology and economics—thereby broadening the base of information on which social anthropology now rests. She rejected some of the rigid techniques of the day, claiming also that is was necessary to "suspend ... one's beliefs and disbeliefs" in order to understand "another reality," Samoa.

Mead lived with the villagers day and night, giving her an advantage in observing and understanding behavior and customs that otherwise would have remained unknowable to a person from the United States. For instance, she discovered

that monogamy (marriage to one person) and jealousy were not valued or understood by the Samoans and that divorce occurred simply by the husband or wife "going home." However, her most important work in Samoa was on courtship patterns in adolescents. *Coming of Age in Samoa,* which was published in 1928 and drew numerous parallels between Samoan and American culture, became a bestseller in the United States and placed Mead squarely in the forefront of American anthropology.

Margaret Mead with some Manus children during her 1928 field trip to the Admiralty Islands.

Publishes important study on New Guinea

Mead made her second field trip in the late 1920s with her second husband, Reo Fortune. Studying the culture of Manus, the largest of the Admiralty Islands off the coast of New Guinea, she observed the fantasy worlds of young children and the development of social behavior. The culmination of her research among the Manus was published in her 1930 volume *Growing Up in New Guinea.* Five years later she published *Sex and Temperament* about her studies of the Arapesh, Mundugumor, and Tchambuli peoples of New Guinea. As a result of her observations she concluded that human values depend on time and environment, not inherited traits.

Takes 38,000 photographs in Bali

In 1936 Mead went to Bali, an Indonesian island, with Gregory Bateson, her third husband, with the plan to study the presence or absence of schizophrenia, a mental disease, in the Balinese people. But Boas had told Mead, "If I were going to Bali I would study gesture," so she and Bateson decided to follow Boas's advice. In fact, they took 38,000 photographs in their study of the Balinese people, which resulted in their innovative 1941 book *Balinese Character: A Photographic Analysis.* Mead was one of the first anthropologists to use still and motion pictures to record the customs and habits of primitive societies.

Raises first "Spock baby"

Although doctors repeatedly told Mead she could never have children, after several miscarriages she gave birth to a daughter, Mary Catherine Bateson, in 1939. Bateson became the first "Spock baby." At the time of her birth Mead was a friend of Dr. Benjamin Spock, a young pediatrician who had innovative ideas about child rearing. Since his theories were directly opposed to the more rigid practices that were being followed at the time, Mead agreed to let him test his ideas with her and newborn Catherine. Seven years later, in 1946, Spock published *The Common Sense Book of Baby and Child Care,* a book that influenced the way American parents brought up their children.

During World War II Mead served on the U.S. Committee on Food Habits and worked on a national character study that examined British and American relations. In 1942 she published *And Keep Your Powder Dry: An Anthropologist*

Looks at America, in which she compares American culture with the cultures of seven other countries.

Promotes changes in gender relations

Always Mead seemed to return to studying the family. Every few years she commented on the problems facing American families amid changing social conditions. She was concerned about the loss of extended families and the isolation felt by people living in cities. An early feminist, Mead wrote in 1946 about the need for changing gender roles. Perhaps her most profound impact was as a counselor to American society. With Rhoda Metraux, she wrote a monthly column in *Redbook* from 1961 to 1978, offering advice to American women. Though married and divorced three times, Mead firmly stated, "I don't consider my marriages as failures. It's idiotic to assume that because a marriage ends, it's failed." Mead was critical of the women's movement when it was anti-male, calling for a truly revolutionary vision of gender relations.

During the 1960s Mead wrote on a number of issues with the hope of influencing the thinking of the American public, particularly on topics such as the generation gap, the environmental crisis, and overpopulation. Rather than increasing the world's population, Mead advocated a philosophy of educating and nurturing all the world's children as our own. She was also an early proponent of birth control, an advocate of the repeal of anti-abortion laws, and a supporter of the right to die. While Mead endorsed civil disobedience, she was also a strong believer in people being morally responsible for their lives.

Receives honors and awards

Margaret Mead lived life fully and tirelessly. "I am glad that I am alive," she said. "I am glad that I am living at this particular very difficult, very dangerous, and very crucial period in human history." Her list of published works is long and her honors numerous. In 1969 *Time* magazine named her

Mother of the Year. She was president of the American Academy for the Advancement of Science and remained active in education for most of her life, teaching at Columbia University and New York University among other schools. Mead's association with the American Museum of Natural History began in 1926, when she became assistant curator. In 1964 she was appointed curator of the museum and named curator emeritus, an honorary title, in 1969. Mead died of cancer on November 15, 1978, in New York City.

During the early 1990s critics began to question Mead's findings in her studies of Samoan society, contending that she had slanted her data to produce preconceived results. This criticism came at a time when the entire field of anthropology was being scrutinized. Nonetheless, Mead is still regarded as an important figure in twentieth-century cultural studies.

Further Reading

Bateson, Mary Catherine, *With a Daughter's Eye,* Morrow, 1984.

Cassidy, Robert, *A Voice for the Century,* Universe Books, 1982.

Cole, John R., and others, "Samoan Hoax, Margaret Mead, and Cultural Relativity," *Skeptical Inquirer,* Summer 1993.

Goode, Stephen, "The Decline and Fall of Anthropology," *Insight on the News,* March 15, 1993.

Howard, Jane, *Margaret Mead: A Life,* Simon & Schuster, 1984.

Ludel, Jacqueline, *Margaret Mead,* Franklin Watts, 1983.

"Margaret Mead: She Visited Other Societies and Showed Us Ourselves," *Life,* Fall 1990.

Mead, Margaret, *Blackberry Winter: My Earlier Years,* Morrow, 1972.

Saunders, Susan, *Margaret Mead,* Viking Kestrel, 1987.

Ziesk, Edra, *Margaret Mead,* Chelsea House, 1990.

Lise Meitner

Born November 7, 1878
Vienna, Austria
Died October 27, 1968
Cambridge, England

Austrian physicist Lise Meitner codeveloped the theory of nuclear fission.

In 1938 Lise Meitner and her nephew Otto Robert Frisch, who were both physicists, developed the theory that explains nuclear fission. Their work would eventually make possible the creation of the atomic bomb. Meitner and her lifelong collaborator, Otto Hahn, made several other key contributions to the field of nuclear physics. At a time when sexism ran rampant in the scientific community, in 1944 Hahn received the Nobel Prize for work he shared with Meitner; Meitner was not invited to share the honor.

Shows early academic promise

Elise Meitner was born on November 7, 1878, to an affluent family in Vienna, Austria. Her father, Philipp, was a lawyer and her mother, Hedwig, traveled in the same Vienna intellectual circles as **Sigmund Freud** (see entry), the founder of psychoanalysis.

Lise Meitner devoted her life to the study of nuclear phenomena. Her first joint publication with Otto Hahn provided a method for producing pure samples of radioactive materials that eventually became a standard procedure. Meitner devoted considerable time to analysis of changes that take place in the atoms of both stable and radioactive isotopes (varieties of the same element). With Hahn she discovered protactinium (element 91) and the phenomenon of nuclear isomers, atoms that have identical nuclear structures but decay (emit atomic particles) by different mechanisms. Meitner's most famous accomplishments, however, will always be associated with her description of the process of nuclear fission, which is considered to have initiated the building of atomic weapons.

During the early years of her life, Meitner gained experience that would later be invaluable in enduring the slights she received as a woman in a field dominated by men. The third of eight children, she expressed interest in pursuing a scientific career, but her practical father insisted she attend the Elevated High School for Girls in Vienna. She earned a diploma that would enable her to teach French, a more acceptable career for a woman. After completing this program, however, Meitner found her desire to become a scientist was greater than ever. In 1899 she began studying with a local tutor who prepared students for the difficult university entrance exam. She worked so hard that she was ready for the test in two years rather than the average four. Shortly before she turned twenty-three, Meitner became one of the few women students at the University of Vienna.

Becomes a physicist

When she entered the university in 1901, Meitner could not decide between physics or mathematics. Later, inspired by her teacher, the well-known physicist Ludwig Boltzmann, she pursued the study of physics. In 1906, after becoming only the second woman ever to earn a Ph.D. in physics from the University of Vienna, she stayed on in Boltzmann's laboratory as an assistant to his assistant. This was hardly a position for a recent doctoral graduate, but Meitner had no other offers, as universities at the time did not hire women faculty members.

Less than one year after Meitner joined the lab, Boltzmann committed suicide, leaving the future of the research team uncertain. In an effort to recruit the noted physicist **Max**

Planck (see entry) to replace Boltzmann, the university invited Planck to visit the lab. Although Planck refused the offer, he met Meitner and talked with her about quantum physics and radiation research. Inspired by this conversation, Meitner left Vienna in 1907 to study with Planck at the Institute for Experimental Physics in Berlin, Germany.

Begins work with Hahn

Soon after her arrival in Berlin, Meitner met a young chemist named Otto Hahn, who worked at the Chemical Institute. Hahn was surrounded by organic chemists (scientists who study the carbon compounds of living beings as well as most other carbon compounds), who did not share his research interests in radiochemistry (the study of radioactive substances). Meitner was not only intrigued by the same research problems, but also had the training in physics that Hahn lacked. Unfortunately, Hahn's supervisor balked at the idea of allowing a woman researcher to enter the all-male institute. Finally, Meitner and Hahn were allowed to set up a laboratory in a converted woodworking shop in the basement, as long as Meitner agreed never to enter the higher floors of the building.

Endures sexism

This incident was neither the first nor the last experience of sexism that Meitner encountered in her career. According to one famous anecdote, she was asked to write an article by an encyclopedia editor who had read a paper she had written on the physical aspects of radioactivity. When Meitner answered the letter, which was addressed to "Herr Meitner," and explained she was a woman, the editor wrote back to retract his request, saying he would never publish the work of a woman. Even in her collaboration with Hahn, Meitner at times conformed to gender roles. When British physicist **Ernest Rutherford** (see entry) visited their Berlin laboratory on his way back from the Nobel Prize ceremonies in 1908, Meitner spent the day shopping with Rutherford's wife while the two men talked about their work.

James Chadwick, English Physicist

Lise Meitner's work in nuclear fission was made possible by James Chadwick (1891–1974), who was awarded the 1935 Nobel Prize for physics for his discovery of the neutron. Chadwick was led to conduct his experiment in the early 1930s, when the German team of Walther Bothe and Hans Becker reported the emission of highly energetic radiation when a beryllium (a light but strong metallic element) target was bombarded with alpha rays (positively charged particles). The radiation behaved somewhat like gamma rays (radiation of very short wavelengths) but had some properties that were uncharacteristic of such radiation. Chadwick suspected that the radiation might consist of uncharged particles.

Soon after the Bothe-Becker experiments, the French physicists Frederic Joliot-Curie and Irène Joliot-Curie showed that the radiation the Germans had observed was able to emit protons from paraffin (a waxy substance). Chadwick decided to repeat the Bothe-Becker and Joliot-Curie experiments in his own laboratory. He found that the new radiation was able to eject protons from a number of materials other than paraffin. He eventually concluded that the radiation was actually a beam of uncharged particles. Chadwick was able to determine that the mass of these particles was about 1.005 AMU (atomic mass units), slightly greater than the mass of the proton, whose mass equals 1.000 AMU. The particles were neutrons.

Becomes first female professor in Germany

Within her first year at the institute, the school opened its classes to women, and Meitner was allowed to roam the building. Meitner and Hahn concentrated their investigations on the behavior of beta rays (streams of particles ejected from atomic nuclei) as they passed through aluminum. By today's standards, the laboratory in which they worked would be appalling. They frequently suffered from headaches brought on by their adverse working conditions. In 1912, when the Kaiser Wilhelm Institute was built in the nearby suburb of Dahlem, Hahn received an appointment in the small radioactivity department and invited Meitner to join him in his laboratory. Soon thereafter, Planck asked Meitner to lecture as an assistant professor at the Institute for Theoretical Physics. As the first woman in Germany to hold such a position, Meitner drew several news reporters to her opening lecture.

At the onset of World War I in 1914, Meitner interrupted her laboratory work to volunteer as an X-ray technician in the Austrian army, and Hahn entered the German military. By arranging coinciding leaves throughout the war, the two scientists returned periodically to Dahlem, where they continued their attempts to discover the precursor of the element actinium. By the end of the war, they announced that they had found this elusive element and had named it protactinium. It was the missing link on the chemical periodic table between thorium (number 90) and uranium (number 92). A few years later Meitner received the Leibniz Medal from the Berlin Academy of Science and the Leibniz Prize from the Austrian Academy of Science for this work. Shortly after she helped discover protactinium in 1917, Meitner accepted the job of establishing a radioactive physics department at the Kaiser Wilhelm Institute. Hahn remained in the chemistry department, and they ceased working together for a time so they could concentrate on research more suited to their individual training.

Receives recognition for radiation work

Throughout the 1920s Meitner continued her work in beta radiation, winning several prizes. In 1928 the Association to Aid Women in Science upgraded its Ellen Richards Prize, calling it a Nobel Prize for women. Meitner and chemist Pauline Ramart-Lucas, who worked at the University of Paris, were the first recipients of the prize. In addition to the awards she received, Meitner acquired a reputation in physics circles for some of her personal quirks as well. Years later, her nephew Otto Robert Frisch, also a physicist, recalled that Meitner adopted some of the mannerisms stereotypically associated with her male colleagues. Among them was absentmindedness. On one occasion a student approached her at a lecture, saying they had met earlier. Knowing she had never met the student, Meitner responded earnestly, "You probably mistake me for Professor Hahn."

Begins work on uranium

Meitner and Hahn resumed their collaboration in 1934, after **Enrico Fermi** (see entry) published his important article on "transuranic" uranium. The Italian physicist announced that when he bombarded uranium with neutrons (uncharged or neutral atomic particles), he produced two new elements—numbers 93 and 94—in a mixture of lighter elements. Joining a young German chemist named Fritz Strassmann, Meitner and Hahn compiled a list of all the substances the heaviest natural elements produced when bombarded with neutrons. Three years later they confirmed Fermi's findings and expanded the list to include ten additional substances that resulted from bombarding these elements with neutrons. In the meantime, French physicists Irène Joliot-Curie and Pavle Savitch announced that they had created a new radioactive substance by bombarding uranium with neutrons.

Joliot-Curie and Savitch speculated that this mysterious new substance might be thorium, but Meitner, Hahn, and Strassmann could not confirm this finding. No matter how many times they bombarded uranium with neutrons, no thorium resulted. Hahn and Meitner finally sent a private letter to the French physicists suggesting that perhaps they had erred. Although Joliet-Curie did not reply directly, a few months later she published a paper retracting her earlier assertions and said the substance she had noted was not thorium.

Smuggled out of Germany

Current events soon took Meitner's mind off professional squabbles. Although her father, of Jewish heritage but assimilated into mainstream European culture, had had all his children baptized as Christians, Meitner was Jewish by birth. Because she continued to maintain her Austrian citizenship, she was at first relatively untouched by the political turmoil in Germany, where laws against Jewish people were being enacted by the racist Nazis who came to power under Adolf Hitler. In the mid-1930s Meitner had been asked to stop lecturing at the university, but she continued her research. When Germany annexed Austria in 1938, Meitner became a German citizen and began to look for a research position in an environment that was not hostile to Jews. Her tentative plans grew urgent in the spring of 1938, when Germany announced that academics could no longer leave the country. Meitner's colleagues devised an elaborate scheme to smuggle her out of Germany to Stockholm, Sweden, where she had made temporary arrangements to work at the Institute of the Academy of Sciences under a Nobel grant. By late fall, however, Meitner's position in Sweden looked dubious: her grant provided no money for equipment and assistance, and the administration at the Stockholm Institute would offer her no help.

Posits theory of nuclear fission

In Germany, Hahn and Strassmann had not let their colleague's departure slow their research efforts. After carefully studying the paper Joliot-Curie had published about her research techniques, they thought they had found an explanation for her confusion: perhaps, instead of finding one new substance after bombarding uranium, as she had thought, she had actually found two new substances! Repeating Joliot-Curie's experiments, they indeed found two substances in the final mixture, one of which was barium. This result seemed to suggest that bombarding uranium with neutrons led it to split up into a number of smaller elements. Hahn immediately wrote to Meitner to share this perplexing development. Meitner received his letter while on Christmas vacation in Kunglav, Sweden, where Frisch was visiting her. Meitner and Frisch set off for a walk in the snowy woods—Frisch on skis, with his aunt trotting alongside—continuing to puzzle out how uranium could possibly yield barium. When they paused for a rest on a log, Meitner began to posit a theory, sketching diagrams in the snow.

Danish physicist **Niels Bohr** (see entry), with whom Frisch worked in Copenhagen, had previously suggested that the atomic nucleus behaves like a liquid drop. Elaborating on this concept, Meitner reasoned that when this drop of a nucleus was bombarded by neutrons, it might elongate and divide itself into two smaller droplets. The forces of electrical repulsion would act to prevent the nucleus from maintaining its circular shape by forming it into a dumbbell shape. As the bombarding forces grew stronger, the nucleus would sever at the middle to yield two droplets, or two completely different nuclei. But one problem still remained. When Meitner added together the weights of the resultant products, she found that the sum did not equal the weight of the original uranium. The only place the missing mass could be lost was in energy expended during the reaction.

Frisch rushed back to Copenhagen, where he shared this revelation with Bohr. After hearing Frisch's description of the splitting of the nucleus, he responded: "Oh, what idiots we have been. We could have foreseen it all! This is just as it must be!" Buoyed by Bohr's obvious admiration, Frisch and Meitner spent hours on a long-distance telephone writing the paper that would publicize their theory. At the suggestion of a biologist friend, Frisch coined the word "fission" to describe the splitting of the nucleus in a process that seemed to him analogous to cell division.

Lays foundation for atom bomb

Meitner and Frisch's paper, "On the Products of the Fission of Uranium and Thorium," appeared in the journal *Nature* in February 1939. Although it would be another five and a half years before the American military would successfully explode an atom bomb over Hiroshima, Japan, many physicists consider Meitner and Frisch's paper to be the initial step in the creation of atomic weapons, which explode and release huge amounts of energy generated by nuclear fission reactions. After moving to Sweden in 1938, Meitner continued her research, first at the Nobel Institute for Physics and later at the Atomic Energy Institute. In 1944 Hahn was awarded the Nobel Prize in chemistry, although, because of the war, he did not accept the prize until two years later. Although Meitner attended the ceremony, she did not share in the honor.

Wins numerous awards

In 1946 Meitner traveled to the United States to visit one of her sisters, whom she had not seen for several years. During her stay Meitner delivered a lecture series at Catholic University in Washington, D.C. In the following years she won the Max Planck Medal and was awarded numerous honorary degrees from both American and European universities. In 1966 she, Hahn, and Strassmann split the $50,000 Enrico Fermi Award given by the Atomic Energy Commission (A.E.C.). By this time Meitner had become too ill to travel, so the chairman of the A.E.C. delivered the prize to her in Cambridge, England, where she had retired in 1960. Meitner died shortly before her ninetieth birthday on October 27, 1968.

Further Reading

Crawford, Deborah, *Lise Meitner, Atomic Pioneer,* Crown, 1969.

Rhodes, Richard, *The Making of the Atom Bomb,* Simon & Schuster, 1988.

Watkins, Sallie, "Lise Meitner and the Beta-Ray Energy Controversy: An Historical Perspective," *American Journal of Physics,* Volume 51, 1983, pp. 551–53.

Watkins, Sallie, "Lise Meitner: The Making of a Physicist," *Physics Teacher,* January 1984, pp. 12–15.

Gregor Mendel

Born in 1822
Heinzendorf, Austria
(now Czech Republic)
Died in 1884

Gregor Mendel was an Austrian priest who made important contributions to the study of heredity.

Because of financial troubles, Gregor Johann Mendel entered a monastery, where he conducted experiments on heredity (the passing of traits from one generation to the next) and the various laws concerning its functions. He conducted countless studies, the results of which he used to formulate the laws of heredity, which, when published, did not receive the credit they deserved. It was not until after his death that Mendel received the acknowledgement for his invaluable contribution to the field of genetics.

Joins monastery

Gregor Johann Mendel was born in 1822 in Heinzendorf, Austria (now the Czech Republic), the son of a peasant farmer and the grandson of a gardener. As a child Mendel benefited from the progressive education provided by the local clergyman, and eventually enrolled at the Philosophical Institute in Olmutz (now Olomouc). However, his worsening financial condition repeatedly forced him to suspend his studies, and in 1843 he entered the Augustinian monastery at Brunn (now Brno).

Although Mendel felt no personal calling to a religious vocation at the time, he believed that the monastery would provide him the best opportunity to pursue his education without financial worries. He took the name Gregor and eventually was placed in charge of the monastery's experimental garden. In 1847 he was ordained as a priest. Four years later he was sent to the University of Vienna to study zoology, botany, chemistry, and physics. Following his studies, Mendel returned in 1854 to the monastery and also began teaching the natural sciences at the Brno Technical School.

Experiments with cross-breeding

Until 1868, in his limited spare time, Mendel performed most of his now-famous hereditary experiments. In the mid-nineteenth century no one had yet been able to make any statistical analysis in breeding experiments. However, Mendel's strong background in the natural sciences and his course work in mathematics prompted him to try. Working mostly with pea plants, Mendel carefully selected pure varieties that had been cultivated for several years under strictly controlled conditions. He crossed different plants until he produced seven easily distinguishable seed and plant variations (for instance, yellow versus green seeds, wrinkled versus smooth seeds, tall versus short stems). Mendel discovered that while short plants produced only short offspring, tall plants produced both tall and short offspring. Since only about one-third of the tall plants produced other tall plants, Mendel concluded that there must be two types of tall plants: those that bred true (that is, more tall plants) and those that did not.

Mendel continued experimenting. He thought that by crossing these different plants, he would find intermediate varieties of the offspring. In other words, if he crossed a tall plant with a short plant, the result would be a medium-sized plant. He soon found that this was not the case. Mendel

Gregor Mendel was the first scientist to deduce correctly the basic principles of heredity. Consequently, the genetic traits carried through the heredity process have come to be known as Mendelian inheritance. Mendelian traits are also called single gene or monogenetic traits, because they are controlled by the action of one single gene or gene pair. More than 4,300 human disorders are known or suspected to be inherited as Mendelian traits, including the disease cystic fibrosis and such sex-linked conditions as color blindness and hemophilia. Overall, incidence of Mendelian disorders in the human population is about 1 percent. Many other ordinary characteristics are also inherited in Mendelian fashion.

crossed short plants with tall plants, planted the seeds from that union, then self-pollinated the plants from this second generation. He followed the results by counting and recording each generation. All of the offspring that sprouted from the short-tall cross were tall, but the offspring from the self-pollination of those tall plants gave him half tall plants (non-pure), one quarter pure tall, and one quarter pure short. Tallness, the more powerful characteristic (the one that shows up the most), he designated the dominant trait. Shortness, the weaker characteristic (the one that is frequently masked), he called the recessive trait. The results were always the same. Mendel's quiet, methodical investigation took over eight years to complete and involved over thirty thousand plants.

Discovers laws of heredity

The results of Mendel's initial plant-breeding experiments formed the basis of his first law of heredity: the law of segregation. This law states that hereditary units (genes) are always in pairs, that genes in a pair separate during division of a cell (the sperm and the egg each receive one member of the pair), and that each gene in a pair will be present in half the sperm or the eggs.

Mendel's further experiments established a second law: the law of independent assortment. This law states that each pair of genes is inherited independently of all other pairs. However, it holds true only if the characteristics are located on different chromosomes. By sheer coincidence, Mendel had indeed selected such characteristics. But genes located on the same chromosome, as the American geneticist Thomas Hunt Morgan later discovered, are usually inherited together.

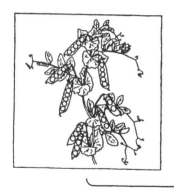
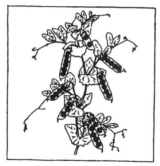
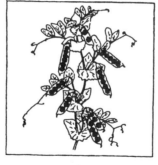

A nineteenth-century diagram illustrating Gregor Mendel's discovery of the patterns of inheritance as shown by sweet peas. The diagram shows the original crossing, the first generation, and the next when recessive traits appear in the proportions discovered by Mendel of 9:3:3:1.

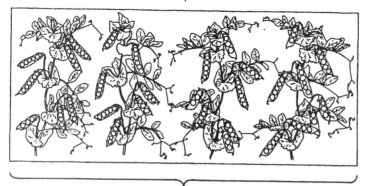

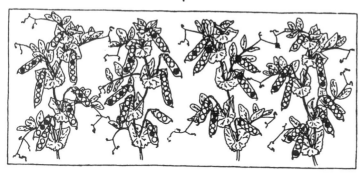

In all, Mendel uncovered the following basic laws of heredity: 1) Heredity factors must exist; 2) Two factors exist for each hereditary characteristic; 3) At the time of sex cell formation, heredity factors of a pair separate equally into the gametes (the sperm or the egg); 4) Gametes bear only one factor for each characteristic; 5) Gametes join randomly, no matter what factors they carry; 6) Different hereditary factors sort independently when gametes are formed.

Hugo de Vries, Dutch Botanist

Gregor Mendel's theories of heredity finally were recognized in the scientific community through the work of Hugo de Vries (1848–1935). Dutch plant physiologist de Vries began experimenting with the evening primrose in 1886, and soon discovered that periodically a dramatically different variety appeared and then would occasionally reappear in later generations. He postulated that hereditary characteristics were therefore independent units, which he called pangenes, that could not be "blended" like two liquids. According to de Vries, pangenes grow and divide into two new pangenes that are passed on to offspring. A pangene can be active or latent (inactive), and some characteristics may be presented by more than one pangene.

Unknown to de Vries, these findings had already been documented by Mendel over thirty-four years earlier. In 1900, while checking the literature for any earlier experiments along these lines, de Vries came across the forgotten work of Mendel and used it to supplement his own experiments. The rediscovery of Mendel's laws created quite a stir among scientists, and many flocked to the field of heredity. But de Vries felt something was missing: while Mendel's laws of segregation explained how existing characteristics were redistributed to create variations, they did not show how new species originated. Relying on his primrose experiments, de Vries termed the new varieties "mutations." He further concluded that a species produces mutants over relatively short time periods throughout its evolutionary life, and only the useful or "progressive" characteristics contribute to the evolution of the species. De Vries documented his theory in *Die Mutationstheorie* ("The Mutation Theory"), completed in 1903.

Theories ignored

During his lifetime Mendel never received recognition for the important contribution he had made to the study of heredity. He carefully documented his experiments and presented his findings to the Brunn Society for the Study of Natural Science in 1865. The following year he published *Experiments With Plant Hybrids.* Yet the scientific community was indifferent. Botanists, including Karl Wilhelm von Nageli (to whom Mendel sent his work), were unaccustomed to statistical analysis, and scientists on the whole were hesitant to accept such novel theories regarding heredity from such an obscure man.

Ironically, because of Mendel's work the evolutionary theory of **Charles Darwin** (see entry) gained support. Prior to Mendel's work, natural selection was believed to be counteracted or compromised by repeated blending of gene characteristics throughout the hereditary cycle. Nearly two decades after his death, when Mendel's pioneering work was rediscovered by the Dutch botanist and geneticist Hugo de Vries (see box) and others in 1900, did Mendel begin to receive the recognition he had earned. He died in 1884.

Further Reading

Olby, Robert C., *The Origins of Mendelism,* 2nd ed., University of Chicago Press, 1985.

Orel, Vieslav, *Gregor Mendel: The First Geneticist,* Oxford University Press, 1995.

Dmitry Mendeleev

Born February 8, 1834
Tobolsk, Siberia
Died February 2, 1907
St. Petersburg, Russia

Russian chemist Dmitry Mendeleev developed the periodic table of the elements.

Dmitry Mendeleev's name will always be linked with the development of the periodic table, a method of organizing and listing known chemical elements. The first chemist who actually understood that the relationship between all elements could be demonstrated through a single ordered system, Mendeleev changed an unfocused and speculative branch of chemistry into a logical science. Although his nomination for the 1906 Nobel Prize for chemistry failed by one vote, he went down in history fifty years later when element 101—mendelevium—was named for him.

Family plagued by tragedy

Dmitry Ivanovich Mendeleev (also transliterated, or spelled in English as, Mendeléev, Mendeleef, Mendeleeff, and Mendeleyev) was born in Tobolsk in western Siberia (a vast, frozen region of Asiatic Russia), on February 8, 1834. He was the youngest child in a family of either fourteen or seventeen children. (Records do not agree.) When Mendeleev was still quite young, his father, a teacher at the Tobolsk gymnasium (high school), became blind and lost his job. Mendeleev's mother tried to support the family by building a glassworks (a place where glass is manufactured) in the nearby town of Axemziansk. Only an average student, Mendeleev learned science from a brother-in-law who had been exiled to Siberia because of revolutionary activities in Moscow.

Mendeleev completed high school at the age of sixteen, but only after the family had experienced more bad luck. His father died of tuberculosis, and his mother's glassworks burned down. Determined that her two youngest children receive a college education, in 1850 she traveled by horseback with the youngsters first to Moscow, then on to St. Petersburg. Through the efforts of a family friend, she was able to enroll Mendeleev at the Central Pedagogical Institute in St. Petersburg. A few months later, exhausted from her efforts, she died.

Becomes government official

After graduating from the Pedagogical Institute in 1855, Mendeleev went to France and Germany for graduate study. While studying at Heidelberg, Germany, with German chemist Robert Bunsen, he discovered the phenomenon of critical temperature, the temperature at which a liquid and its vapor exist in equilibrium. Irish physicist and chemist Thomas Andrews, however, is usually credited with independently making this discovery two years later. In 1861 Mendeleev returned to St. Petersburg, where he became professor of chemistry at the Technological Institute. Six years later he was also appointed professor of general chemistry at the University of St. Petersburg. He remained there until 1890, when he resigned after a dispute with the minister of education. Mendeleev was later appointed Director of the Bureau of Weights and Measures, a post he held until his death in 1907.

Develops periodic law

The achievement with which Mendeleev's name will forever be associated was his development of the periodic law. In

Dmitry Mendeleev is famous for his 1869 formulation of the periodic law and the invention of the periodic table of the elements, which brought order to the science of chemistry. Mendeleev based the periodic table on the atomic weight and other properties of the elements. The table would be slightly revised forty-five years later when, in 1913, English physicist Henry Moseley assigned atomic numbers to the elements. Nonetheless, Mendeleev's periodic table worked remarkably well and even allowed its designer to predict the properties of three missing elements.

1868 he set out to write a chemistry text-book, *Principles in Chemistry,* that would later become a classic in the field. Mendeleev wanted to find a way to organize his discussion of the sixty-three chemical elements that were known at the time. After having attended the Karlsruhe Congress in 1860, he concluded that the atomic weights of the elements might provide a clue. He began by making cards for each of the known elements. On each card he recorded an element's atomic weight, valence (the degree of combining power), and other chemical and physical properties (characteristics). Then he tried arranging the cards in various ways to see if any pattern emerged. Mendeleev was apparently unaware of similar efforts to arrange the elements on the basis of their weights made by English chemist J. A. R. Newlands only a few years earlier.

Mendeleev's system was eventually successful. He saw that when the elements were arranged in ascending order according to their weights, their properties repeated in a predictable, orderly manner. That is, when the cards were laid out in sequence, from left to right, the properties of the tenth element (sodium) were similar to those of the second element (lithium), the properties of the eleventh element (magnesium) were similar to those of the third element (beryllium), and so on. This recurrence of chemical and physical properties when the elements are arranged by ascending order became known as the periodic law.

A glitch in the law

When Mendeleev laid out all sixty-three elements according to their weights, he found a few places in which the law appeared to break down. For example, tellurium and

Henry Moseley, English Physicist

When English physicist Henry Moseley (1887–1915) discovered how to determine atomic numbers in 1913, he found the first real explanation for inversion of elements in the periodic table. He disproved Dmitry Mendeleev's hypothesis that the inverted elements had been misplaced because their atomic weights had been incorrectly determined. Moseley, who is best known today for his study of the X-ray spectra of the elements, used this technique to determine atomic weights. When X rays are beamed at certain crystalline materials, they are diffracted (scattered) by atoms within the crystals, forming a continuous spectrum on which is superimposed a series of bright lines. The number and location of these lines are characteristic of the element being studied. Moseley found that the frequencies of one set of spectral lines differed from element to element in a very consistent and orderly way. He also found that when the elements are arranged in ascending order according to their atomic weights, the frequency of these spectral lines differed from each other by a factor of one.

Moseley proposed that the factor accounting for the regular progression in the spectral line patterns was the charge of its nucleus. The main difference between what Mendeleev had classified the elements by—atomic weight—and what the revised periodic table classifies them by—atomic number—is that the variation in atomic weight between adjacent elements is never consistent, whereas the variation in nuclear charge is always precisely one. Of all the properties of an atom, atomic number has come to be the single most important characteristic by which an atom can be recognized. And the concept of a unique, identifying, and characteristic number of an element—its nuclear charge—provided a new basis for the periodic table. It even allowed Moseley and other scientists to predict the number and location of elements still missing from the periodic table, a search that turned out to be very fruitful in a relatively brief time.

iodine were in the wrong positions when arranged according to their weights. He solved this problem by inverting the two elements, that is, by placing them where they ought to be according to their properties, even if they were no longer in the correct sequence according to their weights. Mendeleev hypothesized that the atomic weights for these two elements had been incorrectly determined. He happened to be wrong in this assumption, and it was not until English physicist Henry

ПЕРИОДИЧЕСКАЯ СИСТЕМА ЭЛЕМЕНТОВ

ГРУППЫ ЭЛЕМЕНТОВ

ПЕРИОДЫ	РЯДЫ	I	II	III	IV	V	VI	VII	VIII	0
1	I	H 1 — 1,008								He 2 — 4,003
2	II	Li 3 — 6,940	Be 4 — 9,02	5 B — 10,82	6 C — 12,010	7 N — 14,008	8 O — 16,000	9 F — 19,00		Ne 10 — 20,183
3	III	Na 11 — 22,997	Mg 12 — 24,32	13 Al — 26,97	14 Si — 28,06	15 P — 30,98	16 S — 32,06	17 Cl — 35,457		Ar 18 — 39,944
4	IV	K 19 — 39,096	Ca 20 — 40,08	Sc 21 — 45,10	Ti 22 — 47,90	V 23 — 50,95	Cr 24 — 52,01	Mn 25 — 54,93	Fe 26 — 55,85 / Co 27 — 58,94 / Ni 28 — 58,69	
	V	29 Cu — 63,57	30 Zn — 65,38	31 Ga — 69,72	32 Ge — 72,60	33 As — 74,91	34 Se — 78,96	35 Br — 79,916		Kr 36 — 83,7
5	VI	Rb 37 — 85,48	Sr 38 — 87,63	Y 39 — 88,92	Zr 40 — 91,22	Nb 41 — 92,91	Mo 42 — 95,95	Ma 43 — —	Ru 44 — 101,7 / Rh 45 — 102,91 / Pd 46 — 106,7	
	VII	47 Ag — 107,88	48 Cd — 112,41	49 In — 114,76	50 Sn — 118,70	51 Sb — 121,76	52 Te — 127,61	53 J — 126,92		Xe 54 — 131,3
6	VIII	Cs 55 — 132,91	Ba 56 — 137,36	La 57 ★ — 138,92	Hf 72 — 178,6	Ta 73 — 180,88	W 74 — 183,92	Re 75 — 186,31	Os 76 — 190,2 / Ir 77 — 193,1 / Pt 78 — 195,23	
	IX	79 Au — 197,2	80 Hg — 200,61	81 Tl — 204,39	82 Pb — 207,21	83 Bi — 209,00	84 Po — 210	85 — —		Rn 86 — 222
7	X	87 — —	Ra 88 — 226,05	Ac 89 — 227	Th 90 — 232,12	Pa 91 — 231	U 92 — 238,07			

★ ЛАНТАНИДЫ 58–71

Ce 58 — 140,13	Pr 59 — 140,92	Nd 60 — 144,27	61 — —
Tb 65 — 159,2	Dy 66 — 162,46	Ho 67 — 164,94	Er 68 — 167,2

Sm 62 — 150,43	Eu 63 — 152,0	Gd 64 — 156,9
Tu 69 — 169,4	Yb 70 — 173,04	Cp 71 — 174,99

Dmitry Mendeleev's periodic table, in which the elements are arranged by atomic weight.

Moseley (see box) discovered atomic numbers (the number of protons in an atomic nucleus) in 1913 that the real explanation for inversion was found.

Makes valid prediction

Mendeleev made one other critical hypothesis. He found three places in the periodic table where elements appeared to be missing. The blank spaces occurred when he insisted on keeping elements with like properties underneath each other in the table, regardless of their weights. He predicted not only that the three missing elements would be found, but also what the properties of those elements would be. Mendeleev's law was soon validated when the three missing elements were discovered: gallium in 1875, scandium in 1879, and germanium in 1886.

Mendelevium

Mendelevium, chemical element 101, was named in honor of Dmitry Mendeleev. The element was artificially produced in 1955 by Albert Ghlorso, Gregory Choppin, Stanley Thompson, and Glenn T. Seaborg at the University of California at Berkeley. The team bombarded a tiny sample of einsteinium-253 with alpha (positively charged) particles in a sixty-inch cyclotron (particle accelerator). The product of the reaction was seventeen atoms of an isotope with mass 256 and a half life of 77 minutes.

Mendeleev is remembered as a brilliant scholar, an inspiring teacher, and a prolific writer. Besides his career in chemistry, he was interested in art, education, and economics. A man who was not afraid to express his strong opinions, even when they might offend others, he was apparently bypassed for a few academic appointments and honors because of his irritable nature. Nonetheless, his development of the periodic table of the elements cemented his reputation in the scientific community.

Further Reading

Kelman, Peter, and A. H. Stone, *Dmitry Mendeleev,* 1970.

Petryanov, I. V., and D. N. Trifonov, *Elementary Order: Mendeleev's Periodic System,* 1985.

Karl Menninger

Born July 22, 1893
Topeka, Kansas
Died July 18, 1990
Topeka, Kansas

"It is easier ... to help a child grow up with love and courage than it is to instill hope on a despondent soul. What a mother and father mean to them is more than any psychiatrist can ever mean."

In 1908 Dr. Charles Menninger, a general practitioner in Topeka, Kansas, visited the Mayo Clinic in Rochester, Minnesota, an innovative facility where doctors worked together to provide patients with the best treatment possible. Greatly impressed by the benefits of such group practice, Menninger dreamed of one day opening a similar facility. In 1919 the dream at last began to take shape when he and his eldest son, Karl, opened a small clinic. The Menninger Clinic has since evolved to become a world-renowned center for psychiatric treatment, education, and research. Its guiding principle—"No patient is untreatable"—reflects the compassionate philosophy of Karl Menninger, who did more than perhaps any other individual to transform the way Americans regard mental illness.

A native and nearly lifelong resident of Topeka, Kansas, Karl Augustus Menninger grew up in a deeply religious and nurturing atmosphere. Both Charles Menninger, his father, and Florence Knisely, his mother, stressed the importance of learning and instilled in their three sons a drive to work hard and be of service to others. Menninger and his brother William followed in their father's footsteps and studied medicine, while the middle son, Edwin, chose a career in journalism. Menninger earned bachelor's and master's degrees at the University of Wisconsin. He then entered the Harvard Medical School in Cambridge, Massachusetts, where he graduated with honors in 1917. He served internships at Kansas City General Hospital and at Boston Psychopathic Hospital. Before returning to Topeka to go into partnership with his father, he taught briefly at Harvard Medical School and Tufts Medical School.

Starts mental health hospital

Menninger was a specialist in neurology (the study of the nervous system) and the relatively new field of psychiatry (a branch of medicine that deals with mental, emotional, and behavioral disorders). He soon convinced his father that their patients' mental health deserved as much consideration as their physical health. At first Topeka residents balked at the idea of having a "maniac ward" in town. But the Menningers were very persuasive, and soon they had solicited enough support to establish a small hospital in a renovated farmhouse. By 1926 William had joined his father and brother in practice. The Menninger facilities had expanded not only to include the clinic and the hospital, but also a sanitarium (an establishment for the treatment of the mentally ill) and a pioneering residential treatment program for children that allowed them to live in a family-like atmosphere and attend school.

Challenges conventional ideas

The Menninger complex continued to expand throughout the 1920s and 1930s, with Karl as the chief of staff and William as the administrative head and fund-raiser. In 1941 they formed the Menninger Foundation, a nonprofit corporation encompassing the many different psychiatric services offered by the Menningers and their associates. At the foundation's core were the hospital and sanitarium. Among the other components were the Karl Menninger School of Psychiatry and the Topeka Institute for Psychoanalysis, both dedicated to training mental health professionals. The Menningers also wielded considerable influence in the affairs of the Topeka Veterans Administration Hospital and the Topeka State Hospital, where they challenged conventional "warehousing" methods for dealing with the mentally ill.

As chief of staff, Karl Menninger exercised a pivotal role in formulating and running programs in treatment and education. He was trained in Freudian theory (see **Sigmund Freud** entry) and accepted its basic principle that mental illness can be traced to a variety of subconscious causes rooted mostly in childhood. Yet he did not ignore the importance of more immediate causes that bring on emotional distress. In fact, he attributed most mental illness to improperly handled feelings of aggression, hostility, and destruction brought on by external (outside) stress. Because he was not committed to any form of therapy, Menninger advocated constantly examining and reexamining successes and failures so that treatment could be adjusted accordingly.

Provides loving environment

One especially innovative approach the Menningers developed went far beyond customary basket-weaving and leather-working, which only helped the patient pass time. Called a "school in practice living," the clinic re-taught patients how to channel their energies into healthy work, play, and learning activities tailored to individual needs and interests. Depending on the patient, the activities might have included dancing lessons, language study, photography, or even scrubbing floors and walls. The Menningers found that active involvement gave patients a feeling of accomplishment, restored a sense of order and discipline in their lives, and improved their relationships with others.

In Karl Menninger's view, a cold and unloving home environment was to blame for most instances of mental illness. With that in mind, his goal was to create at the clinic an atmosphere of caring and kindness in a family-type living situation. His philosophy emphasized that everyone who came in contact with patients—from the doctors to the groundskeepers—was part of the treatment team and had an obligation to offer understanding and support. Menninger also shied away from classifying patients and even avoided using terms like "neurotic" or "psychotic," which he believed could ruin a patient's life.

Shares his vision

Menninger shared his vision in a variety of ways. For example, his bestselling book *The Human Mind* (originally published in 1930 and revised several times since then) effectively explained psychiatry and psychiatric principles to a lay audience and brought its author national prominence. In subsequent years he wrote numerous books and articles, lectured extensively, and served as a consultant. But his greatest impact came as the foundation's director of education and head of the school of psychiatry. Under his supervision, the school trained more psychiatrists than any other facility in the world. Also central to his mission were the seminars held at the institute for other health-care professionals and people outside the field with an interest in human behavior.

IMPACT

Karl Menninger was instrumental in improving the once-dreadful conditions of the American prison system, which he maintained do more harm to the inmates than the inmates have ever done to society. Noting that the crime rate has not decreased as the prison population has increased, he proposed an alternative solution: rehabilitation programs offering a combination of job training and mental health counseling to help prisoners adjust to life. The counseling was especially important, he insisted, because oftentimes crime is the vehicle people use to gain revenge for physical or mental abuse they received as children. Although his views were at one time embraced, within the past few years they have fallen into disfavor among those who advocate longer sentences and less "coddling" of prisoners.

Champions social causes

In his later years Menninger gave up teaching and seeing patients to devote more time to crusading on behalf of such causes as prison reform, neglected and abused children, the rights of Native Americans, and the environment. Believing that mental illness stems from problems linked to society, Menninger felt he could make a better impact by preventing situations that result in mental problems. The president of the American Psychoanalytic Association and a founding member of similar organizations, Menninger was honored with many awards during his life. Among them was the Medal of Freedom in 1981. He remained actively involved in social reform efforts until shortly before his death in 1990 at the age of ninety-six. The institute Menninger began with his father and brother has now expanded to more than three dozen buildings on two separate campuses in Topeka.

Further Reading

"The Kansas Moralist," *Time,* July 30, 1990.

"Karl A. Menninger: Psychiatrist as Moralist," *Christian Century,* August 22–29, 1990, pp. 758–59.

Menninger, Karl, *Sparks,* edited by Lucy Freeman, Crowell, 1973.

New York Times, November 13, 1975; July 19, 1990.

U.S. News & World Report, July 30, 1990.

Marvin Minsky

Born August 9, 1927
New York, New York

American computer scientist Marvin Minsky is a pioneer in the field of artificial intelligence. Since the 1950s he has tried to define and explain the thinking process and design a machine that can duplicate it. His 1987 book *The Society of Mind* puts forth a detailed theory of how the mind works and how it might be duplicated by a machine.

Marvin Lee Minsky was born in New York City on August 9, 1927, to Dr. Henry Minsky and Fannie Reiser. His father was an eye surgeon and an artist, and his mother was active in the Zionist movement (an organization devoted to establishing a Jewish nation in Israel). Minsky attended the Bronx High School of Science, then graduated from the Phillips Academy in Andover, Massachusetts, in 1945. After a year of service in the U.S. Navy, he entered Harvard University in 1946.

Although at Harvard Minsky majored in physics, he also attended classes in a wide variety of subjects, including genetics, mathematics, and the nature of intelligence. Minsky was

"It's so thrilling not to be able to do something."

665

Marvin Minsky believes that the field of artificial intelligence has not progressed significantly over the years. No major steps toward developing—or even defining—a truly intelligent machine have been made in decades. Minsky believes this could change if more researchers would pay attention to his theory of the mind. Whether or not artificial intelligence does advance, it is very likely that Minsky will be somewhere nearby, giving it a push.

associated briefly with the researchers in the psychology department, but he questioned the current theories of what happens deep inside the mind. For instance, he became interested in the theories of behavioral psychologists such as **B. F. Skinner** (see entry) but ultimately disagreed with his concept that humans are governed by learned behavior patterns.

Minsky viewed human intelligence not only according to purely behavioral principles (that is, human consciousness is based entirely on responses to stimuli from the environment) but also from the perspective of the deep biological processes of the mind. Skinner had enjoyed considerable success with his theories, yet Minsky felt there must be a better explanation of how the human mind works. Using his knowledge of mathematics he formulated a model of a "stochastic neural network" in the brain. He also switched his major from physics to mathematics in his senior year, graduating from Harvard in 1950.

Builds the "Snarc"

From Harvard Minsky moved to Princeton University in New Jersey to begin his doctoral studies. At Princeton he began working on artificial intelligence, a branch of computer science dealing with the simulation of intelligent behavior in humans, and built his first electronic learning machine, which he called the "Snarc." The Snarc had to learn how to trace a path through a maze using a programmed "reward" system. Minsky's accomplishments with the Snarc were limited. Even though he thought he was on the right track with the "reward" principle, the Snarc was not versatile enough for his purposes.

Seeking a more complex machine, Minsky began to explore how a machine might use memory to "remember" and use past experience. He elaborated on this idea in his doctoral dissertation, in which he tried to show the ways a learning machine can predict the results of its behavior based on its knowledge of past actions. There was some question at the time whether this line of inquiry properly belonged in a program that appeared to be about mathematics. This is a recurring problem for Minsky, whose interests typically draw from so many disciplines that it becomes difficult to determine exactly what to label them. Nonetheless, Minsky received his Ph.D., then accepted a three-year junior fellowship at Harvard, where he continued to pursue his theories about intelligence.

Founds MIT Artificial Intelligence Laboratory

In 1958 Minsky joined the staff of the Lincoln Laboratory at the Massachusetts Institute of Technology (MIT) in Cambridge, Massachusetts, as an assistant professor of mathematics. A year later he and a colleague, John McCarthy, founded the MIT Artificial Intelligence Project, which eventually became the Artificial Intelligence Laboratory. Minsky was the director of the laboratory from 1964 until 1973. The following year he was promoted to Donner Professor of Science in the Department of Electrical Engineering and Computer Science. In 1989 he moved to the media laboratory at MIT, where he became Toshiba Professor of Media Arts and Sciences.

Proposes his theory

Minsky has made it his life's work to finalize an overall theory of how minds work. He has disturbed, and perhaps alienated, many of his coresearchers by insisting that what we think of as "consciousness" or "self-awareness" is actually a myth, a convenient fallacy that allows us to function as a society. According to Minsky's theory (which he has outlined in *The Society of Mind* as well as in numerous articles in popular magazines), there is no difference between humans and machines.

Minsky believes humans are machines whose brains are made up of many semi-autonomous (partially self-directed)

Raymond Kurzweil, American Inventor

Raymond Kurzweil (1948–) is prominent in the field of artificial intelligence and is one of the leading inventors in the United States today. He unveiled his groundbreaking invention, a reading machine that scans written text and turns it into synthesized speech, in 1976, when he was only twenty-eight years old. The system has been hailed as the most significant reading aid for the blind since the Braille system of writing was introduced in the mid-nineteenth century. The Kurzweil Reading Machine is recognized as the world's first consumer product that successfully incorporates artificial intelligence technology.

In 1984, at the suggestion of blind musician Stevie Wonder (who had used one of the first Kurzweil Reading Machines), Kurzweil turned his energies to music. The result was an electronic synthesizer (computerized music keyboard) that reproduced the rich sounds of orchestral instruments. The Kurzweil Music System makes use of artificial intelligence-based pattern-recognition techniques to analyze and create sound models for musical instruments. The sound models can be stored in computer memory and used to recreate a desired sound at will. In the late 1980s Kurzweil produced the first commercially marketed speech recognition technology, developing such devices as the Kurzweil VoiceWriter, which can recognize approximately ten thousand words. He has founded three companies to develop and market these and his other products: Kurzweil Computer Products, Inc., Kurzweil Music Systems Inc., and Kurzweil Applied Intelligence, Inc.

but unintelligent "agents," or specialized mini-computers. Humans mistakenly consider themselves to be intelligent individuals, he contends. Some scientists have expressed concern that Minsky's mechanistic view of the mind, by ignoring established knowledge in the fields of biology and psychology, contradicts what we seem to perceive about ourselves. But Minsky dismisses such objections, maintaining that most research on how the mind works has been crippled by researchers who simply ask the wrong questions.

Continues developing his theory

Minsky continues to hold a professorship at the Artificial Intelligence Laboratory. For the past few years, he has devoted himself to private research, fleshing out his Society of Mind theory. Minsky often writes for such publications as *Omni* and *Discover.* He has also coauthored a science fiction novel (not surprisingly based on his theory) with Harry Harrison titled *The Turing Option.* In 1953 Minsky married Gloria Rudisch, a doctor. They have three children: Margaret, Henry, and Juliana. Among the honors Minsky has won for his pioneering work are the Donner professorship, the Turing Award in 1970, and the prestigious Japan Award in 1990.

Further Reading

Current Biography, H. W. Wilson, September 1988, pp. 398–402.

Discover, October 1989; June 1992; July 1993.

Scientific American, August 1994.

McWilliams, Gary, "The Father of AI Says His Child Has Gone Astray," *Business Week,* March 2, 1992.

Minsky, Marvin, "NASA Held Hostage," *Ad Astra,* June 1990.

Minsky, Marvin, "Will Robots Inherit the Earth?" *Scientific American,* October 1994.

Minsky, Marvin, and Harry Harrison, *The Turing Option,* Warner Books, 1992.

Alfred Nobel

Born in 1833
Stockholm, Sweden
Died December 10, 1896
San Remo, Italy

Alfred Nobel, the inventor of dynamite, left a fund to be used for the annual awarding of the Nobel Prizes for achievement in a variety of fields.

Owner of more than 350 patented inventions during his lifetime, Alfred Nobel is best known as the inventor of dynamite. Appalled that his invention—which revolutionized the mining industry—was being used for military purposes, Nobel attempted to promote peace and beneficial advances in technology by bequeathing a portion of his estate to the establishment of the Nobel Foundation. The foundation awards the annual Nobel Prizes for accomplishments in physics, chemistry, physiology or medicine, literature, economics (which was added later), and the promotion of peace.

Improves use of explosives

Alfred Nobel was born in Stockholm, Sweden, in 1833. As a youth he was privately tutored and undertook various apprenticeships. Like his father, a manufacturer of torpedoes, mines, and other explosives, Nobel displayed an avid interest in engineering and chemistry. As a young man he worked for a time in the laboratory of French chemist Theophile Jules Pelouze, who is regarded by some as the inventor of guncotton (an explosive nitrate product). After extensive travels, through which he acquired the sharp skills of a businessman and the distinct advantages of a multilinguist (a person who speaks several languages), Nobel returned to Sweden in 1863 to develop a process for safely manufacturing nitroglycerin (a powerful form of chemical explosive).

Almost two decades earlier Italian chemist Ascanio Sobrero had invented this oily liquid, but it proved so volatile (unstable) that it could not be widely used. Instead, gunpowder (an explosive mixture of powder substances used in gunnery) and guncotton, which also presented problems, dominated the explosives industry. Through his own studies and experiments, begun as early as 1859, Nobel had familiarized himself with Sobrero's compound of glycerin treated with nitric acid. He had even exploded small quantities of it under water. Sharing his son's interest, the elder Nobel designed a method for the large-scale production of the explosive. In Nobel's mind, all that remained was to devise a special blasting charge to ensure a predictable detonation of the nitroglycerin by shock, rather than heat, which he already knew to be a dangerously imperfect firing method. The result was Nobel's first important invention, the mercury fulminate cap.

Patents dynamite

Around 1963 Nobel established a factory to produce liquid nitroglycerin. But when the facility blew up the following year, killing his younger brother Emil, Nobel determined to find safe handling methods for the substance. He hoped to discover a benign (harmless) substance to absorb the liquid explosive, thereby making it safe for manipulation and transportation, without seriously reducing its explosive capacity. After exhaustive experimentation, Nobel found a nearly perfect substance, kieselguhr. When saturated with nitroglycerin, this porous clay became a highly desirable explosive, which Nobel termed dynamite and patented in 1867.

Although Alfred Nobel's invention of dynamite revolutionized mining and he grew rich from the industry it spawned, it is for the Nobel Prizes that the inventor and philanthropist is best remembered. Mortified that dynamite was being used for military purposes, to promote peace and advances in science and medicine Nobel provided the funds to establish the Nobel Foundation that awards the prizes every year on December 10, the anniversary of his death.

Virtually overnight, Nobel's invention of dynamite revolutionized the mining industry. Five times as powerful as gunpowder, it was relatively easy to produce and reasonably safe to use. Nobel acquired a vast fortune from this invention, which spawned an intricate network of factories, sales representatives, and distributors in several industrialized countries around the world.

Despite the enormous demands of his business ventures, which required him to travel almost continuously and engage repeatedly in legal battles, Nobel persevered with his scientific research, creating new inventions and improving his existing ones. (Indeed, he would come to patent more than 350 inventions.) For instance, he was not satisfied with the qualities of kieselguhr, which occasionally leaked nitroglycerin and somewhat reduced the power of the liquid. Consequently, he experimented with nitroglycerin and collodion (a low-nitrogen form of guncotton), finding that these two substances formed a gelatinous (jelly-like) mass that, with modifications, possessed a high resistance to water and an explosive force greater than that of dynamite. The invention, perfected in 1875, became known by a variety of names, including blasting gelatin, Nobel's Extra Dynamite, saxonite, and gelignite.

Seeks smokeless powder

One of Nobel's last significant discoveries was closely related to his work with blasting gelatin. Like a number of other inventors, he was in search of a smokeless powder to replace gunpowder. In 1888 he introduced ballistite, a mixture of nitroglycerin, guncotton, and camphor (a gummy, volatile crystalline compound), which could be cut into flakes and used as a propellant. The substance was particularly valuable for its ability to burn ferociously without exploding. A year later two British scientists invented a smokeless powder based on ballistite, called cordite. To Nobel the invention represented an infringement on his patent, but his suit to recover damages was unsuccessful.

Starts Nobel Foundation

Nobel was a lifelong pacifist and for some time had misgivings about his family's business. He wished his explosives to be used solely for peaceful purposes, and he was greatly embittered by their military use. Before he died in 1896, Nobel composed a handwritten will that, while problematic and fiercely contested, led to the creation of the Nobel Foundation. He arranged for annual prizes to be awarded through the foundation for outstanding achievement in physics, chemistry, physiology or medicine, peace, and literature (economics was added later). Each prize consists of a gold medal, a sum of money, and a certificate of award. The amount of money for each prize varies yearly. Presented on December 10, the anniversary of Nobel's death, Nobel Prizes are awarded without regard to nationality. According to Nobel's will, the judges are the Royal Swedish Academy of Science, the Swedish Royal Caroline Medico-Surgical Institute, and a committee elected by the Norwegian parliament. The first prizes were given in 1901.

Further Reading

Crawford, Elisabeth, *The Beginnings of the Nobel Institution: The Science Prizes, 1901–1915,* Cambridge University Press, 1987.

Fant, Kenne, *Alfred Nobel: A Biography,* Little, Brown, 1993.

Robert Noyce

Born December 12, 1927
Burlington, Iowa
Died June 3, 1990

American physicist and inventor Robert Noyce invented an improved integrated circuit (computer chip or microchip), an electronic component that is considered to be among the twentieth century's most significant technological developments. The laptop computer, the ignition control in a modern automobile, the "brain" of a VCR that allows for its programming, and thousands of other computing devices all depend for their operation on the integrated circuit. Noyce was not only a brilliant inventor, credited with more than a dozen patents for semiconductor devices and processes, but a forceful businessman who founded the Fairchild Semiconductor Corporation and the Intel Corporation. He later became president and chief executive officer of Sematech.

Exhibits talent for math and science

Robert Norton Noyce was born on December 12, 1927, in Burlington, Iowa, the third of four sons of Ralph Noyce and

674

Harriet Norton Noyce. Growing up in Grinnell, a small town in central Iowa, Noyce was gifted in many areas. While in high school he excelled in sports, music, and acting, and showed a talent for math and science. During his senior year he took the Grinnell College freshman physics course. Noyce went on to receive his baccalaureate degree in physics from Grinnell, graduating with Phi Beta Kappa honors in 1949.

Introduced to the transistor

At Grinnell in the mid-1940s Noyce was introduced to the transistor, a device that is used to control the flow of electricity in electronic equipment. He was excited by the invention, seeing it as freeing electronics from the constraints of the bulky and inefficient vacuum tube. After he received his Ph.D. in physics from the Massachusetts Institute of Technology in Cambridge, Massachusetts, in 1954, and having no interest in pure research, he started working for Philco in Philadelphia, Pennsylvania, where the company was making semiconductors (materials whose conductivity of an electrical current puts them midway between conductors and insulators).

After three years Noyce became convinced Philco did not share his enthusiasm for transistors. By chance, in 1956 he was asked by **William Shockley** (see entry), Nobel Prize winner and coinventor of the transistor, to work for him in California. Shockley had assembled an electrical engineering team to research and develop better transistors and diodes (an electronic device that has two electrodes or terminals and is used to convert alternating current into direct current). Each day his "Ph.D. production line," as he called his group of young scientists, baked germanium (a metallic element that resembles silicon and is used as a semiconductor) and silicon (a nonmetallic element that is used in electronic devices) in kilns. They created crystals that could be cut into slices that would then be wired together to create transistors.

Moves to Silicon Valley

Excited by the opportunity to develop state-of-the-art transistor technology, Noyce moved to Palo Alto, which is located in an area that came to be known as Silicon Valley (named for the silicon compounds used in the manufacture of computer chips). But Noyce was no happier with Shockley than he had been with Philco; both Shockley's management style and the direction of his work, which ignored transistors, were disappointing. In 1957 Noyce left with seven other Shockley engineers to form a new company, financed by Fairchild Camera and Instrument, to be called Fairchild Semiconductor. At age twenty-nine, Noyce was chosen as the leader of the new corporation.

Invents the integrated circuit

The Fairchild firm spent about two years conducting research before Noyce invented the integrated circuit. Although he did not know it, a young engineer with Texas Instruments named Jack Kilby had invented a similar device about six months earlier. However, Kilby's circuit, which was made of germanium, was less efficient and harder to produce than Noyce's, which was constructed of silicon. Noyce's thumbnail-sized innovation soon became the industry's standard. Transistors were etched onto the silicon chips, thus eliminating the costly and time-consuming wiring together of chips. This made possible tremendous reductions in the size of circuit components with a corresponding increase in the speed of their operation. Gone forever were the huge computers such as ENIAC (Electronic Numerical Integrator and Calculator), a computer created by the U.S. Army in 1946 to calculate missile trajectories. The integrated circuit, or "microchip" as it became commonly known, had been born.

Forms Intel

Both technological advances and competition in the new microchip industry increased rapidly. The number of transistors that could be put on a microchip grew from ten in 1964 to one thousand in 1969 to thirty-two thousand in 1975. (By 1993 up to 3.1 million transistors could be put on a 2.15-inch-square microprocessor chip.) The number of manufacturers eventually grew from two (Fairchild and Shockley) to dozens. During the 1960s Noyce's company was the leading producer of microchips, and by 1968 he was a millionaire. However, Noyce still felt constricted at Fairchild. Wanting more control, he joined Gordon Moore to form the Intel Corporation, a new company in Santa Clara, California.

In Intel's first year, Noyce and Moore invested primarily in research, for they had decided to explore the most underdeveloped area of computer technology at that time: memory. They searched for a more efficient mechanism in which computers could store data, hoping to replace the ceramic cores then in use. These cores, which resemble spirals, could store only one piece of information each at any one time. After two years they developed the 1103 memory chip that was made of silicon and polysilicon. It quickly replaced the ceramic cores.

Intel followed its success in memory with the introduction of the microprocessor in 1971. A revolutionary discovery made by one of Intel's young engineers, Ted Hoff, the microprocessor allowed a single silicon chip to contain the circuitry for information storage and processing. This invention propelled Intel into the forefront of the industry. By 1982 Intel could claim to have pioneered 75 percent of the advances in microtechnology during the previous decade.

Dubbed "Mayor of Silicon Valley"

Noyce's management style could be called "roll up your sleeves." He shunned fancy corporate cars, offices, and furnishings in favor of a less-structured, relaxed working environment in which everyone contributed and no one benefited from luxuries. Becoming chairman of the board of Intel in 1974, he left the work of daily operations behind him, founding and later becoming chairman of the Semiconductor Indus-

IMPACT

With his invention of the integrated circuit, Robert Noyce helped usher in the age of the computer. Changing forever the lives of millions, his miniscule invention revolutionized nearly every field of engineering and made possible space travel, microcomputers, digital watches, pocket calculators, home computers, robots, and missile guidance systems.

try Association. In 1980 Noyce was honored with the National Medal of Science and in 1983, the same year that Intel's sales reached $1 billion, he was made a member of the National Inventor's Hall of Fame.

Noyce was called the "Mayor of Silicon Valley" during the 1980s, not only for his scientific contributions but also for his role as a spokesperson for the industry. He spent much of his later career working to improve the international competitiveness of American industry. At the outset he had recognized the strengths of foreign competitors in the electronics market and the corresponding weaknesses of U.S. companies. In 1988 Noyce took charge of Sematech, a consortium (group) of semiconductor manufacturers working together and with the United States government to increase American competitiveness in the world marketplace.

Noyce had many interests. He enjoyed reading Ernest Hemingway, flying his own airplane, hang gliding, and scuba diving. He believed that microelectronics would continue to advance in complexity and sophistication well beyond its current state, and that the question would finally arise as to what use society would make of the technology. Noyce was married twice, first to Elizabeth Bottomley and then to Ann Bowers, who was the Intel personnel director. Noyce died on June 3, 1990, of a sudden heart attack.

Further Reading

Adams, Robert McC., "Smithsonian Horizons," *Smithsonian,* December 1989.

Bonner, M., W. L. Boyd, and J. A. Allen, *Robert N. Noyce, 1927–1990,* Sematech, 1990.

Chamberlain, Gary, "Polishing the Engineer's Image," *Design News,* February 12, 1990.

Fifty Who Made the Difference, Villard Books, 1984, pp. 270–303.

Kehoe, Louise, "Robert N. Noyce: 1990 Award for Achievement," *Electronics,* December 1990.

Miller, Michael J., "Lifetime Achievement: Jack St. Clair Kilby and Robert N. Noyce," *P. C. Magazine,* December 21, 1993.

Moore, Gordon, "Robert Noyce," *Physics Today,* January 1991.

Palfreman, Jon, and Doron Swade, *The Dream Machine,* BBC Books, 1991.

Slater, Robert, *Portraits in Silicon,* MIT Press, 1987.

J. Robert Oppenheimer

Born April 22, 1904
New York, New York
Died February 18, 1967
Princeton, New Jersey

American physicist J. Robert Oppenheimer headed the Manhattan Project, a collaboration of scientists who built the first atomic bomb.

Theoretical physicist J. Robert Oppenheimer was a pioneer in the field of quantum mechanics. As head of the weapons lab at Los Alamos, New Mexico, he led the U.S. effort, called the Manhattan Project, to build the first atomic bomb that was dropped to hasten the end of World War II. In the postwar years, however, he staunchly opposed the proliferation of nuclear weapons. This stance brought him before Congress during the McCarthy era and cost him his security clearance as a government consultant.

Grows up in New York

Julius Robert Oppenheimer was born in New York City on April 22, 1904, to a wealthy and cultured family. His father, Julius Oppenheimer, who emigrated from Germany as a young man, had a successful business importing textiles. His mother, the former Ella Friedman, was a painter and a great lover of the arts. Oppenheimer, his parents, and his younger brother, Frank, divided their time between a spacious New York apartment overlooking the Hudson River and a summer house on Long Island.

Graduates from Harvard

It became apparent when Oppenheimer was quite young that he had a quick mind, a huge appetite for learning, and a wide range of interests. At age eleven he was the youngest person ever admitted to the New York Mineralogical Society, and at the age of twelve he presented a paper to the organization. He attended the Ethical Culture School in New York, and after graduating he spent the summer in Europe. During the trip he contracted dysentery (a severe intestinal infection) and needed a whole year to recuperate.

Oppenheimer entered Harvard University in 1922. He studied a broad curriculum, which included several languages as well as chemistry and physics. Despite his course load, Oppenheimer graduated from Harvard *summa cum laude* (with highest honors) in just three years, and in 1925 he left the United States for Europe to study theoretical physics.

Explains molecular activity

In Europe during the 1920s the most important advances were being achieved in quantum mechanics (the study of the energy of atomic particles). Several brilliant theoreticians were formulating theories about quantifying and predicting the movement and location of atomic particles. Oppenheimer initially went to the Cavendish Laboratory in Cambridge, England. Within just a few months he had submitted his first paper, which used some of the most recent theoretical advances in nuclear physics to explain aspects of the behavior of the molecule (the smallest particle of a substance that retains all the properties of that substance and is composed of one or more atoms).

In 1926 Oppenheimer left Cavendish for the University of Göttingen in Germany. He did independent research on radiation at Göttingen and also collaborated with the physicist Max Born in a further investigation of molecular activity. The two scientists tackled variations in the vibration, rotation, and electronic properties of the molecule. Their results led to the so-called "Born-Oppenheimer method," which deals with quantum mechanics at the molecular rather than the atomic level. After receiving his doctorate in 1927, he left Göttingen for Leiden, Holland, and then went on to Zurich, Switzerland, where he worked with another distinguished physicist, Wolfgang Pauli. Throughout this period Oppenheimer consistently demonstrated his ability to synthesize ideas, draw connections between theories, and detect their inherent contradictions.

Earns reputation as charismatic teacher

In 1928 Oppenheimer obtained teaching positions at the University of California at Berkeley and at the California Institute of Technology (Cal Tech) in Pasadena. For the next thirteen years he taught and did research at these schools during alternating semesters and became a fine teacher. Although many students complained that he set an impossible pace in the classroom, he interested a number of students and even some colleagues in theoretical physics. Oppenheimer's social life was very much involved with his teaching; he would often discuss subjects such as astrophysics and cosmic rays or nuclear physics and electrodynamics for hours on end.

Does work in particle physics

Some of Oppenheimer's best work in particle physics (the study of elementary particles) was also done during his years as a teacher. In 1930 he was able to demonstrate that the proton is not the antimatter equivalent of the electron (antielectron) as had then been supposed. Oppenheimer's earlier work on radiation led to his contribution to the discovery that cosmic ray particles could break down into another generation of particles, a phenomenon commonly called the "cascade process." In 1935 he discovered it was possible to accelerate deuterons, which are composed of a proton and a neutron, to much higher energies than neutrons alone. Deuterons, as a consequence, could be used to bombard positively charged atomic nuclei at high energies, enabling further research into atomic particles.

Scientists experiment with "nuclear fission"

For years physicists had been aware of the possibility of manipulating the splitting of the nucleus of the atom. In 1934 the Italian physicist **Enrico Fermi** (see entry) succeeded in bombarding a type of uranium (a radioactive metallic element) with neutrons, particles from the nucleus of an atom. Fermi reported the reaction, which in 1938 was called "nuclear fission" by German scientists **Lise Meitner** (see entry) and Otto Robert Frisch.

The scientists recognized the importance of nuclear fission. Uranium is itself a source of free neutrons. When one uranium atom gives off a neutron, the neutron might split the nucleus of a nearby atom. When that nucleus is split, it releases some of its neutrons, producing large amounts of heat energy. Some of the released neutrons bombard other nuclei, splitting them as well. If enough of the right kind of pure uranium (U-235) is present, a quantity called "critical mass," the process will continue by itself.

This chain reaction, the scientists realized, could result in a vast, instant explosion of energy. In the United States and Germany scientists were rushing to work on a weapon that could harness this energy—the atomic bomb. At the Radiation Laboratory at Berkeley scientists began working with uranium, since it was the chemical element most likely to lend itself to nuclear fission for military purposes. However, no coordinated effort to design and fabricate an actual atomic weapon was made.

Leads the Manhattan Project

The Manhattan Project began when President Franklin D. Roosevelt, after learning that the Germans might construct an atom bomb, created a U.S. atomic research program. According to Oppenheimer's colleague Victor Weisskopf, "many physi-

≡IMPACT≡

While J. Robert Oppenheimer is best known for leading the Manhattan Project, the U.S. effort to build the first atomic bomb, he also conducted important research in the field of quantum physics. His research on protons and their relation to electrons led directly to the discovery of a new particle, the positron. Furthermore, his later work shed light on deuterons, the nuclei of heavy hydrogen atoms.

Joseph Rotblat, Polish-born British Physicist

Joseph Rotblat (1908–) was the only scientist who quit the Manhattan Project for moral reasons. Rotblat left the secret laboratory at Los Alamos, New Mexico, in 1944, only nine months after he had started working on the atomic bomb. He later said he came to the realization that Germany was not an atomic threat to the United States and that the bomb was actually being developed to subdue the Soviet Union. U.S. security officers suspected Rotblat of being a Russian spy, but they could find no evidence against him.

Returning to England, where he had worked as a physicist, Rotblat remained silent about his doubts about atomic research until after the United States dropped bombs on Hiroshima and Nagasaki, Japan. Then he began speaking out about radioactive fallout and the potential dangers of nuclear testing. In 1957 Rotblat joined the German-born American physicist **Albert Einstein** and American chemist **Linus Pauling** (see entries) to form the Pugwash Conferences on Science and World Affairs, which was named for the Canadian town where the organization held its first meeting.

During the cold war period (when the United States and the Soviet Union were hostile to one another but not openly warring), from the late 1950s through the early 1990s, the Pugwash movement successfully campaigned for nuclear disarmament. For instance, the group was instrumental in bringing about the 1963 ban on the testing of nuclear weapons in the sea and atmosphere. Rotblat was awarded the 1995 Nobel Prize for peace for his efforts in curtailing the development of weapons for mass destruction. He and his colleagues continue their work, most recently criticizing China for conducting underground nuclear testing for so-called peaceful purposes.

cists were drawn into this work by fate and destiny rather than enthusiasm," and Oppenheimer was one of them. For two years the program made little progress because the scientists encountered many obstacles. However, Oppenheimer emerged as an innovative problem-solver, and the program soon evolved into the Manhattan Project at the lab at Los Alamos, New Mexico.

One of the problems the scientists discovered was that, even though they had already concluded that uranium was the ideal chemical element for nuclear fission, they had not yet determined how much should be used. After working on the calculations, Oppenheimer solved the problem. On October

21, 1941, he presented his results. Critical mass, he concluded, was about 220 pounds.

Another problem the scientists encountered was that purifying enough U-235 would require not only research but also massive plants, which would have to be built. Similarly, putting together the bomb itself would require special facilities as well as physicists and other experts to do the work. Furthermore, all of this work would have to be top secret. Oppenheimer suggested it might be best to create a single laboratory where all the scientists could work together. That way, they could discuss their ideas freely, without worrying so much about security, because the laboratory could be protected from the outside world. Early in 1942 Oppenheimer brought together a group of theoretical physicists—many of whom had been working in separate laboratories as part of the Manhattan Project—and became director of the new research lab at Los Alamos to develop the first nuclear weapon.

Approves implosion method

In early 1943 Oppenheimer's main challenge was assembling critical mass—that is, how to bring together two pieces of U-235 quickly enough to create a chain reaction that would produce the explosion. Earlier, he had settled on the "gun method," in which one piece of uranium would be fired like a bullet into another sphere-shaped uranium target.

A young scientist named Seth Neddermeyer had a different idea, called implosion. Neddermeyer pictured a hollow ball of uranium surrounded by explosive material. When the explosive went off, the hollow center would collapse, and the now compacted sphere would become critical. Most rejected the idea—the explosion would have to be perfectly even all around the sphere, which seemed impossible—but Oppenheimer told Neddermeyer to go ahead with research on his own.

Encounters more problems

Oppenheimer continued to work under very difficult conditions. He had to develop an atomic weapon without enough

Andrei Sakharov, Soviet Physicist

Andrei Sakharov (1921–1989) occupied a position in the Soviet Union comparable to that of J. Robert Oppenheimer in the United States, both as a leading developer of nuclear technology and later as an advocate of nuclear disarmament. Sakharov first gained international fame in the 1950s as one of the developers of the Soviet Union's hydrogen bomb. A premier physicist, he was the youngest person ever elected to the Soviet Academy of Sciences and was decorated three times with the Soviet's highest civilian honor, the Order of the Red Banner of Labor. During the 1960s, however, Sakharov became disenchanted with the nuclear arms movement. "Civilization," he wrote, "is imperiled by universal thermonuclear war." By the early 1970s, a time when most dissenters in the U.S.S.R. were immediately exiled or imprisoned, he began a mounting dissent against Soviet nuclear proliferation and political suppression. Only internationally known Soviet figures who expressed these opinions —such as Sakharov, writer Aleksandr Solzhenitsyn, and a few others—were tolerated because of the worldwide disgrace that would follow their censure. In recognition of his efforts to bring about greater political freedom in the U.S.S.R., Sakharov was awarded the Nobel Prize for peace in 1975.

radioactive material (material made up of atoms with the type of nucleus that gives off neutrons on its own) to properly test possible designs. By early 1944, huge factories with tens of thousands of employees had been built at Oak Ridge, Tennessee, and Hanford, Washington. Some were based on particle accelerators; others used different methods to refine the uranium to the high level of purity needed. One mission of the Hanford plant was to produce plutonium (a man-made radioactive material), but production was slower than expected. None of the methods for refining uranium seemed to work well, and machines at the plants kept breaking down. As for plutonium, Oppenheimer and his team were not even sure it would be useful.

Settles on implosion method

By the summer of 1944, both problems—material and assembly—had become connected. Uranium would work with the gun method, but production had become so slow that only enough material for one bomb would be ready by mid-1945. This meant that if Oppenheimer wanted to test a bomb, there would not be one available for use in war. Furthermore, tests of plutonium showed it would work, but the gun method would be too slow. A plutonium bomb would have to use Neddermeyer's implosion method. The factories could produce plenty of plutonium, but could Oppenheimer perfect implosion in time to use it? So far, Neddermeyer had made no progress. It simply seemed impossible to create a perfectly even explosion around the bomb's core.

Approves the explosive lens

The answer came when British scientists joined the project. Among them was a young Englishman named James Tuck, who suggested using an explosive lens to direct the force just as a regular lens directs light rays. If such lenses were focused around the core, Tuck suggested, it should be possible to produce an even explosion. In the late summer and fall of 1944, Oppenheimer completely reorganized the implosion team, adding hundreds of scientists and speeding up tests and research.

Experiences the fateful moment

Gradually, the implosion bomb began to take shape. In early 1945 the U.S. Army took over land in the New Mexico desert for a test of the bomb, uprooting the few ranchers in the area (some of whom had to be forced to leave). On the morning of July 16, 1945, Oppenheimer stood silently, awaiting the detonation of the test bomb. He later wrote in his *Letters and Recollections* that, upon seeing the power it unleashed, he thought the play of the light had the "radiance of a thousand suns," but he was also reminded of a dark, foreboding line from the Hindu *Bhagavad-Gita:* "I am become death, the Shatterer of Worlds."

Regrets decision to use bomb

Oppenheimer was one of a panel of four scientists, including Ernest Orlando Lawrence, Enrico Fermi, and Arthur Compton, who were asked to formulate an opinion regarding the use of the atomic bomb to end the war against Japan. They were told there was a choice between a military invasion of Japan, which was certain to cost many American lives, and a nuclear attack on a military target that would also kill many civilians. Confronted with this choice, the panel voted to use the bomb. Oppenheimer later regretted his decision, saying the intentional slaughter of civilians had been unnecessary and wrong.

The ultimate authority belonged to President Harry S Truman, who decided to use the bomb. On August 6, 1945, the atomic bomb, code-named "Little Boy," was dropped on the city of Hiroshima, with devastating results. From 78,000 to 200,000 people were killed, with over 60,000 buildings destroyed. The entire center of the city was wiped out in a fraction of a second. Thousands began dying of radiation sickness, the results of the bomb's radioactive fallout (the radioactive particles resulting from a nuclear explosion). Only three days later, on August 9, the second bomb, "Fat Man," was dropped on the city of Nagasaki. Over 100,000 were killed that day, again with more dying later of radiation sickness. On August 14, Japan surrendered.

Achieves fame

As news of the secret work at Los Alamos became public, Oppenheimer was suddenly one of the most famous scientists in America, the "Father of the A-Bomb," as the press

called him. For most of the next decade he acted as scientific advisor at the highest levels of government, helping politicians try to deal with the awesome new power that had been unleashed. He served on several committees that worked out U.S. policy on both atomic energy and atomic weapons. In 1947 he was appointed director of the Institute for Advanced Study at Princeton University. Oppenheimer single-handedly built the institute into a top-notch physics research center.

Accused of being a communist

Despite his success, by the early 1950s Oppenheimer had made some powerful enemies. In particular, his opposition to the "H-Bomb" (a more powerful nuclear bomb that uses hydrogen rather than uranium or plutonium) angered both scientists and air force commanders. As anticommunist hysteria, spurred by Senator Joseph McCarthy, swept the nation, they saw their chance to damage Oppenheimer. In 1953 they used Oppenheimer's past ties to communism to convince President Dwight D. Eisenhower to take away his security clearance. In the 1930s, to many Americans it seemed that communism was the best hope of fighting the fascism of Adolf Hitler, and of improving life for workers in industrial nations. While Oppenheimer was a member of several communist front organizations, he had never actually joined the party itself.

In 1954 a month-long hearing, which in effect put Oppenheimer on trial as a communist spy, ended in a refusal to return his security clearance. It was thought that he might have helped pass information to the Soviets while working on the Manhattan Project. He would never again be called on to advise the government, although his academic career at Princeton would continue. In response to the hearing, the scientific community rallied around Oppenheimer.

Receives Fermi Award

In 1963 the Atomic Energy Commission and President Lyndon Johnson—as if making up for past injustice—presented Oppenheimer with the highly regarded Fermi Award for his contributions to theoretical physics. Soon after, his health began to fail. Oppenheimer died of cancer on February 18, 1967, at the age of sixty-two.

Further Reading

Broad, William., "Joseph Rotblat: Still Battling Nuclear Weapons 50 Years After Manhattan Project," *New York Times,* May 21, 1996, pp. B5, B7.

Driemen, J. E., *Atomic Dawn: A Biography of Robert Oppenheimer,* Dillon Press, 1989.

Goodchild, Peter, *J. Robert Oppenheimer: Shatterer of Worlds,* Fromm, 1985.

Kunetka, James W., *Oppenheimer: The Years of Risk,* Prentice-Hall, 1982.

Oppenheimer, J. Robert, *Letters and Recollections,* edited by Alice Kimball Smith and Charles Weiner, Harvard University Press, 1980.

Picture Credits

Jane Goodall

The photographs appearing in *Scientists: The Lives and Works of 150 Scientists* were received from the following sources:

On the cover (clockwise from top right): Luis Alvarez, Robert H. Goddard (**AP/Wide World Photos. Reproduced by permission.**); Margaret Mead (**The Bettmann Archive. Reproduced by permission.**). On the back cover (top to bottom): Edwin H. Land (**AP/Wide World Photos. Reproduced by permission.**); George Washington Carver (**The Bettmann Archive. Reproduced by permission.**).

Courtesy of the Library of Congress: pp. v, 11, 30, 66, 82, 96, 98, 102, 135, 137, 185, 188, 197, 200, 203, 206 (top and bottom), 208, 211, 224, 244, 260, 267, 275, 296, 308, 316, 339, 371, 374, 395, 399, 405, 441, 444, 487, 490, 506, 524, 527, 529, 568, 573, 599, 616, 620 (top and bottom), 648, 654, 680, 686, 693, 723, 726, 746, 759, 772, 787, 794, 803, 822, 855, 858, 905, 908, 945, 959, 990, 996, 1004, 1023; **AP/Wide World Photos. Reproduced by permission.:** pp. xv, xliii, 7, 19, 34, 72, 92, 105, 121, 124, 128, 141, 142, 233, 236, 239, 242, 254, 258, 273, 280, 282, 283, 320, 326, 333, 335, 367, 376, 384, 389, 397, 408, 415, 418, 422, 425, 432, 438, 466, 468, 474, 478, 483, 498, 502, 512, 523, 556, 575, 581, 585, 588, 642, 652, 660, 665, 674, 733, 735, 737, 738, 743,

693

769, 783, 797, 801, 814, 838, 845, 862, 882, 901, 917, 921, 957, 962, 969, 980, 992, 999, 1012; **The Bettmann Archive. Reproduced by permission.**: pp. xxix, 65, 144, 174, 181, 226, 458, 609, 631, 670, 728, 750, 810, 889, 923, 926, 995; **UPI/Corbis-Bettmann. Reproduced by permission.**: pp. xxxi, 112, 115, 117, 178, 251, 378, 448, 454, 515, 593; **Courtesy of Keiiti Aki**: p. 1; **Photograph by Robert T. Eplett. California Governor's Office of Emergency Services.**: p. 3; **The Granger Collection, New York. Reproduced by permission.**: pp. 27, 37, 41, 85, 168, 184, 217, 249, 392, 543, 607, 628, 651, 658, 753, 805, 825, 876, 893, 948, 987, 1017; **UPI/Bettmann. Reproduced by permission.**: pp. 48, 51, 56, 75, 95, 127, 131, 150, 155, 292, 341, 412, 463, 493, 495, 578, 603, 604, 622, 635, 639, 695, 755, 757, 836, 867, 933, 936, 951, 1010, 1025; **AT&T Bell Laboratories. Reproduced by permission.**: p. 62; **UPI/Bettmann Newsphotos. Reproduced by permission.**: pp. 80, 134, 149, 161, 780, 819, 832, 870; **Washington University Photographic Services. Reproduced by permission.**: p. 165; **From** *Undersea World of Jacques Cousteau.* **American Broadcasting Company. Reproduced by permission.**: p. 171; **Courtesy of Francisco Dallmeier**: p. 192; © **Zefa Germany, Stock Market. Reproduced by permission.**: p. 195; **Los Alamos National Laboratory**: p. 285; **Illustration by Robert L. Wolke. Reproduced by permission.**: p. 289; **Archive Photos, Inc. Reproduced by permission.**: p. 313; **Photri/Bikderberg. Stock Market. Reproduced by permission.**: p. 329; **Reuters/Bettmann. Reproduced by permission.**: pp. 363, 508, 565; **U.S. National Aeronautics and Space Administration (NASA)**: p. 437; **J. W. Cappelens Forlag. Reproduced by permission.**: p. 451; **Courtesy of Louis Keith**: p. 549; **Photograph by Yousuf Karsh. Reproduced by permission of Woodman Camp**: p. 536; © **1990 Peter Menzel. Reproduced by permission.**: p. 562; **Mary Evans Picture Library. Reproduced by permission.**: p. 591; **Anthony Howarth/Science Photo Library. Reproduced by permission.**: p. 596; **Courtesy of Raymond Kurzweil**: p. 668; © **Scott Camazine, The National Audubon Society Collection/Photo Researchers, Inc. Reproduced by permission.**: p. 689; **Conservation International. Reproduced by permission.**: p. 767; **Royal Institute of Technology. Reproduced by permission.**: p. 791; **Photograph by Allen Furbeck. Reproduced by permission.**: p. 827; **Courtesy of Dr. Susan Leeman.**: p. 851; © **The Alan Mason Chesney Medical Archives of The Johns Hopkins Medical Institutions. Reproduced by permission.**: p. 897; **Courtesy of New York Public Library Picture Collection**: p. 911; **Courtesy of Dr. Levi Watkins**: p. 929; **Photograph by Brent Clingman.** *Time* **Magazine. Reproduced by permission.**: p. 973.

Index

Italic type indicates volume numbers;
boldface *type indicates
entries and their page numbers;
(ill.) indicates illustrations.*

James D. Watson

Galileo Galilei *1:* 267;
2: 444–46, 490; *3:* 789
Gallagher, John *1:* 272
Galle, Johann Gottfried *2:* 373
Game theory *3:* 962
Gates, Bill *2:* **363–70,** 363 (ill.)
Gauss, Carl Friedrich *2:*
371–75, 371 (ill.)
Gayle, Helene D. *2:* **376–79,**
376 (ill.)
Gay-Lussac, Joseph *1:* 215
Geiger counter *3:* 808; *3:* 920
Geiger, Hans *3:* 808–11,
810 (ill.)
Geissler, Heinrich *3:* 1020
Gelfond, A. O. *2:* 458
Geller, Margaret *2:* **380–83,**
380 (ill.)
*Genes and Genomes: A Changing
Perspective 3:* 874
Genes, Mind and Culture 3: 977
Genetic code *1:* 78, 179, 209
Genetic engineering *1:* 76–78,
80; *3:* 870, 873–74
Genetic transposition *2:* 622,
624–25, 627
Geodesic dome *1:* 333–34,
336–37
George III (of England)
2: 443–47
Germ theory *3:* 726
Gilbert, Walter *1:* 81;
2: **384–91,** 384 (ill.)
Glaser, Donald *1:* 11
Glashow, Sheldon L.
3: 832, 835, 836 (ill.)
Glass, nonreflecting *1:* 92, 94
Glaucoma *2:* 531
Gliders *3:* 989–93
Global warming *2:* 597
Goddard, Robert H. *2:* **392–98,**
392 (ill.), 397 (ill.)
Gödel, Kurt *2:* 372, 461
Goeppert-Mayer, Maria
2: **399–404,** 399 (ill.)
Gold, Lois Swirsky *1:* 21–22
Gold, Thomas *1:* 71
Golka, Robert *3:* 891
Gombe Stream Reserve, Tanzania
2: 405, 407, 409

Gondwanaland *3:* 956
Goodall, Jane *2:* **405–14,** 405
(ill.), 412 (ill.)
Gorillas in the Mist 2: 408
Gosling, Raymond *1:* 304–06
Gough, John *1:* 198
Gould, Gordon *2:* 601, 604,
604 (ill.)
Gould, Stephen Jay *2:* **415–21,**
415 (ill.); *3:* 976
Gourdine, Meredith *2:* **422–26,**
422 (ill.), 425 (ill.)
Grand unification theory *2:* 435
Graphophone *1:* 62, 67
Gray, Elisha *1:* 64, 66, 66 (ill.)
The Great Train Robbery
1: 250
Greenhouse effect *1:* 30, 33–35
*The Greenhouse Effect, Climate
Change, and Ecosystems 1:* 34
Green Revolution *1:* 105,
107–09
Greylag geese *2:* 589
Growing Up in New Guinea
2: 636
Guillemin, Roger *3:* 1009,
1010 (ill.)
Gutenberg, Beno *3:* 781, 784
Guyots *3:* 954
Gypsum *2:* 569

H

Hadar, Ethiopia *2:* 519–20, 523
Hadrons *2:* 500
Hahn, Otto *1:* 289; *2:* 401,
641–42, 644–45, 647
Hale, George E. *2:* 489
Half-life, radioactive *3:* 807, 809
Hall, Lloyd A. *2:* **427–31**
Hardy, G. H. *3:* 960
Hardy-Weinberg law *2:* 552
Hargreaves, James *1:* 24–25
Harrar, George *1:* 107
Harris, Geoffrey W. *3:* 1009
Hawkes, Graham *1:* 239–41
Hawking, Stephen *2:* **432–40,**
432 (ill.)

M

MacArthur, Robert H. *3:* 971
Macrophage *1:* 284
Magic numbers *2:* 403
Magnetic core memory
   3: 923, 925
Magnetohydrodynamics *2:* 424
Maiman, Theodore *2:* **601–06**
Mall, Franklin P. *3:* 823
Manhattan Project *1:* 7, 10,
   103, 268–69, 285, 289–91;
   2: 399, 402; *2:* 680, 683–85;
   3: 779, 1002
Manus (people) *2:* 635, 635 (ill.)
*The Man Who Mistook His Wife
   for a Hat* *3:* 827, 830
Marconi, Guglielmo *1:* 218–19;
   2: **607–15,** 607 (ill.), 609 (ill.);
   3: 806, 896
Mark I *3:* 924, 926
Marriage and Morals *3:* 802
Marsden, Ernest *3:* 809, 811
Martin, Pierre-Emile *1:* 86
Marx, Karl *3:* 797
Maser *2:* 602
A Matter of Consequences *3:* 880
Mauchly, John William *2:* 367,
   367 (ill.)
Maury, Antonia *1:* 133
Maxam, Allan *2:* 387
Max Planck Society *3:* 765
Maxwell, James Clerk *2:* 610,
   616–21, 616 (ill.); *3:* 789,
   906, 908
Maybach, Wilhelm *1:* 227
Mayer, Joseph E. *2:* 400–01
Mayer, Julius *2:* 527
McCarthy, Senator Joseph
   2: 690
McClintock, Barbara *2:*
   622–27, 622 (ill.)
McCoy, Elijah *2:* **628–32,**
   628 (ill.)
Mead, Margaret *2:* **633–38,**
   633 (ill.), 635 (ill.)
Meaning of Evolution *2:* 416
*The Mechanism of Mendelian
   Heredity* *2:* 626
Meiosis *2:* 624–25

Meitner, Lise *1:* 288; *2:* 401,
   639–47, 639 (ill.)
Meltdown, nuclear *1:* 127
Mendel, Gregor *1:* 209; *2:* 626,
   648–53, 648 (ill.)
Mendel, Lafayette B. *3:* 857
Mendeleev, Dmitry *2:* **654–59,**
   654 (ill.)
Menlo Park, New Jersey *1:* 248
Menninger, Charles *2:* 660
Menninger Clinic *2:* 660–61
Menninger, Karl *2:* **660–64,**
   660 (ill.)
Menninger, William *2:* 661
Mental illness *2:* 660–62;
   3: 827, 830
Mercalli scale *1:* 3; *3:* 781–82
Mesometeorology *1:* 331
Mesoscaphe *3:* 758
Metric system *2:* 569
Michelson, Albert *2:* 620–21,
   620 (ill.)
Microbursts *1:* 326, 328, 331
Microchips *2:* 674, 676–77
Microsoft *2:* 363–64, 368
Microwaves *2:* 603, 614; *3:* 943
Mid-oceanic ridges *3:* 954
Migraine *3:* 829
Milky Way *2:* 445, 447
Minkowski, Hermann *2:* 455
Minsky, Marvin *2:* **665–69,**
   665 (ill.)
Mirowski, Michel *3:* 931
The Mismeasure of Man *2:* 419
*Miss Goodall and the Wild
   Chimpanzees* *2:* 410
*Missile Envy: The Arms Race and
   Nuclear War* *1:* 129
Moi, Daniel Arap *2:* 585
*The Molecular Biology of the
   Gene* *3:* 937
Monod, Jacques Lucien *2:* 386
Monterey One *1:* 335 (ill.)
Morgan, Lewis Henry *3:* 719
Morgan, Thomas Hunt *2:* 626
Morgenstern, Oskar *3:* 962
Morley, Edward *2:* 620–21,
   620 (ill.)
Morse code *2:* 611; *3:* 983–84

W

Walden Two *3:* 878–79
Wang, An *3:* **923–28,** 923 (ill.)
Wang Laboratories *3:* 923–25, 927
War Crimes Tribunal *3:* 804
War of the Worlds *2:* 393
Washkansky, Louis *2:* 506
Wassermann, August von *2:* 465
Water frame *1:* 25, 27 (ill.)
Water pollution *3:* 734–36
Watkins, Levi, Jr. *3:* **929–32,** 929 (ill.)
Watson, James D. *1:* 174, 176, 178, 180, 302, 304–06; *2:* 384–85, 469; *3:* **933–38,** 933 (ill.), 936 (ill.)
Watson, Thomas A. *1:* 63–65
Watson-Watt, Robert *3:* **939–44**
Watt, James *3:* **945–50,** 945 (ill.)
Weak force *1:* 287; *3:* 833
Weber, Wilhelm *2:* 373
Webster, Arthur Gordon *2:* 393
Wegener, Alfred *3:* **951–58,** 951 (ill.)
Wegener's granulomatosis *1:* 281
Weinberg, Steven *3:* 832, 834–35, 836 (ill.)
Weinberg, Wilhelm *2:* 552
Weizenbaum, Joseph *2:* 566
Weller, Thomas *3:* 818, 841, 843
Wells, H. Gideon *3:* 857
Westinghouse, George *3:* 892; *3:* 1020
What Mad Pursuit: A Personal View of Scientific Discovery *1:* 179–80
Wheat *1:* 107–09
Wheatstone, Charles *2:* 375
Wheelwright, George *2:* 558
Whitehead, Alfred North *3:* 796–97, 797 (ill.), 799
Whitehouse, E. O. W. *3:* 909
Whiting, Sarah Frances *1:* 132

Why Men Fight: A Method of Abolishing the International Duel *3:* 800
Wien, Wilhelm *3:* 762–63
Wiener, Norbert *3:* **959–63,** 959 (ill.)
Wigner, Eugene Paul *2:* 403
Wiles, Andrew J. *2:* 460
Wilkins, A. F. *3:* 941
Wilkins, Maurice *1:* 176–77, 302, 304, 306; *3:* 933–36
Williams, Robin *3:* 828
Williamson, James S. *3:* **964–68**
Wilson, Edward O. *3:* **969–79,** 969 (ill.)
Wilson, Woodrow *3:* 801
Wind shear *1:* 326, 330–31
Wireless receiver *2:* 609, 609 (ill.)
Women Who Run with the Wolves *2:* 540
Wonderful Life: The Burgess Shale and the Nature of History *2:* 420
Wong-Staal, Flossie *1:* 283, 283 (ill.)
Woods, Granville T. *3:* **980–86,** 980 (ill.)
Woods Hole Oceanographic Institute *1:* 49; *2:* 544, 547
Woodwell, George M. *1:* 142, 142 (ill.)
Worlds in the Making *1:* 35
Worldwatch Institute *1:* 258
Wozniak, Stephen *2:* 508–11, 513
Wright, Almroth *1:* 293
Wright Flyer I *3:* 993
Wright Flyer III *3:* 994
Wright, Orville *3:* **987–98,** 987 (ill.), 992 (ill.)
Wright, Wilbur *3:* **987–98,** 987 (ill.), 995 (ill.)
Wu, Chien-Shiung *3:* **999–1003,** 999 (ill.), 1012, 1015

X

X-ray crystallography *1:* 177;
  2: 474–76, 478
X-ray diffraction *1:* 175–76,
  303–04, 306
X-ray imaging *1:* 44–45, 47
X-ray photograph *3:* 791 (ill.)
X rays *2:* 483; *3:* 776–77, 779,
  787, 789–93, 807
X-ray spectroscopy *2:* 657
X-ray telescope *1:* 45

Y

Yalow, Rosalyn Sussman *3:*
  1004–11, 1010 (ill.), 1004 (ill.)
Yang, Chen Ning *3:* 999, 1002,
  1012–16, 1012 (ill.)
The Year of the Greylag Goose
  2: 592

Yerkes Observatory (University
  of Chicago) *2:* 489
Young, Thomas *2:* 617
Yukuna (people) *3:* 768

Z

Zero Population Growth *1:* 257
Zinjanthropus *2:* 579–80
Zion, Élie de *3:* 747
Zionist movement *1:* 269
Zoological Institute, University
  of Munich *1:* 321, 324
Zoological Philosophy *1:* 208
Zooplankton *1:* 15, 17–18
Zwicky, Fritz *1:* 156
Zworykin, Vladimir
  3: **1017–22,** 1017 (ill.)